What Every Silver Dollar Buyer Should Know.

by Steve Ivy and Ron Howard

The Ivy Press
Dallas, Texas

Published by
The Ivy Press, Inc.
7950 Elmbrook Drive, Suite 100
Dallas, Texas 75247

Dedication

To our Lindas.

Contents

Acknowledgements i
Foreword iii
A Word About Mintages iv
Mint State Grading Standards vi
Mintage Table for Morgan and Peace Dollars viii
Technique For Grading Mint State Morgan Dollars x
1878 Eight Tail Feathers 1-2
1878 Seven Over Eight Tail Feathers 3-4
1878 Seven Tail Feathers 5-6
1878 Seven Tail Feathers, Round Breast 7-8
1878-S 9
1878-CC 10
1879 11
1879-O 12-13
1879-S 14
1879-S Concave Breast 15-16
1879-CC 17-19
1880 20-21
1880-O 22
1880-S 23
1880-CC 24
1880-CC Concave Breast 25
1881 26
1881-O 27
1881-S 28
1881-CC 29
1882 30
1882-O 31
1882-S 32
1882-CC 33
1883 34
1883-O 35-36
1883-S 37-38
1883-CC 39
1884 40
1884-O 41
1884-S 42-43
1884-CC 44-45
1885 46
1885-O 47
1885-S 48-49
1885-CC 50
1886 51

(CONTENTS, continued)

1886-O	52-53
1886-S	54
1887	55
1887-O	56
1887-S	57
1888	58
1888-O	59-60
1888-S	61
1889	62-63
1889-O	64-65
1889-S	66
1889-CC	67-68
1890	69
1890-O	70
1890-S	71
1890-CC	72
1891	73-74
1891-O	75
1891-S	76
1891-CC	77
1892	78-79
1892-O	80
1892-S	81-82
1892-CC	83-84
1893	85
1893-O	86-87
1893-S	88-89
1893-CC	90-91
1894	92-93
1894-O	94
1894-S	95
1895	96-97
1895-O	98-99
1895-S	100-101
1896	102-103
1896-O	104
1896-S	105
1897	106
1897-O	107-108
1897-S	109
1898	110
1898-O	111
1898-S	112
1899	113-114
1899-O	115

(CONTENTS, continued)

1899-S 116
1900 117-118
1900-O 119
1900-O over CC 120
1900-S 121
1901 122-124
1901-O 125
1901-S 126-127
1902 128
1902-O 129
1902-S 130
1903 131
1903-O 132
1903-S 133-134
1904 135-136
1904-O 137
1904-S 138-139
1921 Morgan 140-141
1921 Peace 142-143
1921-D 144
1921-S 145-146
1922 147
1922-D 148
1922-S 149
1923 150
1923-D 151
1923-S 152
1924 153
1924-S 154
1925 155
1925-S 156
1926 157
1926-D 158
1926-S 159
1927 160
1927-D 161
1927-S 162
1928 163
1928-S 164
1934 165
1934-D 166
1934-S 167-168
1935 169
1935-S 170
Bibliography 171

Acknowledgements

Many people contributed to the completion of this book. Numerous conversations, on the phone or at coin shows, and years of learning from those more experienced cannot be properly credited here. However, the authors would like to specifically thank Brian Beardsley, Jeff Garrett and Dean Tavenner for providing photographed coins; for valuable assistance regarding pedigrees, our thanks to Bruce Amspacher, Jim Jelinski, Mark Thornton, Harlan White, Ray Merena, Julian Leidman and Vince Filpi; and for editing, Fred L. Reed, III. Photography by Bryan Renfro, Heritage Numismatic Auctions, Inc. Typesetting by Karen Cleek; cover by Marsha Cathey, Heritage Capital Corporation. Our apologies for any omissions.

Foreword

The fact that you are reading this book proves that you are interested in United States Silver Dollars. And who isn't? Who can resist the lure and romance of the obsolete but beloved "cartwheels?" Who can avoid excited speculation of a windfall fortune when he discovers a cigar box full of old Morgan Dollars in a long-unexplored bureau? Who can heft a handful of Silver Dollars made from real silver and clink them together without exclaiming "Now that's when money *felt* like money!?"

In a way, the old Silver Dollars symbolize America's fondly regarded past. Although nostalgic reminiscences are often more of fantasy than realism, there is much to be said for the days when a dollar was worth something, and many things in life were more important than getting more material things than anyone else. The dollars covered by this book were minted during the years 1878-1935, an era that generally covers the time in which our modern way of life was shaped. The Depression, world wars, the growth of American business and industry, labor revolution, women's rights and the settlement of the Western frontier all occurred during those 57 years. A Silver Dollar personifies all of these things and more in an ounce of precious metal.

The authors intend this work to be interesting and enriching to all Silver Dollar enthusiasts, whether you have only a casual interest or whether you are an experienced collector. Grading and the date-by-date discussion of the Morgan and Peace Dollar series are very important sections to those who have reached or passed the point of contemplating the purchase of Silver Dollars, whether for collection or investment or, as is most often the case, for both purposes. While the discussions of the individual dates may appear somewhat technical to the beginner, experience will familiarize, and repeated referrals to the information will increase its clarity and value.

There are 103 different discussions of individual issues of Morgan Dollars included, and 24 of Peace Dollars. Each date is introduced by a photographic illustration and a written description of the typical mint state, or uncirculated example.

To the limits of affordability and availability, collectors prefer to own coins in mint state condition. More so than most series of United States coins, Morgan and Peace Dollars can vary drastically in quality and still be defined as mint state. It is imperative that the serious dollar investor or collector be familiar with the typical quality of the dates he wants to own. To convey this information, the authors selected the photographed coins from the tens of thousands of examples they encountered during the evolution of this book. The typical numerical grade and the four major characteristics affecting value are listed under each photograph. The four characteristics, and the terms used to describe them, are:

1. Strike - weak, average, above average, sharp.
2. Bagmarks - light, moderate, heavy.
3. Surfaces - frosty, semiprooflike, prooflike.
4. Luster - poor, good, excellent.

The terms used to describe bagmarks refer to the overall density of the marks and not to the severity of an individual mark. Since the surfaces of each issue of Peace Dollars are typically frosty, item three is omitted for that series.

Following the delineation of the typical mint state characteristics of each issue is a general discussion section that examines the availability of that particular date in mint state and circulated grades, expounds on the mint state characteristics, details auction records and pedigrees of specific examples and discusses major varieties. Other information that the authors' deemed helpful to the reader also was included.

In order to provide a comprehensive treatment of each issue, a list of the most frequently asked questions concerning individual dates of dollars follows the general discussion. How rare is this issue with prooflike surfaces? How rare is it in superb condition? Was it included in the Redfield Hoard? Were there proofs minted, and if so, what are their characteristics? What investment potential does this particular issue possess, and in what condition should it be purchased for the highest appreciation? All of these questions are answered for each issue of Morgan Dollars. Since prooflike Peace Dollars are extremely rare, the prooflike topic is omitted for this series. All known or alleged proofs of the Morgan series struck at the branch mints are included, as are the only dates of Peace Dollars struck in proof, 1921 and 1922.

The authors earnestly recommend that the reader be satisfactorily versed in the terms used, and with the grading of dollars in general before he attempts to study the individual date analyses. Reference to the grading chapter of this work will help, but reading other Silver Dollar books, grading guides and the invaluable experience of personally grading and examining Silver Dollars are the best ways for the dollar collector to expand his scope and knowledge. Most dollar dealers and experienced collectors love to share their knowledge; if you can adopt a tutor, by all means do it. But be wary of the person who professes to know it all. One thing that knowledgeable dollar collectors agree on is that it is impossible to learn everything that these fascinating coins have to offer. And, while you are learning, remember that the education process ceases when the student presumes that there is nothing left to learn.

A word about Mintages

While the total number of coins of a certain denomination manufactured at a certain mint during a certain year is of significant importance to numismatists, the crucial question is "How many coins of a particular issue survive today?" In some of the series of United States coins, the original mintage figures may be a somewhat consistent way to compare relative rarity of the members of that series. Not so with Morgan and Peace Dollars.

Mintage figures are not a reliable source of information from which to estimate the relative rarities of either Morgan or Peace type Silver Dollars. An advertiser that notes a certain issue's "low mintage" is not justified in increasing the coin's price for that reason alone. In fact, the mintage figure for Silver Dollars is incidental in determining values. The original number minted often has little relationship with the total number of mint state pieces, or circulated pieces, for that matter, extant.

Obviously there is some consistency between mintages and present day supply. As an extreme example, the 1895, with only 880 pieces made (all of those were proofs), is thousands of times rarer than the 1889, which has a mintage of over twenty million. But there are many more inconsistencies in the Morgan and Peace series than there are consistencies. The number of comparisons to support this point is almost limitless, as the perusal of a current price list and a table of mintage figures will confirm.

Some of the more glaring examples of issues with relatively low mintages but are nonetheless in readily available supply in mint state condition are the Carson City issues from 1882 through 1885, inclusive, 1899 and 1928. A high percentage of each of these issues survived in mint state condition.

Some examples of issues with high original mintages but which are scarce in mint state are 1883-S, 1884-S, 1886-O, 1892-S, 1896-O, 1896-S, 1897-O and 1901.

Silver Dollars were like puppets, with strings attached to economic and political influences. Sharp increases and decreases in dollar production were common and usually tied to crucial economic issues that affected the entire nation, such as the Panic of 1873, which indirectly caused the cessation of dollar coinage for five years; the Free Silver movement of the 1890's, which ranked as the primary election issue in the presidential campaign of 1896; and World War I, which precipitated the Pittman Act of 1918.

The Pittman Act authorized the melting of over 270,000,000 silver dollars. No records of the dates melted were kept. A total of 333,022,048 were melted by the U.S. Treasury department from 1883 to 1964. The huge silver dollar melts are a primary reason for the uselessness of mintage figures as an indication of rarity.

Another reason silver dollar mintages should be ignored by investors is the inconsistency with which dollars were placed into circulation. Some issues were bagged and secreted for years, with very few coins entering general circulation. An excellent example of this case is the 1884-CC, of which nearly 85% of the entire mintage was discovered in Treasury vaults in the early 1960's! On the other hand, the 1892-S issue, which has a similar mintage to that of the 1884-CC, was placed almost in its entirety into circulation. Thus, circulated examples of 1892-S are very common; mint state examples are extremely rare.

Of less importance, but of undeniable significance, is private hoarding. LaVere Redfield accumulated over 400,000 silver dollars, most of them in mint state condition, and stored them in the walls of his Reno, Nevada, home. His holdings of some dates was extensive enough to materially effect the percentage of original mintages previously thought to have survived in mint state condition. Other hoards may exist, but the likelihood of their significance relative to the Redfield Hoard is remote.

Proof coins were minted especially for collectors, and thus have been preserved in numbers roughly proportional to their mintages. The mintage figures for proof Morgan Dollars are a reliable source for estimation of the comparative rarity of different dates as proofs.

Mint State Grading Standards

MS 70 A flawless coin, exactly as it was minted, with no trace of wear or injury. Must have full mint luster and brilliance, or light toning. Must be fully struck. An MS 70 Morgan Dollar may not exist.

MS 69 A near perfect dollar that shows no marks or injuries of any kind upon the obverse portraits (Ms. Liberty's) face or neck, or upon the eagle's breast on the reverse. A tiny mark or two is permissible in the fields, among the letters, or amid Ms. Liberty's hair or the eagle's wings or legs. None of these marks can be singularly detracting from the dollar's overall appearance, i.e., no longer than the width of a single denticle at its midpoint (about 0.5mm). There can be no noticeable nicks or dents on the rims. The strike must be full. Toning will not reduce the grade, but, if present, a notation indicating its density and location should be made. The mint luster must be full, vibrant and uninterrupted across the surfaces. An MS 69 Morgan must appear perfect at first glance; any flaws it possesses should not be immediately apparent, but should require careful examination with the unaided eye to locate.

MS 67 A dollar with no significant marks or abrasions on the portrait of Liberty on the obverse or on the eagle's breast on the reverse. Several widely scattered, tiny contact marks may be found in the fields, among or on the letters, or amid Ms. Liberty's hair or the eagle's wings or legs. None of these marks can be singularly detracting from the dollar's overall appearance, i.e., no longer than the width of a single denticle at its midpoint. There can be no noticeable nicks or dents on the rims. There can be no slide marks on Ms. Liberty's cheek. There may be no details absent due to insufficient strike. Any toning that may be present should be noted. The mint luster must be fully vibrant and uninterrupted across the surfaces.

MS 65 A dollar that may have small bagmarks widely scattered across the surfaces, or several bagmarks longer than the width of a single denticle, but not both. The cheek of Ms. Liberty may have some small marks, but cannot have any major injuries, such as a deep scratch or a prominent milling mark. The breast of the eagle should be perfect or very nearly so. The rims may have one or two imperfections, but they must not extend more than halfway between the edge of the coin and the bottom of the denticles. The luster must be full and unbroken. If there are slide marks, they must be minor, and be virtually the only defect on the obverse of the coin. A dollar with slide marks and more than a few sparse bagmarks cannot be graded MS 65. Any toning will not reduce or improve the grade, but should be mentioned when describing the coin. An MS 65 dollar should be pleasant in its overall appearance. A single major mark can be enough to remove a dollar from the MS 65 level. An MS 65 dollar must be fully struck.

MS 63 A dollar with numerous small bagmarks (those no longer than the width of a single denticle at its midpoint), or a few serious bagmarks, but not both. Liberty's cheek should not have any serious injuries, nor should the eagle's breast, though both of these areas may show some bagmarks and/or abrasions. The rims may have some nicks and dents, but none should extend into the denticles. The luster must be unbroken, although it may not be as intense and vibrant as that on an MS 65 or better coin. An MS 63 dollar must be fully struck unless it otherwise qualifies as an MS 65. Any significant toning should be mentioned.

MS 60 A dollar that may be densely bagmarked or a dollar with a particularly serious problem, such as a deep scratch on the cheek or a large (the width of three or more denticles), distracting rim bump. An MS 60 dollar must have no rubbing on the high points; the luster must be complete, even on Liberty's face and hair curls and the eagle's breast. The luster may not be as intense and vibrant as on coins of superior grades. An MS 60 dollar may or may not be fully struck. Abnormal weakness in striking or deep toning should be mentioned.

The above standards can be applied to Peace Dollars with only slight modification, i.e., liberalization of the reverse standards with regard to the eagle's breast. The entire eagle on the reverse of a Peace Dollar need not be "perfect or very nearly so" to qualify for MS 65.

Since the area involved is several times larger than on a Morgan Dollar, a few moderate marks can be tolerated. However, an MS 67 Peace Dollar, as a Morgan, should be expected to have no significant marks or abrasions on the portrait of Liberty or on any portion of the eagle.

Although an effort has been made to minimize the use of vague and imprecise terms in the above standards, a certain amount of subjective interpretation is inevitable. It is also often possible for one person to see a mark, defect, weakness, etc., that another person misses. Thus, an honest difference of opinion regarding a coin's grade can, and will, occur from time to time.

If a dollar exceeds all the requirements of one mint state grade, but does not quite meet all the requirements of the next highest mint state level, the lower grade should be assigned.

Mintage Table For Morgan and Peace Silver Dollars

Morgan Dollars

Date	Proof Mintage	Business Mintage	Date	Proof Mintage	Business Mintage
1878 - 8TF	500	750,000	1885	930	17,787,767
1877 - 7TF	500	9,759,550	1885-CC		228,000
1878 - 7/8TF	500	9,759,550	1885-O		9,185,000
1878-CC		2,212,000	1885-S		1,497,000
1878-S		9,774,000	1886	886	19,963,886
1879	1,100	14,807,100	1886-O		10,710,000
1879-CC		756,000	1886-S		750,000
1879-O		2,887,000	1887	710	20,290,170
1879-S		9,110,000	1887-O		11,550,000
1880	1,355	12,601,355	1887-S		1,771,000
1880-CC		591,000	1888	832	19,183,333
1880-O		5,305,000	1888-O		12,150,000
1880-S		8,900,000	1888-S		657,000
1881	975	9,163,975	1889	811	21,726,811
1881-CC		296,000	1889-CC		350,000
1881-O		5,708,000	1889-O		11,875,000
1881-S		12,760,000	1889-S		,700,000
1882	1,100	11,101,100	1890	590	16,802,590
1882-CC		1,133,000	1890-CC		2,309,041
1882-O		6,090,000	1890-O		10,701,000
1882-S		9,250,000	1890-S		8,230,373
1883	1,039	12,291,039	1891	650	8,694,206
1883-CC		1,204,000	1891-CC		1,618,000
1883-O		8,725,000	1891-O		7,954,529
1883-S		6,250,000	1891-S		5,296,000
1884	875	14,070,875	1892	1,245	1,037,245
1884-CC		1,136,000	1892-CC		1,352,000
1884-O		9,730,000	1892-O		2,744,000
1884-S		3,200,000	1892-S		1,200,000

Morgan Dollars (continued)

Date	Proof Mintage	Business Mintage	Date	Proof Mintage	Business Mintage
1893	792	389,792	1899-O		12,290,000
1893-CC		677,000	1899-S		2,562,000
1893-O		300,000	1900	912	8,830,912
1893-S		100,000	1900-O		12,590,000
1894	972	110,972	1900-S		3,540,000
1894-O		1,723,000	1901	813	6,962,813
1894-S		1,260,000	1901-O		13,320,000
1895	880	12,880	1901-S		2,284,000
1895-O		450,000	1902	777	7,994,777
1895-S		400,000	1902-O		8,636,000
1896	762	9,976,762	1902-S		1,530,000
1896-O		4,900,000	1903	755	4,652,755
1896-S		5,000,000	1903-O		4,450,000
1897	731	2,822,731	1903-S		1,241,000
1897-O		4,004,000	1904	650	2,778,650
1897-S		5,825,000	1904-O		3,720,000
1898	735	5,884,735	1904-S		2,304,000
1898-O		4,440,000	1921		44,690,000
1898-S		4,102,000	1921-D		20,345,000
1899	846	330,846	1921-S		21,695,000

Peace Dollars

Date	Business Mintage	Date	Business Mintage
1921	1,006,473	1926-D	2,348,700
1922	51,737,000	1926-S	6,980,000
1922-D	15,063,000	1927	848,000
1922-S	17,475,000	1927-D	1,268,900
1923	30,800,000	1927-S	866,000
1923-D	6,811,000	1928	360,649
1923-S	19,020,000	1928-S	1,632,000
1924	11,811,000	1934	954,057
1924-S	1,728,000	1934-D	1,569,500
1925	10,198,000	1934-S	1,011,000
1925-S	1,610,000	1935	1,576,000
1926	1,939,000	1935-S	1,964,000

Technique For Grading Mint State Morgan Dollars

To aid consistency, the grader should duplicate lighting conditions as much as possible each time he examines a group of coins. The authors recommend a 75 watt lamp in an otherwise dim room. Sunlight or fluorescent lighting should be avoided. If magnification is used, no more than a 5x should be utilized.

1. Scan the obverse for just a few seconds, making a mental note of the severity of the bagmarks on Liberty's cheek, the detail in the hair curls above her ear, and the quality of the coin's luster.

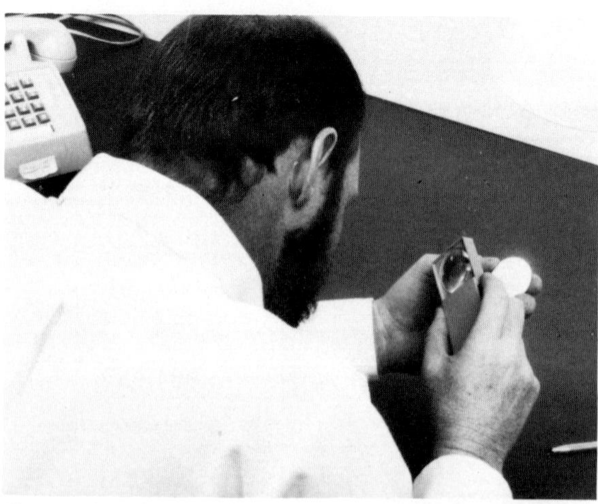

Coins should be held by the edge, and observed using a single incandescent bulb light source.

2. Scan the reverse in a similar fashion, looking first at the eagle's breast to check for bagmarks and the sharpness of the strike. Register your initial impression of the luster. You should, at this point, have the grade tentatively determined, or at least reduced to two possibilities among MS 60, 63, 65, 67 and 69.

3. Reexamine the obverse, this time more closely. Check for bagmarks that may be camouflaged under toning or by details of the coin's design. Sometimes, other large marks can be deceptively concealed

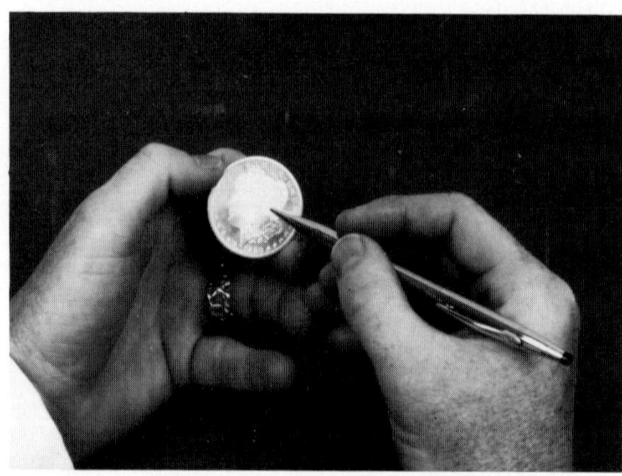

Scan the obverse and reverse checking for obvious marks, making note of their severity.

among the intricate lines of Liberty's hair. A scratch could be concentric to, and between, the denticles and the lettering, and thus not be immediately noticeable. Make sure you haven't missed any mark or defect that affects the coin's grade. Examine the rims closely for nicks and bumps.

4. Inspect Liberty's cheek for rubbing (wear) and slide marks. To do this, hold the dollar perpendicular to your line of vision and positioned so that the fact of Liberty is well illuminated. Focus your sight on a point created by the intersection of a hypothetical line drawn vertically from the corner of Liberty's eye and another extended horizontally from her mouth. Slowly tilt the coin toward the light and then return it to its original position. Do this at several different angles, riveting your attention to the area surrounding the focal point. If there is any rubbing on the obverse, it will interrupt the luster in this area. The rubbing may not be noticeable in one ·position, but be obvious in another. Therefore, the rotation of the coin beneath a proper light source is essential. This method is very effective in revealing slide marks. Slide marks are very thin, hairline scratches on Liberty's face. They are most often the result of a plastic panel from a coin album being pulled across the surface of the dollar. These slide marks are usually between one eighth and one quarter inch long and parallel to one another. They are usually roughly horizontal and may vary in number from a single mark to a dozen or more. If the dollar is held and tilted, as prescribed in the preceding paragraph, the light will reveal the slide marks to the viewer. They are not at all similar to bagmarks, but rather appear as very bright, thin scratches on the surface.

5. Reexamine the reverse, this time more closely. Check for camouflaged bagmarks and hidden scratches. Examine the rims carefully. Look at the wreath – some weakness in striking will often be evident in the details of this device.

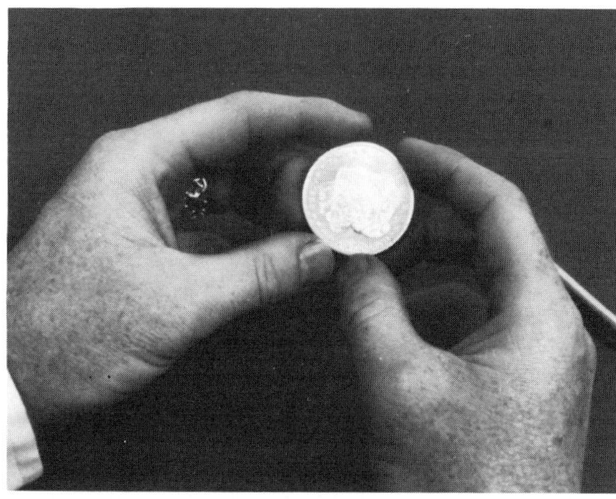

Reexamine the obverse more closely, rotating the reflection of the light off the surface of the coin.

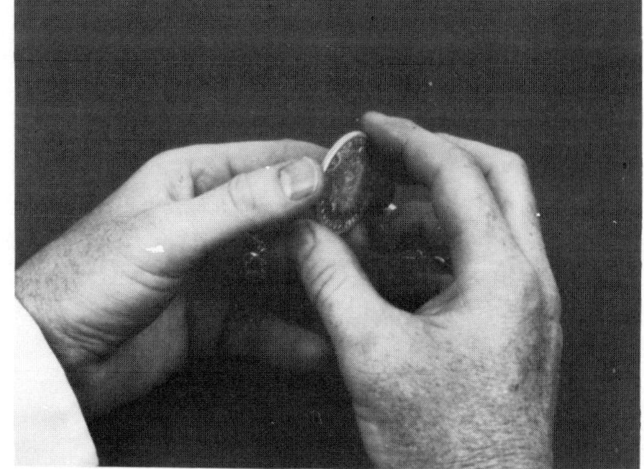

Examine the rims of the coins for edge bumps or nicks.

Reexamine the reverse looking "through" any dark toning to see the surfaces of the coin.

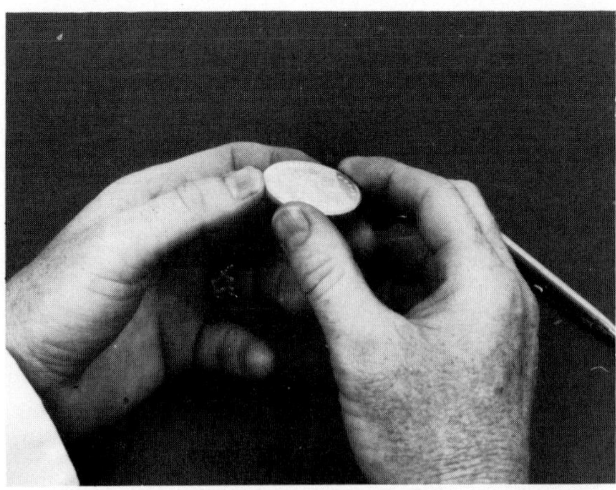

Tilt the coin several times away from you then back to a perpendicular line of sight, always watching for luster breaks.

6. Recheck the eagle's breast for rubbing (wear). Focusing upon the center of the eagle's breast, proceed as you did when you examined the obverse for rubbing (Step 4). If there is any rubbing on the reverse, it will appear on the highest portion of the eagle's breast.
7. Using the standards set forth for mint state Morgan Dollars, assign the proper grade.
   Note: If any rubbing exists, the coin is not in mint state condition, but is in Almost Uncirculated condition.

The seven steps listed above should provide an accurate and thorough method of grading Mint State Morgan Dollars. However, each collector will ultimately develop his or her own procedure for grading. The authors strongly feel that this procedure should incorporate all of the steps, and that all of the pitfalls mentioned in the grading standards and the technique for grading should be covered.

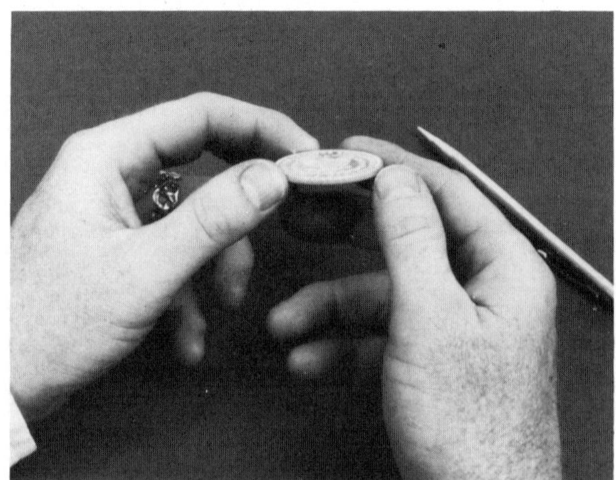

Watch closely for slide marks or other luster disturbances.

The authors certainly do not propose that the grader sit down with a copy of this book and count off steps one through seven for every mint State dollar that is examined. With experience, precise grading will become second nature! However, occasional referral to the standards and techniques may prove helpful to even the most knowledgeable specialist.

It is not always necessary to follow each of the seven steps in order to arrive at a grade. Scrutinization of an obvious MS 60 dollar will not make the bagmarks any less severe. The procedure outlined above becomes more critical as the potential grade of the dollar being examined increases.

Grades exist because differences in value exist among coins of the same issue. As utopian as it would be, a state of perfect consistency will never exist among graders of coins. If, for some reason, a person is determined to set himself apart from his peers by being so critical and demanding in his standards that he relegates Morgan and Peace Dollars with a few normal bagmarks to the MS 60 category, that person is apt to place some seemingly very high values upon some of his "MS 60" dollars. Similarly, a person who ignores generally accepted standards and overgrades his dollars by five points or more may seem to value his coins far below the going rate.

It is the authors' sincere hope that the standards and procedures set forth in this book will enable an increased level of consistency to be reached in the grading of Morgan and Peace Dollars.

1878

Eight Tail Feathers

Typical Mint State Example
MS (63), above average strike,
moderate bagmarks, frosty surfaces,
good luster.

GENERAL DISCUSSION: Although elementary arithmetic often leads to the seven tail feather variety of this year being listed first, the correct chronology is eight feathers, followed by seven over eight feathers, then seven feathers (all of which refer to the number of feathers of the eagle's tail). Naturalists must have been at least somewhat influential upon government even in those days, for some alert ornithologists promptly pointed out that the eagle on the new dollar sported an incorrect number of tail feathers. After striking an estimated (probably *under*estimated) three-quarters of a million pieces, the design was changed so that seven feathers were displayed.

If the mintage figure of 750,000 is correct, then an inordinate number of mint state dollars of this date exist today. This is possible, however, since many first year of type coins were saved in considerable quantities by those intrigued by the appearance of a new design on their money (e.g. 1883 No Cents Liberty Nickels, 1909 V.D.B. Lincoln Cents, 1916 Mercury Dimes, etc.). Because the design change from the previous Liberty Seated Type was a radical one, and because no Silver Dollars had been minted since 1873, some hoarding was to be expected. Probably few common folk kept their prizes long, for a dollar was a lot of money in 1878, and the decades immediately following replete with hard times. The fact remains that roll and occassional bag quantities of mint state coins surface. Circulated examples are relatively scarce and always command a premium.

The reverse design employed for virtually all 1878 Dollars used an ill-conceived, concave eagle's breast. The shallow breast and unclearly defined feathers should not be confused with a weakly struck coin. Most 1878 eight feather dollars are well struck. The obverse device, the bust of Liberty, also differs slightly from that of following years. Several minor modifications were made until a refined design, apparently satisfactory to all, was attained as production for the calendar year 1879 approached.

Most Morgan Dollar collectors prefer the design of subsequent years to that of 1878.

The authors have always maintained that the eight-feather variety was overpriced relative to the seven-feather. The overrated mintage factor is no doubt primarily responsible for this disparity. Our opinion was verified during the Morgan Dollar's one hundredth birthday. When this anniversary occurred in 1978, several major rare coin firms promoted a "One Hundredth Anniversary Special Collection" or similarly titled groupings of dollars, most often one uncirculated coin from each mint. As a result of the increased demand for these coins, and because they were eagerly received, the price of each increased significantly. Needless to say, the dealers sought the more inexpensive seven feather variety to fulfill the Philadelphia Mint's representative in the collection. Frequently, however, the exasperated promoters discovered that the more expensive eight feather variety was the commoner one, and had to use it to fill orders.

RARITY IN PROOFLIKE: A peculiar characteristic of 1878 eight-feather dollars is the frequency of one side exhibiting prooflike surfaces. The surfaces of that side usually are deeply mirrored, while the opposite side is totally frosty. While it is possible that every date of the series may have some one-sided prooflikes, this variety and few others are particularly noted for that characteristic. A two-sided prooflike specimen of this issue is only moderately scarce, and commands little attention from prooflike collectors.

RARITY IN SUPERB CONDITION: The 1878 eight-feather is quite scarce in grades above MS (65). Bagmarks, some often severe, plague the obverses of the majority of surviving mint state examples. The authors have examined original roll and bag quantities and found very few coins that deserved a true MS (65) classification, let alone exceeded it.

REDFIELD: No.

PROOFS: Seven hundred proofs were struck, making this date the fifth scarcest Morgan in proof. It is surprising that a nice Proof (65) example does not command more respect, value wise, than it does, because it is a very difficult item to acquire, and it is technically a one year of type coin. Most seen have been toned, often attractively so. Some are weakly struck as proofs go, although the resulting effect is exaggerated by the previously discussed concave breast design. Beware of first strike prooflikes that are offered as proofs.

INVESTMENT POTENTIAL: Investment in this issue should be restricted to truly superb MS (65) or better examples, whether they are prooflike or frosty. One-sided prooflikes should carry little or no premium over frosty coins. Because strongly struck coins are available, weak ones should be ignored. It is doubtful that this issue will perform well in the future relative to other Morgans. The most important factor in investment performance is how the misleadingly low published mintage figures influence potential buyers.

1878

Seven Over Eight Tail Feathers

Typical Mint State Example
MS (63), above average strike,
moderate bagmarks, frosty surfaces,
good luster.

GENERAL DISCUSSION: When the design of the new Morgan Dollar was changed so that the eagle would display seven tail feathers instead of eight, the correction of the reverse dies failed to obliterate the old design entirely. Varying degress of the old design remained and were reproduced on the new coins. Below the seven-feathered eagle's tail can be seen from three to seven tips of the original eight-feather design. The coins with five or more sharp tips visible are more desirable than those with fewer or fainter tips showing. A glass (5x is sufficient) is helpful, but not essential, in studying this interesting phenomenon. The 1878 seven-over-eight-feather dollar is the most widely known Morgan variety, and was the first major variety to be discovered and publicized. The stronger undertips are somewhat sheltered by the design, and therefore are clearly in evidence even on circulated coins. Therefore, circulated examples in as low as Very Fine condition command a significant premium over common dates.

A number of sub-varieties exist. Two that have consistently realized a significant premium in price are the doubled "LIBERTY" (VAM 38) and the "doubled legs" (VAM 43). The easiest way to discern a "doubled legs" coin is to examine the field to the right of the eagle's left leg. Extra wrinkles will be visible in the field. Comparison with a normal coin is helpful.

This variety is, of course, here to stay. It is listed in the Guide Book and is widely accepted and sought by collectors. However, the future may well see a definite trend away from the very weak varieties (i.e., those with few and/or indistinct undertips) and toward those with diagnostic characteristics readily apparent. Within these parameters, the 1878 seven-over-eight-feather dollar will no doubt persist in being the most valuable of the three major categories of Morgans of this year.

Note: To save time and space, coin dealers' advertisements usually use the abbreviations 8F, 7/8F and 8F to denote the varieties.

RARITY IN PROOFLIKE: Although sometimes available for a nominal premium, an 1878 seven-over-eight feather dollar with prooflike surfaces is a legitimately difficult coin to locate. When described as "prooflike," the surfaces are most often deeply reflective. In other words, stretching the term is not usually a problem with this issue. Prooflikes are normally moderately bagmarked and are of the weaker undertips varieties.

RARITY IN SUPERB CONDITION: Bagmarks are the key factor in locating a superior example. Strike is rarely a problem. As a percentage of total surviving mint state examples, a superb MS (67) or better eight-feather is slightly scarcer than a seven-over-eight-feather because of its popularity and greater overall rarity, the seven-over-eight will undoubtedly maintain a considerable edge in value.

REDFIELD: No.

PROOFS: None reported nor rumored. Wouldn't it be interesting if one were?

INVESTMENT POTENTIAL: One of the few non-key Morgans that is salable in all mint state conditions. The investor need not feel that he has to wait for a superb coin; he should be quite secure with nice MS (65) specimens. The most important future factor will be the sharpness of the diagnostic feather tips. Coins with a sharp six or seven tips showing are rapidly disappearing from the marketplace. Prooflikes are very underrated.

1878
Seven Tail Feathers

Typical Mint State Example
MS (63), sharp strike, moderate
bagmarks, frosty surfaces, good
luster.

GENERAL DISCUSSION: Although comparative prices and estimated mintages indicate otherwise, the 1878 seven-tail-feather dollar is scarcer than the 1878 eight-feather. At every price level during the last ten years, the seven-feather has been more challenging to locate in gem uncirculated condition than the eight-feather. More accumulations of eight-feather varieties have come upon the market as well.

As on the eight-feather variety, the shallow breast and indistinctly defined feathers should not be confused with a weakly struck coin. These are characteristics of this particular design.

Because the seven-feather version was minted and released in the last eight months of the year, fewer were saved as novelty items. Thus, these coins circulated freely and today are not particularly scarce in non-mint state grades.

As discussed previously, only those seven-over-eight-feather varieties with strong evidence of the old feathers beneath the eagle's tail should be actively sought. This trend will inevitably affect the seven-feather market as well. Seven-over-eights may become even less desirable than a strong seven-feather of the same grade. It may take decades for this trend to be reflected in the relative values of the two varieties.

This issue is often seen with significant bagmarks, though not quite to the extant as is its eight-feather cousin.

RARITY IN PROOFLIKE: At present, a deep mirror 1878 seven-feather dollar can be located with little difficulty. The surfaces on dollars of this issue are usually found either wholly frosty (that is, with no reflective properties, but with a full, original mint luster) or entirely prooflike.

RARITY IN SUPERB CONDITION: Although by no means common, MS (67) examples arise occasionally. As with most dates of the series, such outstanding quality invariably demands a commensurate price.

REDFIELD: No.

PROOFS: Proof specimens of the 1878 seven-feather dollar are extremely scarce (mintage: 300), and superb proofs are very rare. The most outstanding example seen by the authors was a splendidly toned, nearly perfect coin sold privately to a Texas collector in 1977. As a proof, it is many times rarer than the 1895, and is third in rarity only to the 1878 round breast (see the discussion under the following date) and a true, non-Zerbe proof 1921 (see discussion under 1921). Another superb, beautifully toned specimen surfaced in the summer of 1981, and was offered in a Steve Ivy Rare Coin Company fixed price list. Another was sold in a 1982 Southeby's sale.

INVESTMENT POTENTIAL: The price of 1878 seven-feather dollars should continue to increase relative to the 1878 eight-feather. A minor factor to consider is the date's inclusion in *all* Morgan Dollar collections. Some albums, notably the Dansco series, omit the eight feather and seven over eight varieties, and list merely "1878." It is also popular with date set (one coin of each year) collectors. Both these considerations are negligible, however, when compared to the overall future performance of Morgan Dollars as a series.

1878

Seven Tail Feathers, Round Breast

Typical Mint State Example
MS (65), strong strike, light to
moderate bagmarks, semiprooflike
surfaces, excellent luster.

GENERAL DISCUSSION: This major variety is also known as 1878, third reverse, or 1878, reverse of 1879. Van Allen and Mallis refer to it as 1878 7 TF SAF (1878 seven-tail feathers, slanted-arrow-feather). But Miller uses round breast, and we have followed suit, because it seems the simplest and most descriptive.

The round breast used on this issue and on all subsequent issues, save one, until 1921, is not the only difference from that used on other 1878 dollars, as Van Allen and Mallis point out:

> The number of tail feathers remained at seven but the eagle's breast was rounded and the top arrow feather was slanted. In addition, the A of AMERICA no longer touched the eagle's wing, the eagle's beak was less hooked, the rim was wider, and the wing feathers near the eagle's body were slightly changed.

Obviously, the rounded breast is the most notable change, and is the reason for the variety's widespread distinction today.

Because today's sophisticated collectors and investors are more observant and knowledgeable then those of yesteryear, there is considerbly greater demand for a major variety such as the 1878 round breast. Thus, many thousands of these coins have emerged "from the woodwork," in the last decade or so. The appearance of more coins has subsequently encouraged a brisker market and increased transactions. In turn, more collectors have been created. As the chicken created the egg (or was it vice versa?), so the appearance of more coins can create an increased demand for them.

The Philadelphia minters exercised their coining skills well with the new dies. Poorly struck examples of this issue are scarce. If only later crews of workers had endeavored to match this performance!

This variety is very important and popular, since it marks a significant transition in the development of the design of the Morgan Dollar.

RARITY IN PROOFLIKE: Unlike its 1878 predecessors, this issue is more often seen with semiprooflike surfaces than with reflective, mirrorlike fields. A coin with deep mirror surfaces on both sides should garner the utmost respect from experienced prooflike collectors. When such a specimen is located, it is usually refreshingly well struck and exhibits relatively light surface contact marks. Perhaps the finest known prooflike is a coin that our good friend Bruce Amspacher fondly recalls selling in the early 1970s for the then awesome price of $250. "And it was a good deal then," he asserts.

RARITY IN SUPERB CONDITION: Since this issue's comparative quality is a cut above the average Morgan, MS (67) examples can be located with some regularity. Any superior to that level are numismatic treasures.

REDFIELD: No.

PROOFS: A proof 1878 round breast is one of the greatest rarities of the Morgan series. If more collectors included proofs in their sets, the 1878 round breast proof could be the most valuable coin in the entire collection. Numismatic *extraordinaire* Walter Breen, in his exhaustive work entitled *ENCYCLOPEDIA OF UNITED STATES AND COLONIAL PROOF COINS*, lists three known specimens, but indicated the third coin may be a repeated offering of one of the first two. The third piece is definitely not the example listed as number two, which was sold in Bowers and Ruddy's Stanislaw Herstal Sale (February, 1974) for $4,600 to California dealer Harlan White, a specialist in proof Morgans. At one time, Mr. White also owned the third example, and has seen one or two others. He maintains that the Herstal coin, which ultimately sold for a five-figure price, is the finest known. So the minimum number known is three, and the true number is more likely about five. The authors would not be surprised if there is not an equal number hidden in old collections, bringing the estimated specimens to ten.

Only time will tell if others will emerge. When and if they do, they will surely command the utmost respect from serious Morgan Dollar enthusiasts.

INVESTMENT POTENTIAL: There is no indication that the popularity of this major variety will decrease in the future, so its investment outlook is bright. Also, a high percentage of surviving mint state examples are MS (65) or better, enabling an above average number of transactions to take place. Since the natural tendency of any numismatic transaction is to drive the price upward, this date should do very well indeed.

1878-S

Typical Mint State Example
MS (63), sharp strike, moderate to
heavy bagmarks, frosty or semiprooflike surfaces, excellent luster.

GENERAL DISCUSSION: The 1878-S has never been a difficult coin to locate in mint state condition. In circulated grades it is regarded as a common date. It should carry very little premium over common coin values in MS (60) or even MS (63). In grades of MS (65) or better, however, the buyer can expect to pay a substantial premium over common price.

Branch mint coins of San Francisco and Carson City did not undergo the same variety changes and design modifications as did their Philadelphia counterparts. All 1878-S Dollars have seven tail feathers in the eagle's tail and a concave eagle's breast, the same design used on the 1878 seven-feather described earlier. Perhaps problems of transportation and communications prevented the western mints from following suit in modifying the designs. In fact, as we will learn later, the San Francisco and Carson City Mints each employed a reverse die used in 1878 to strike coins bearing later dates.

Although one would think that eager westerners would have necessitated the release of virtually all of the 1878-S dollars as they were produced, many thousands of coins have been stored in bag quantities over the decades. Even before the appearance of the coins included in the Redfield hoard, bags of this date caused no appreciable impact when they were traded. Like many dates that were commonly traded and stored in bags, 1878-S is seen with more than its fair share of bagmarks.

RARITY IN PROOFLIKE: The 1878-S is quite common with semiprooflike or fully prooflike surfaces. However, since this issue so often is heavily bagmarked, the fragile fields on a prooflike specimen often appear horribly abraded. A gem, MS (65) or better example with mirror surfaces can be considered a mild challenge to locate.

RARITY IN SUPERB CONDITION: A collector can expect to acquire an MS (67) example with relative ease. Superior specimens occasionally arise, with a greater frequency than the vast majority of other Morgans with relatively low price tags. Some of these special coins are spectacularly toned and command a huge premium when sold. One of the harbingers of the quality craze in Morgan Dollars was a beautiful, nearly perfect 1878-S offered in the Stanford Sale (Steve Ivy Numismatic Auctions, July, 1977). It brought a then impressive $135.

REDFIELD: Yes, and among the very worst group of coins in the entire hoard. Scarcely a roll of MS (65) coins could have been assembled from the bags the authors personally examined. There might have been a few prooflikes, but the degree of bagmarks present made the status of the surfaces immaterial.

INVESTMENT POTENTIAL: This issue was given a mild shot in the arm by the promoters of 1878 anniversary sets of Morgan Dollars. Thus a small percentage of its future potential can be regarded as having been used in advance. All things considered, the date should perform in an average fashion relative to the rest of the series.

Heavily bagmarked coins should be treated as common bulk mint state dollars. If possible, investment should be restricted to MS (65) or better examples, whether they be prooflike or frosty.

1878-CC

Typical Mint State Example
MS (63), sharp strike, moderate bagmarks, frosty surfaces, good luster.

GENERAL DISCUSSION: Before the discovery and sale of the U.S. Treasury-held Carson City Silver Dollars from 1972-1974 and 1980-1981, 1878-CC was the most common CC dollar. The enormous quantities of 1882, 1883 and 1884 dollars from the same mint included in the General Service Administration's sale of the Treasury dollars has now made 1878-CC the fourth most common Carson City cartwheel in mint state condition. In circulated grades, it remains the most common.

All examples of this issue utilize the seven-feathered eagle with the concave breast as the reverse device. Some 1880-CC dollars were struck using the reverse die of 1878.

Silver Dollars from the Carson City Mint have always held a unique fascination for collectors and non-collectors alike. The nostalgia and *wanderlust* caused by daydream fantasies of the Old West can be held in an ounce of minted silver when one is the owner of a CC dollar. Thus, all silver dollars from this mint are subject to an extra measure of demand from the CC collector. The authors have seen hundreds of the Nevada-shaped plastic holders containing one each of the thirteen years of CC Morgans.

RARITY IN PROOFLIKE: As a percentage of the total surviving mint state examples, prooflike 1878-CC's are not scarce. Some prooflike pieces have very broad rims that almost seem to frame the mirrored fields. New England Rare Coin Galleries purchased and subsequently sold, on an individual basis, a small hoard of 1878-CC dollars that contained at least several dozen of these superb prooflikes. Each of the coins examined possessed some degree of lavender toning on each side. These were atypical of the issue, since most coins with reflective surfaces are considerably bagmarked. A respectable percentage of prooflike coins have at least some cameo effect.

RARITY IN SUPERB CONDITION: Bagmarks prohibit all but a scant proportion of mint state examples of this date from being classified in the MS (67) or higher levels. Strike and luster seldom are problems.

REDFIELD: No.

INVESTMENT POTENTIAL: The GSA sales contained about 50,000 1878-CC's. The winning bid for the date was $16; the minimum bid set by the government was $15. Because all of the coins were sold individually, no large quantities known to the authors overhang the market at this time.

Like all inexpensive Carson City dates, 1878-CC is one of the exceptions to the rule of the saleability of MS (60) or MS (63) Morgans. Even moderately bagmarked examples enjoy considerable demand. Of course, superb examples are in greater demand, and are the coins that should be added to investment portfolios.

1879

Typical Mint State Example
MS (63), average strike, light to
moderate bagmarks, frosty surfaces,
good luster.

GENERAL DISCUSSION: Long considered virtually a common date in mint state condition, the 1879 has undergone a notable adjustment in price in recent years. This upward alignment of value was entirely appropriate, since far fewer uncirculated coins of this date can be found than the amount of common, or even slightly better, dates. Although bag quantities were no doubt saved, they have undoubtedly nearly all been dispersed by now. This date is valued as a common date in circulated grades.

Many examples begin to exhibit some softness on the breast and on the hair curls above Liberty's forehead. The surfaces can exhibit the spectrum of possibilities; some coins have fully frosty surfaces while others may be semiprooflike or deeply reflective. The late William Hall held a dozen or more rolls of mirrored-surfaced coins that he sold to eager dealers at the September, 1977, coin show at the Jack Tar Hotel in San Francisco. None of those coins were as superb as the cameo prooflike example that sold for a then unbelievable $200 at the Long Beach show the following month.

One of the finest known examples of this date is the fantastic cameo prooflike that Wayne Miller used as the plate coin on his popular book.[1] After spirited bidding, the piece brought $855 on the floor of the Roger M. Turner Sale (Steve Ivy Numismatic Auctions, November, 1978).

RARITY IN PROOFLIKE: Coins of this date are often seen with only one side bearing prooflike surfaces. These coins should bear little or no premium over frosty coins, since two-sided prooflikes are available. Occasionally, spectacularly contrasted cameo prooflike specimens come to light, and are quickly spirited away.

RARITY IN SUPERB CONDITION: For the patient collector, an MS (65) or superior 1879 will be among the least of his worries. Unfortunately, some of the least bagmarked specimens seen have a tendency to be softly struck.

REDFIELD: No.

PROOFS: The Guide Book lists the mintage at 1,100, but Breen corrects that figure to 650, which seems much more in line with the frequency of appearance. As far back as the 1890s and as recently as the 1950s, 1879 carried a premium in proof. Since all but a few Morgans in proof are today priced as type coins, this is no longer the case.

An unimpaired proof 1879 is usually a beautiful coin with excellent contrast between frosted devices and deep fields.

INVESTMENT POTENTIAL: Investment in this issue is neither particularly risky nor exceptionally promising. While some nice prooflike and/or superb, MS (67) specimens are available for the time being, present price trends already indicate that such coins will bring the highest premiums in the future. Inferior graded pieces below the MS (65) level should not be considered for investment purposes.

---

[1] All references to Wayne Miller plate coins mean those used in his book's original edition.

1879-O

Typical Mint State Example
MS (65), above average strike, light
to moderate bagmarks, frosty
surfaces, excellent luster.

GENERAL DISCUSSION: In characterizing the typical mint state example, the authors had to be careful to take into account all of the thousands of uncirculated coins they have examined in their experience. With the increased emphasis on quality Morgan collectors are exerting upon the market today, many of the superior, mark free examples that were relatively commonplace years ago have all but disappeared. What remains today are a group of bagmarked, average strike coins, and many unmarked examples that are a slight rub away from mint state. The fact is that 1879-O's are one date that are either all there or they aren't. That is, they are usually found in either MS (65) or better or in AU (55) or MS (60).

The reader should not infer from the above paragraph that a quantity of superb 1879-O's are apt to come upon the market at any given time — such is not the case at all. The MS (67) coins once prevalent were secreted away usually one or two at a time. Even if there were a large hoard of superb pieces unleashed upon the market, the net effect would be a stimulating, not depressing, one. Redfield and other occasions for wholesale promotion of coins (not only dollars) have taught that one sure way for a specific issue to increase in price is for a large quantity to ''come out of the woodwork'' and fall into dealers' hands.

But back to the issue at hand — 1879-O dollars. They are generally well struck, although some may be seen with a soft eagle's breast. The surfaces are typically frosty, but may be semiprooflike or prooflike with regularity.

This is the first Morgan Dollar struck at the New Orleans Mint. The mintmark ''O'' would continue to be placed upon coins of the denomination and design for twenty-five uninterrupted years. Although the New Orleans Mint performed excellent workmanship during its first year of Morgan production, the quality of its output soon began to deteriorate. As we will discuss later, the New Orleans Mint unwittingly peeved the collectors of today by striking the worst examples of this noble series produced by any of the five mints.

RARITY IN PROOFLIKE: Although scarce, prooflike 1879-O's represent a relatively high percentage of the surviving mint state specimens of the date. Nonetheless, they have been known to command substantial premiums. This phenomenon of overrating a relatively common coin because it comes from a relatively tough mint will be discussed in connection with several dates of Morgans, typically from the New Orleans Mint. As a percentage of surviving mint state coins, prooflike 1879-O's are the most common New Orleans dollar with prooflike surfaces.

RARITY IN SUPERB CONDITION: Although a superb MS (67) or better coin may not be easy to find at any given point in time, rest assured that they do exist. Some of the nicest, frostiest Morgans emanated from New Orleans in 1879, and survive somewhere today. It was not at all unusual in the early seventies to see solid rolls of predominantly MS (67) 1879-O. Even the most fastidious collector, with patience, can find a pleasing, affordable representative.

REDFIELD: No.

PROOFS: At least four *bona-fide* branch mint proofs of this date are known. An unknown number were struck on the occasion of the reopening of the New Orleans Mint on February 20, 1879. As Breen states, "They compare well with Philadelphia proofs."

INVESTMENT POTENTIAL: As more and more superb coins are removed from numismatic circulation, the price of these MS (67) and better coins should continue to rise. No matter what the Morgan series does as a whole in the future, the performance of the 1879-O should favorably compare.

1879-S

Typical Mint State Example
MS (65), sharp strike, light
bagmarks, semiprooflike surfaces,
excellent luster.

GENERAL DISCUSSION: This issue is a refreshing departure from the norm for the Morgan Dollar series. Skillfully manufactured and stored in roll and bag quantities during the decades, many thousands of superb 1879-S's have survived for numismatists' pleasure today. No matter what budget a collection of Morgans is based upon, chances are that it will include an 1879-S in at least MS (65) condition.

This date is readily available with either frosty or semiprooflike surfaces. Many semiprooflikes are offered as "prooflike." Contrary to popular belief, true, deep mirror prooflikes are not so very common. Such deeply reflective coins command substantial premiums.

The 1879-S is considered a common date in circulated condition.

RARITY IN PROOFLIKE: The 1879-S is not rare in prooflike condition, and is quite common with semiprooflike surfaces. These semiprooflike coins have such abundant luster that dealers often stretch the term "prooflike" just a little and classify them as such. Deeply mirrored and/or cameo prooflike examples are not as common as generally thought. While not especially difficult to locate, they are much scarcer than 1880-S or 1881-S Morgans in the same condition.

RARITY IN SUPERB CONDITION: Fortunately for collectors of the Morgan Dollar series, a few dates can be easily located in superb condition for a modest price increment over average coins. The 1879-S is certainly one of these.

REDFIELD: Yes. The Redfield Hoard contained multiple bags of 1879-S's. They were fairly typical in quality, and were distributed very quickly, primarily through Paramount International Coin Corporation. Once the common date coins reached retail distributors such as Paramount, they were received eagerly by collectors and investors who wanted some inexpensive representatives of the highly publicized accumulation of silver dollars. Paramount soon sold its initial allotment, and reordered until all of the available 1879-S's were depleted through Phase I of A-MARK's marketing plan.

INVESTMENT POTENTIAL: Bagmarked or otherwise sub-par coins of this date should be ignored for investment purposes, unless one wishes to invest in common bulk silver dollars. Examples of 1879-S in MS (63) or lesser quality should not sell for a premium over any other common date dollar.

It is highly likely that bag quantities of 1879-S still exist, but the number of surviving mint state examples is so high and so well distributed that no possible quantities released on the market in the future could have a negative effect upon the price.

While superb examples are available, they should be strongly considered for long term investment potential. The authors believe that superb Morgans are a disappearing breed. Less than one percent of the extant uncirculated population of this series can be graded as MS (67) or better. The investor who has any of these superior coins in his safety deposit box should feel confident in his selection.

1879-S
Concave Breast

Typical Mint State Example
MS (63), sharp strike, moderate
bagmarks, semiprooflike surfaces,
excellent luster.

GENERAL DISCUSSION: This major variety is also known as 1879-S flat breast; 1879-S second reverse; 1879-S, reverse of 1878; and 1879-S 7 TF PAF (seven tail feathers, parallel arrow feathers). To be consistent with our description of the 1878 seven-tail feather, round breast, and since the word "flat" in silver dollar vernacular most often refers to the quality of strike rather than a variety, we have chosen "concave breast" to denote this variety.

Prior to the release of the coins of this issue from the LaVere Redfield estate, there was not a sufficient quantity available to maintain an active market. Although, as Miller points out, the variety became widely known in the 1960s, it wasn't until 1976 that it really gained a foothold in the Morgan series.

Still, it is not nearly as popular as the 1878 round breast. One factor that causes its relative unpopularity is the poorer quality of the 1879-S coins. Most of the pieces offered today no doubt emanated from the Redfield Hoard. Like many dates contained therein, this issue was considerably bagmarked. The overall quality of the 1879-S concave breast is about two-and-one-half points below that of the 1878 round breast. This variety is exactly parallel to the 1878 round breast and is of equal importance. Time will inevitably bring about an equalization in acceptance by collectors.

This variety is uncommon in circulated condition.

RARITY IN PROOFLIKE: The 1879-S concave breast is scarce in prooflike condition, although a relatively high percentage of mint state examples exhibit semiprooflike surfaces.

RARITY IN SUPERB CONDITION: Since most of the supply of this issue originates from the Redfield estate, it is very uncommon to find an MS (67) or better piece.

REDFIELD: Yes. At least two bags were sold to Leon Hendrickson (SILVERTOWNE) of Winchester, Indiana. There is no doubt that these bags came from the Redfield Hoard. More might have been included. The bags that Mr. Hendrickson bought were quickly wholesaled and subsequently distributed evenly through retail outlets. Unless more remain unreleased from Redfield, there are no known significant quantities that may potentially affect the market.

The Redfield 1879-S concave breast coins were consistent in their quality, and closely resemble the typical mint state example.

INVESTMENT POTENTIAL: As Morgan Dollar collectors continue their inexorable growth in both numbers and knowledge, varieties such as the 1879-S concave breast can only grow in popularity. Thus, keeping in mind these collectors' thirst for high quality coins, solid MS (65) or better specimens of this date have the potential to perform very well. If such lofty quality proves impractical to obtain, keep in mind that this is one of the few Morgan issues that enjoys considerable demand in any mint state condition. It is very easy for authors and "investment specialists" to recommend only the highest quality coins available. It is quite another story to implement this philosophy and to fill a portfolio with superb pieces at affordable prices. The over-cautious investor may pass up reasonable buys in an unreasonable attempt to obtain only nearly perfect coins. While we also recommend buying the highest quality coins as is practical, we do not recommend that good investments be sacrificed in the process.

1879-CC

Typical Mint State Example
MS (60), average strike, heavy
bagmarks, frosty or semiprooflike
surfaces, poor to good luster.

GENERAL DISCUSSION: Chronologically speaking, 1879-CC is the first key date in the Morgan series. Unlike its 1878 predecessor, the 1879-CC issue was almost entirely released into circulation. Once in circulation, the coins were heavily used in the everyday business and commerce of the Old West. This use is evident in the price structure of circulated examples: Coins that grade Very Fine or worse are readily available at a modest premium; those Extremely Fine or Almost Uncirculated are in more precious supply.

A few bags of 1879-CC dollars were not released into circulation and were held apparently as reserves for paper money. Four bags made their way to the U.S. Treasury in Washington, D.C., where they were discovered, along with thousands of other bags of Carson City dollars, during the Treasury's liquidation of its silver dollar holdings in 1964. When the numismatic and historic value of the CC's was discovered, they were segregated from other coins (mostly New Orleans minted dollars) and eventually sent to West Point, New York. There they awaited their eventual promotion and sale by the General Services Administration.

At the time of the initial GSA sale in 1972, a frequent topic of discussion among dollar enthusiasts was the effect that the sale would have upon the hobby in general, and, in particular, what the reaction would be in the marketplace to the hoard of 4,000 1879-CC's. When the government's marketing plans were learned, many experts believed that the 1879-CC's would "go begging" because of the $300 minimum bid placed upon this key date. The minimum bid conservatively approximated the 1972 wholesale price for a gem specimen. The same experts generally agreed that the net effect of the entire sale upon the dollar hobby would be a positive one, with many thousands of new dollar collectors being launched. They were right about the new dollar collectors; they were wrong about the 1879-CC's.

Those who placed their bids at the minimum $300 level were left out — no 1879-CC's for them. In fact, a bid of $360 was necessary to procure a specimen. The price of 1879-CC's has been increasing ever since. Not only did the simultaneous appearance of nearly 4,000 coins not depress the price, but the additional stimulus of more transactions, plus the increased number of potential buyers created by the sale itself, drove the price upward. This trend has been repeated time and time again in the coin business. (There is a limit to everything, though, as evidenced by the release of thousands of 1903-O dollars in 1964. That coin went from a thousand dollar coin to a forty dollar coin very quickly. The number of existing 1903-O dollars in mint state was just too small, and the number released too large for the market to do anything else. Also, the demand for uncirculated dollars then was probably only about ten percent of what it is today.)

In general, the 1879-CC issue is seen in very poor mint state quality. Because key dates are generally overgraded more often than less expensive coins, many 1879-CC's that have been advertised as "GEM BU," "Superb," MS (67) etc. technically have actually been of a lower grade. The *typical* mint state example is only MS (60), but *any* 1879-CC dollar in uncirculated condition is a very scarce coin and one that any collector should not be ashamed to own.

Most coins of this production were well struck, but many emanated from badly worn dies. Thus, no matter what pressure was exerted upon the surfaces of the planchets when they were minted, not all of the intended details were produced. Although a "weakly struck" coin might be technically not the same as one "struck from worn dies," the net effect is essentially the same, and numismatists' vocabularies have evolved to make the two categories coincident. In any case, it is unusual to examine an 1879-CC with full, sharp breast feathers on the eagle and full hair detail above Liberty's ear.

Bagmarks plague the issue. These telltale signs of contact with other coins, ever-present to some degree on all non-proof Morgans, are usually small but numerous on 1879-CC's. Many coins of this issue have a "peppered" look to their surfaces, a result of hundreds of tiny bagmarks. It is not unusual for a large milling mark (a mark incurred when the reeded edge of one dollar is impressed with considerable force into the surface of another) or two to be present as well.

There is one important variety of 1879-CC dollars. Van Allen and Mallis refer to it as a large CC over small CC. It is more commonly advertised by dealers as "capped dies," "crumbled dies" or "crumbled mintmark." Van Allen's and Mallis' inferred explanation of the variety is that a larger CC mintmark was punched into the die over an existing smaller one. The result was a mintmark that appears to be doubled and surrounded in the immediate vicinity by some porosity or pitting. The VAM book makes no mention of crumbled, capped nor rusted dies. The authors have never heard a plausible explanation of the origin nor exact numismatic meaning of the word "capped" with reference to this coin. We assume it refers to the appearance that the larger mintmark covers, or "caps," as in a hat, the smaller one. Because the terminology is widely accepted, we will employ it.

EXPLODING A MYTH

For decades, the capped die 1879-CC has been spurned by collectors, investors and, consequently, by dealers. Coins that exhibit the variety may be worth fifty percent or less of non-capped specimens in similar conditions. The explanation for this is simple and understandable.

Before dollars were as popular as they are today, little was known about varieties and diagnostic characteristics of the various dates and mints. Unfortunately, counterfeiting and altering dollars preceded the knowledge to combat these practices. Thus, when a collector of yesteryear examined an 1879-CC (a valuable key since the early 1900s) with the capped mintmark characteristic, he was prone to suspect the worst — that the owner of the coin was trying to dupe him into buying an 1879 Philadelphia dollar with an added CC mintmark. Of course, he refused to buy the coin and insisted upon owning a "genuine" piece. Because this scene was repeated hundreds of times during dollar collecting's history, it is not surprising that the capped CC's became less valuable than their uncapped peers.

What *is* surprising is that the disparity in values created in the "Dark Ages" of numismatics persists in today's sophisticated market. Modern dealers and experienced collectors know that not only does the presence of the capped mintmark variety upon an 1879-CC *not* indicate an altered coin, but it guarantees the coin's authenticity! He who is concerned about buying an altered coin should consider this diagnostic characteristic on his prospective purchase a boon and not a bane.

As it happens, the capped-die 1879-CC's, as a group, are inferior in mint state quality to non-capped 1879-CC's. This is not to say that all capped-die coins are poor quality. Some of the nicest examples of this key date examined have been of the capped die type; we are merely stating a general tendency. Certainly, a capped-die specimen should be worth less than a non-capped specimen if it is inferior in quality but it is ludicrous to reduce the value of an 1879-CC by fifty percent merely because it is a specific variety. Some 1909-S VDB Lincoln Cents have a grainy texture beneath the mintmark, but no outcry is heard from specialists in that series when they see such a coin. All genuine 1909-O Half Eagles, a very rare coin, have a doubled mintmark, and gold collectors thank their lucky stars for that; otherwise there would surely be a greater number of bogus coins sold as genuine ones.

Our point is this: The wise collector or investor should not pass up a nice 1879-CC because it has the capped dies. In fact, as we will discuss under INVESTMENT POTENTIAL below, the wise investor may wish to seek out such coins while the present price disparity is so great.

RARITY IN PROOFLIKE: The aforementioned bagmarks that are often present on coins of this issue are compounded by the more vulnerable surfaces of a prooflike piece. The fragile mirror surfaces are more prone to exhibit evidence of contact with other coins than are frosty surfaces. Prooflike 1879-CC dollars are not particularly rare as a percentage of surviving mint state examples, but a nice MS (65) prooflike is a tough act to book. Relative to other key dates of the series, 1879-CC should bring a modest premium for prooflike surfaces.

RARITY IN SUPERB CONDITION: Although there are more than a dozen Morgans that outrank the 1879-CC in terms of overall rarity in mint state condition, very few are as difficult to obtain in superb MS (67) condition. The existence of a superior example is, at the optimum, a remote possibility.

REDFIELD: Yes. The Redfield Hoard contained about four hundred pieces, all of which were of the capped-die variety. None of the coins graded better than MS (63), and none were prooflike. It is unlikely that the hoard contained any further quantities of this date.

INVESTMENT POTENTIAL: This date has a positive price history despite one major (GSA Sale) and one minor (Redfield) influx of coins into the market. Because of the near impossibility of locating a sufficient number of superb pieces to satisfy today's quality conscious collectors, MS (65) and even top-of-the-line MS (63) pieces should perform the best in the future. As mentioned previously, some consideration should be given to seeking out MS (65) examples with the "capped die" characteristic. Time will surely lessen, though it will probably never close completely, the price gap between capped and non-capped coins of the same grade. Investment in typical, MS (60) capped die coins is not recommended.

1880

Typical Mint State Example
MS (63), average strike, moderate
bagmarks, frosty surfaces, good
luster.

GENERAL DISCUSSION: In many ways, this issue represents a good overall average of the Morgan series. Most specimens are fairly well struck, though slightly soft strikes are commonplace. The luster is always good but hardly ever exceptional. Bagmarks are usually of average size and density. One out-of-the-ordinary characteristic of the 1880 is its scarcity in prooflike condition.

In mint state condition 1880 is a slightly better date. In MS (65) condition or better, it carries a premium of roughly three times greater than a common date. This issue is readily available in circulated grades and carries very little or no premium as such.

The 1880 was saved to some extent in bag quantities. A bag was sold on the West coast in December, 1978. A notable bag, consisting primarily of prooflikes, surfaced in 1971. Wayne Miller states that "Specimens from this hoard ... were gorgeous cameos." A Texas collector who is well known to the authors was fortunate enough to have cherry-picked a roll of cameo prooflikes from this bag. He has repeatedly rejected generous offers for the purchase of that roll.

One-sided prooflikes are often seen. Usually the obverse has full-mirror fields while the reverse is completely frosty.

It is interesting to note that the Philadelphia Mint generally did excellent work in 1880. Such issues as the Shield Nickel, Liberty Seated Dime, Quarter and Half Dollar and the Gold Dollar are particularly outstanding in their average quality. The Mint struck more dollars this year than any other denomination besides the Cent piece. Apparently overworked dies account for the lack of craftsmanship accorded the other denominations.

Overdates have been discovered and are listed as 1880, 8-over-7. Their characteristics are quite weak, however, and the coins have not been well received by collectors. Published catalog prices seem exorbitant.

RARITY IN PROOFLIKE: This date, despite the appearance of the prooflike bag in 1971, is still quite scarce on today's market in gem prooflike condition. It ranks slightly behind 1889, and thus is the second toughest Philadelphia issue of the 1880s to locate with mirror surfaces.

RARITY IN SUPERB CONDITION: While difficult to acquire, the persistent searcher can still locate superb MS (67) examples of 1880 Morgan Dollars. Unfortunately, it seems that many of the coins that are superior in the bagmark category are deficient in quality of strike. A specimen that exhibits both sharp strike and minimum bagmarking can be considered a challenge to find. As with the vast majority of Morgans, coins better than MS (65) are rare.

REDFIELD: No.

PROOFS: More proof Morgans were minted this year than during any other. Despite the larger number of coins produced, the personnel responsible performed their jobs quite admirably. Many of the proofs from 1880 are gorgeous cameos. As with every date of proof

Morgan Dollar, most have been cleaned or at least lightly mishandled at some point in their history.

INVESTMENT POTENTIAL: This date, along with other non-common coins in the 1880s from Philadelphia, has undergone considerable price increases during the last four years. Although this increase was long overdue, it is difficult to assess what further movements may be expected. Suffice it to say, the 1880 should perform in at least an average fashion relative to the performance of the series as a whole. Superb MS (67) examples will be in great demand and in short supply in the future, as they are now.

1880-O

Typical Mint State Example
MS (65), above average strike,
moderate bagmarks, frosty surfaces,
excellent luster.

GENERAL DISCUSSION: The 1880-O is similar to the 1879-O. Mint state specimens that reached the (65) and (67) levels were once almost commonplace; as the popularity of silver dollar collecting grew, these specimens were, naturally, the ones that were removed from the market first. They still exist somewhere, though, and must be taken into account when one enumerates the qualities of the typical mint state example.

Like the 1879-O, very lightly circulated, AU (55) or (58), 1880-O's are abundant, and can appear deceptively gem uncirculated to the novice. Good advice to follow when buying this issue (or any other, for that matter) is to either know and trust your dealer, or be sure you know how to tell the difference between a gem coin and a slider (a choice, almost uncirculated coin). To exercise both precautions is best. To exercise neither is an invitation to disaster.

Coins from this particular date and mint in less than almost uncirculated condition are regarded and valued as common dates.

Note: Some readers may disagree with the authors' assignment of an MS (65) rating to the typical mint state example of this date. This may be because of the abundance of coins that are very close to but not quite mint state. Once those coins are eliminated from consideration, it is our feeling that the typical *mint state* example reaches this level.

Some overdate varieties have been discovered and are listed in the current catalogs, but collectors are reluctant to include them in their sets.

RARITY IN PROOFLIKE: The 1880-O is very scarce with reflective surfaces. When found, however, the fields are often very deeply mirrored, and the devices are frosted. With the drastically increased interest in prooflike Morgan Dollar collecting in the last decade, more prooflike examples have recently come on the market. It remains a popular and high-priced prooflike. The fabulous Miller plate coin brought $1,000, the highest price ever paid for a coin of this date until that time, in the William C. Kerr Sale (Steve Ivy Numismatic Auctions, February, 1979). The piece was described therein as:

"Superb! A fully struck, cameo prooflike, and thus one of the finest known. The all-important cheek of Liberty is virtually mark-free..."

The successful bidder was quite pleased to buy the coin at the thousand dollar figure, for he would have bid considerably more to get it!

RARITY IN SUPERB CONDITION: Although certainly not prevalent on today's market, superb MS (67) examples exist in modest quantities. When found, such pieces are splendidly frosty and lustrous and only very lightly bagmarked.

REDFIELD: No. Except among the circulated and mixed uncirculated bags, no New Orleans Mint dollars are known to have been a part of the Redfield estate.

INVESTMENT POTENTIAL: The fact that this date has undergone considerable increases in value in MS (65) or better condition during the last two years should not deter the wise investor. He should keep in mind that there has been little resistance on the buyer's part to the new prices.

1880-S

Typical Mint State Example
MS (65), sharp strike, light
bagmarks, semiprooflike surfaces,
excellent luster.

GENERAL DISCUSSION: In terms of condition of the extant mint state population, this issue is one of the most outstanding of the entire series. No collection need be without a nice MS (67) example; the collector has either frosty or prooflike coins at his disposal.

Needless to say, 1880-S is a common date in circulated condition. Mint state coins that have been bagmarked to less than MS (65) quality should be regarded as common, bulk mint state dollars which are best suited for speculation rather than investment.

The strike on this issue is invariably bold and the luster is full. As a cameo prooflike, it is the most common of all Morgans on today's market. Despite the relative availability, superb examples continue to post high auction records. This alone is ample testimony to how beautiful an 1880-S can be.

A coin reputed to have been MS (70) apparently traded hands for $750 at a Long Beach convention in fall 1978. One of the authors had seen the coin in a dealer's case at a New York coin show a couple of weeks earlier. It had a price tag of $1,000. The table was unattended at the time and a proper examination of the piece was never possible. Its present whereabouts is unknown. We report the story as we heard it — strictly through the grapevine and unconfirmed. We will say this: if a truly perfect Morgan Dollar exists, it could well be an 1880-S.

Overdates have been reported for this issue. Only the variety referred to as 1880-S, 0-over-9 is detectable with the naked eye; the "9" appears to be a filled portion of the zero of the date. This variety has met with mild acceptance by collectors.

RARITY IN PROOFLIKE: The 1880-S is readily available in prooflike condition. Many prooflikes are beautiful coins with a high degree of contrast between deep mirror fields and frosty white devices.

RARITY IN SUPERB CONDITION: The 1880-S is available in superb MS (67) condition. Such examples are scarce but can still be cherry-picked from original rolls, or purchased from dealers as single pieces.

REDFIELD: The Redfield collection contained several bags of typical uncirculated 1880-S dollars and they were quickly distributed, primarily through Paramount International Coin Corporation.

INVESTMENT POTENTIAL: The potential of this date lies with superb MS (67) or better pieces. Any superb Morgan of particular beauty transcends the customary desire of numismatists to own one coin of each date and mint of a given series. Thousands of people collect superb dollars regardless of date and independent of how many they may already own. Not to be forgotten are basic type collectors. Coins such as superb 1880-S dollars are *apropos* for their collections as well. While 1880-S dollars in outstanding condition may be available for generations to come, we see no reason why the demand cannot keep pace with or surpass the supply.

1880-CC

Typical Mint State Example
MS (63), above average strike,
moderate bagmarks, frosty surfaces,
good luster.

GENERAL DISCUSSION: Because of the sizable number (about 110,000) of 1880-CC dollars distributed by the General Services Administration's sales of the government-held Carson City dollars, and the extent of different overdates and varieties found therein, this date has become the most complicated of all Morgans. This dubious distinction has not altered a basic fact of today's dollar market: The collector generally is more interested in the quality of the coin than he is in its variety.

About ninety percent of the 1880-CC dollars in existence are in mint state condition. Thus, circulated examples command a price that is inordinately high relative to the value of uncirculated pieces.

The number of coins sold through the GSA sales of 1972-74 was huge, but the method by which they were sold (A minimum bid that approximated the then current wholesale price was set for each date of the coins offered; for the 1880-CC, that minimum bid was $60), and the even manner in which they were consequently distributed helped prevent a drastic drop in price. Most of the 1880-CC's in the GSA sale were considerably bagmarked. The surfaces of the coins ranged from frosty to semiprooflike, with very few fully prooflike pieces. Overdates were commonplace, and Van Allen and Mallis painstakingly classified a large sampling of the coins while they were still in Treasury vaults. Their accounts of this research, and of the GSA sales in general, are both educational and entertaining to read.

Of all the overdates reported for 1880 dollars from the four mints that produced them, the ones from Carson City have received the most widespread acceptance among collectors.

RARITY IN PROOFLIKE: The 1880-CC is definitely scarce in prooflike, especially considering the large number of mint state examples extant. It is significantly rarer than the similarly priced 1881-CC and 1885-CC.

RARITY IN SUPERB CONDITION: When a superb 1880-CC dollar emerges, one can safely wager that it did not originate in the GSA holdings. Although statistics dictate that some superb coins had to be present among the more than 100,000 pieces, the ratio is negligible. Nonetheless, MS (67) examples surprisingly are frequently available, although they can by no means be construed common.

REDFIELD: No.

INVESTMENT POTENTIAL: Obviously, ordinary examples of this issue might have a relatively low ceiling on their upward price mobility. By the same token, there is also little risk involved. Superb pieces have the best potential, and nice prooflikes get a hearty vote of confidence. And here's a question to think about: Will there ever be a demand for the GSA dollars in their original, sonically sealed plastic holders? Thousands of these holders and their accompanying Richard Nixon-signed boxes are destroyed every year. It's only a thought; again, the most important consideration is the quality of the merchandise.

Investors should restrict their purchases of this date to MS (65) or better examples and avoid paying significant premiums for varieties at this time. This is not to say that the varieties won't be good investments; they simply do not require a large premium in price in the present market.

1880-CC
Concave Breast

Typical Mint State Example
MS (63), sharp strike, moderate to
heavy bagmarks, frosty surfaces,
good luster.

GENERAL DISCUSSION: Though not listed as a separate, major variety as often as the 1878 round breast or the 1879-S concave breast, the 1880-CC with the concave breast, also known as 1880-CC reverse of 1878, 1880-CC flat breast or 1880-CC 7 TF PAF, meets the same criterion as those two varieties. Each is a numismatic anomaly: an obverse matched with a reverse design that was predominantly used on coins of other years.

Compared to normal 1880-CC's, mint state examples of this issue are marginally inferior in overall quality. Circulated coins of this type are very rare.

Auction records are sketchy, because many catalogers do not differentiate between varieties of 1880-CC dollars. Available records indicate that the true value of this variety is approximately in line with current published prices.

A high percentage, perhaps more than half, of the examples seen of this variety have been overdates.

RARITY IN PROOFLIKE: Although many collectors and specialists still have much to learn about dollar varieties and their relative scarcity in various states, it is already evident that the 1880-CC concave breast is quite scarce, if not rare, in prooflike.

RARITY IN SUPERB CONDITION: At this time, this relatively recently publicized variety appears to be very rare in conditions above MS (65).

REDFIELD: No.

INVESTMENT POTENTIAL: The outlook for this issue can only be bright. If purchased at minimal premiums to the price of a normal, round breast 1880-CC, the investor can enjoy owning a commodity with an extremely low risk factor and an extremely high potential gain. Increased acceptance in the future seems inevitable. The only possible detraction is a "too many cooks spoil the soup" syndrome. If collectors become too confused and frustrated by the multitude of overdates and varieties of 1880-CC, they may reject them entirely. If one survives, however, this will be it.

1881

Typical Mint State Example
MS (63), average strike, moderate
bagmarks, frosty surfaces, excellent
luster.

GENERAL DISCUSSION: This is one of those dates that might sound common enough, but is not easy to locate in MS (65) or better condition. For the time being, however, collectors should have little trouble in locating a specimen that suits them.

Moreso than any of its Philadelphia predecessors, the 1881 can be very weakly struck. At the 1977 American Numismatic Association Convention in Atlanta, nearly a bag of 1881's was wholesaled by a prominent West Coast dealer. Most of these coins were semiprooflike or prooflike, and approximately one-third of them were poorly struck, with no breast feathers on the eagle and virtually no hair curls visible immediately above Ms. Liberty's ear.

In circulated condition, this date is common. In MS (60) or (63), it should command only a small premium over common bulk mint state dollars. In MS (65), however, one can expect to pay a price almost triple that of a common date.

One-sided prooflikes are often seen, and should command little premium unless the obverse is a superb cameo.

RARITY IN PROOFLIKE: The appearance of the bag mentioned above gave many collectors an opportunity to acquire a scarce prooflike example of this date. Although prooflike, few of the coins exhibited either deep mirror surfaces of any appreciable cameo effect. Coins with either of these virtues are scarce; pieces with both attributes are highly desirable.

RARITY IN SUPERB CONDITION: This date is legitimately scarce in grades above MS (65). Occasionally, a superior strike that emits abundant luster can have what collectors refer to as the ''apple cheek'' look. This descriptive term refers to the full, rounded contour of Liberty's cheek on absolutely fully struck Morgan Dollars. Such coins will also exhibit full, pointed breast feathers on the reverse. They invariably command premiums of at least triple the price of an MS (65) coin, and sometimes much more.

REDFIELD: Although a quantity of coins appeared from the West Coast in a timely fashion relative to the dispersal of the Redfield coins, it is unconfirmed any 1881's were included in the original hoard.

PROOFS: The proofs of this year, while slightly scarcer than 1880, are generally not as nice. They lack the cameo effect that is valued so highly on proof Morgans. However, one of the most spectacular cameo Proof Morgan Dollars ever offered at public auction sale was purchased by Wayne Miller from Steve Ivy Numismatic Auctions' 1980 ANA Sale. That piece was dated 1881.

INVESTMENT POTENTIAL: In grades of MS (65), this date should perform on or slightly above a par with the rest of the series. In superb MS (67) condition, the outlook is even brighter.

1881-O

Typical Mint State Example
MS (60), average strike, moderate to
heavy bagmarks, frosty or
semiprooflike surfaces, good luster.

GENERAL DISCUSSION: The 1881-O was withheld from circulation in substantial quantities. Mint state rolls are relatively commonplace. It carries no premium as a circulated dollar, and should cost little or no more than common bulk mint state dollars in MS (60) condition.

This sizable New Orleans issue is consistently impaired by numerous bagmarks. Also distracting from the overall appearance of the coins is a frequent absence of contrast between fields and devices. The abundant semiprooflike examples have exactly the same color, luster and reflectivity over every square millimeter of their surfaces. This characteristic is not as desirable to most dollar enthusiasts as are a frosty white portrait of Liberty and the defiant eagle set against a deep gray metallic background.

Superb MS (67) or better specimens are quite scarce and very underrated. This opinion is well supported by the infrequent auction appearances of truly superb coins, and by the high price realized when one does sell under the hammer.

There are no significant varieties of 1881-O dollars.

RARITY IN PROOFLIKE: While abundant in semiprooflike condition, 1881-O's with deep mirror surfaces are decidedly uncommon, and are highly respected by experienced prooflike collectors. Generally, this is a heavily abraded issue, and the fragile surfaces of a prooflike coin are ever more susceptible to injury than those of a frosty piece.

A superb roll of cameo prooflikes was proudly purchased by a New England collector in early 1979.

RARITY IN SUPERB CONDITION: Superb MS (67) coins seldom appear. MS (69) coins are almost unheard of, and will possess record price potential each time a strictly graded specimen is offered for sale.

REDFIELD: No.

PROOFS: The only known proof was discovered by dealers Mike Follett and Kevin Lipton in the Spring of 1982, and was reportedly sold by them for a high four figure price. That piece was viewed by the authors and definitely exhibited all the characteristics of a proof Morgan. It was very lightly hairlined but presented an excellent overall appearance. The occasion for its minting is not known.

INVESTMENT POTENTIAL: Although not as easy to obtain as one might expect, MS (65) coins are available, and collectors need not settle for anything less. Therefore investment should be directed toward MS (65) or better specimens. The buyer who pays particular attention to bagmarks may be amply rewarded in the future. Coins that are relatively free of bagmarks are scarce, and are constantly being removed from the dollar marketplace.

1881-S

Typical Mint State Example
MS (65), sharp strike, light
bagmarks, semiprooflike surfaces,
excellent luster.

GENERAL DISCUSSION: This issue is plentiful in all mint state grades up to and including MS (67). Any collection that has received any attention from its owner includes a gem MS (65) or better 1881-S.

Circulated examples of this date are valued only because they are silver dollars. Uncirculated examples in MS (60) or (63) should be valued only as common bulk mint state dollars.

The coins of this date often have semiprooflike surfaces, although some excellent frosty specimens are not too difficult to locate. Fully reflective, deeply mirrored coins are available, but not as frequently as 1880-S's. A relatively plentiful number of 1881-S's are sharply contrasted cameos.

Private sales of deep-mirror cameos in superb grades have approached the four hundred dollar level. The incredible MS (69) example photographed by Wayne Miller for use in his outstanding work, *An Analysis of Morgan and Peace Dollars*, was sold for $975 in the C.T. Briggs Sale (Steve Ivy Numismatic Auctions, May, 1979).

RARITY IN PROOFLIKE: The 1881-S is one of the most common Morgan Dollars with prooflike surfaces.

RARITY IN SUPERB CONDITION: The 1881-S is readily available in superb MS (67) condition. Occasionally, an MS (69) specimen is offered and invariably commands a healthy premium.

REDFIELD: Yes. Multiple bags of typical mint state 1881-S's were included in Mr. Redfield's holdings.

INVESTMENT POTENTIAL: This issue is so easily obtainable in nice condition that even MS (65) coins should be primarily regarded as a means to speculate in the short term market. Long range investment plans should seek only MS (67) or better examples. The highly contrasted cameos that are presently offered with some regularity may become harder to get in the future. Coins of this issue will always be widely collected as type coins.

1881-CC

Typical Mint State Example
MS (63), sharp strike, light
bagmarks, frosty or semiprooflike
surfaces, good to excellent luster.

GENERAL DISCUSSION: This issue represents one of Carson City's finest efforts. The overall quality of 1881-CC's is high for any issue of Morgan Dollar, let alone for a production of this branch mint.

A very high percentage of the total 1881-CC population survives in mint state. Therefore, the scarce circulated examples, always in demand by collectors who either want to save a little money or who prefer to assemble well-matched sets of dollars, are priced unusually close to mint state coins.

The General Services Administration's sales of Carson City dollars contained more than 120,000 examples of this date.

Although a substantial number of coins were sold through the government's sales, the millions of dollars spent in promoting the dollars assured a widespread distribution. The minimum bid in the original GSA offering was $60.

RARITY IN PROOFLIKE: The 1881-CC is by no means rare in prooflike condition. The premium associated with a prooflike coin is small compared to that charged for other Carson City prooflikes, with the exception of 1885-CC. Occasionally, highly contrasted, cameo 1881-CC's can be located. These prized coins are the finest representatives available bearing the historic CC mintmark.

RARITY IN SUPERB CONDITION: Very few of the coins sold in the GSA auctions were better than MS (65). Nonetheless, quantities were so huge that a few superb specimens are inevitably available at any given time. Superb pieces usually have semiprooflike surfaces; a wholly frosted MS (67) or better coin is very scarce.

REDFIELD: No.

INVESTMENT POTENTIAL: The impact of the GSA sales will always have an effect on how investors regard the potential of this date. Therefore, the upper limit of this issue's price range has some restrictions not imposed on most other dates. Investors may be wise to seek only superb pieces, and thus be assured of adequate future demand by increasingly quality conscious collectors.

1882

Typical Mint State Example
MS (63), above average strike,
moderate bagmarks, frosty surfaces,
good luster.

GENERAL DISCUSSION: This issue has been preserved in bag quantities of mint state examples. Although original bags are now rare, original mint state rolls are not unusual. Heavily abraded, MS (60) examples should be considered as common bulk mint state dollars. The 1882 carries no premium as a circulated coin.

Coins of this production are usually well struck, and can be among the sharpest Morgans from the Philadelphia Mint. Collectors need not settle for a weakly struck coin.

Several 1882 Morgans of notable quality have been sold at auctions during the last few years. Two of them were in consecutive sales conducted by Steve Ivy Numismatic Auctions. The Turner specimen, sold in November, 1978, was a golden toned, frosty jewel that brought $420, a very strong price for a non-prooflike. The following February, a coin of slightly lesser quality, but with prooflike surfaces, brought $380.

The same company cataloged an MS (65) prooflike specimen in the R.C. Matthews Sale (March, 1980) with the description: "As deeply mirrored as any of several spectacular examples of this date we have offered in past sales. Fully struck. Worth several hundred dollars." The coin realized $850. Almost exactly one year later, the piece reappeared as lot 941 of the University Park Sale (SINAI, March, 1981), and sold for $1,100.

RARITY IN PROOFLIKE: The 1882 is quite scarce with prooflike surfaces. Advertised specimens normally produce multiple orders if the price is consistent with current market conditions. One-sided prooflikes are fairly common, and should not command a substantial premium unless the obverse is a deep cameo and the coin is high in overall quality. Unlike the 1880 and the 1881, no quantities of prooflike pieces have come onto the market in the last decade.

RARITY IN SUPERB CONDITION: Superb 1882 dollars can be especially beautiful, and have realized some impressive prices from both auction and private sales. The buyer should be certain that the dollar he purchases exhibits a full strike and minimal bagmarks.

REDFIELD: No.

PROOFS: While generally excellent as far as surfaces and overall eye appeal are concerned, 1882 proof Morgans can be quite weakly struck. How this could happen to such supposedly meticulously manufactured coins has not been explained. Fully struck, unhairlined cameo gems are rare.

INVESTMENT POTENTIAL: All indications are that this date will continue to emerge from its sleeper role. Superb specimens are occasionally available now, but look for that to change in the future. MS (65) coins are acceptable for long term investment, although MS (67) or better quality may increase in value at a faster rate.

1882-O

Typical Mint State Example
MS (60), average strike, moderate to
heavy bagmarks, frosty or
semiprooflike surfaces, good luster.

GENERAL DISCUSSION: This issue is readily available in roll quantities of mint state coins, and it would not be surprising to hear reports of bags of uncirculated coins. Most coins in original rolls or bags are of Mint State (63) quality or less. Such coins should be valued only as common bulk mint state dollars. The 1882-O commands no premium as a circulated coin.

Dollars of this particular date and mint usually come either with a full, sharp strike or with virtually no high point details; an "in-between" striking is scarcely found. Whether sharply struck or not, 1882-O's are notoriously bagmarked. Bags of this issue must have been transported and roughly handled for many years. A high percentage of the bagmarked coins of this issue may have originated from the Treasury's release of hoards of primarily O-Mint dollars in 1964. The chances are good that most superb pieces were already in collectors' hands by that time, or at least stored in rolls.

In 1882, a reverse die that was intended for use in San Francisco, and thus punched with an "S" mintmark, was rerouted to New Orleans. Before it left the Philadelphia Mint, where all mintmarks were applied to the dies, the appropriate "O" was superimposed on the "S". The result was the first Morgan overmintmark variety. It is referred to as 1882-O-over-S. As Morgan varieties go, it has met with positive acceptance by collectors. Overmintmarks of all series have recently enjoyed considerable publicity and increased demand.

RARITY IN PROOFLIKE: The 1882-O is not particularly scarce in prooflike condition. The aforementioned bagmark problem is magnified on coins with mirror fields. Consequently, attractive prooflikes are difficult to acquire. Approximately 30 rolls of sharply struck, prooflike examples surfaced at the February, 1982, Long Beach, California, numismatic convention. No gems were included.

RARITY IN SUPERB CONDITION: This issue is vastly underrated in superb MS (67) or better condition. We should carefully point out, however, that a lack of marks alone does not qualify a dollar for a runaway price. It must have correspondingly superior strike, luster and an intangible quality that can be best described by the term "character."

REDFIELD: No.

INVESTMENT POTENTIAL: The future price potential for strictly graded MS (65) or better specimens should be good, with a dramatic increase in potential as the quality increases. Only sharply struck coins should be purchased for investment purposes.

1882-S

Typical Mint State Example
MS (65), sharp strike, light
bagmarks, semiprooflike surfaces,
excellent luster.

GENERAL DISCUSSION: This year marks the last of a quartet of consecutive outstanding production efforts by the San Francisco Mint. The 1882-S closely parallels the 1879-S, 1880-S and 1881-S in terms of the quality of the typical mint state example. In terms of availability, the 1882-S is slightly scarcer.

In grades of MS (63) or less, this issue is among the most common of Morgans and should carry no premium.

Bag quantities, disregarding the Redfield Hoard, are probably still extant. Original rolls that contain some superb coins are not unusual.

RARITY IN PROOFLIKE: The 1882-S is common with prooflike surfaces, though examples with deep mirror fields and frosted devices are scarce. Such coins are many times scarcer than the often similarly priced 1880-S and 1881-S.

RARITY IN SUPERB CONDITION: Most collections of Morgans contain a superb example of this date. MS (67) coins are available and can often be cherry-picked from dealers' rolls at a small premium. An MS (69) coin is another story — it is quite scarce and can command a premium of more than five times that of an MS (65).

REDFIELD: At least several bags of 1882-S's were included in Redfield.

INVESTMENT POTENTIAL: For investment potential, this is one of the best of all inexpensive Morgan Dollars. Solid MS (65) or MS (67) coins are available, so nothing of inferior quality need be considered. Original rolls should be examined coin by coin to insure that each piece is of gem quality.

1882-CC

Typical Mint State Example
MS (60), above average strike,
moderate to heavy bagmarks, frosty
surfaces, good luster.

GENERAL DISCUSSION: The 1882-CC will always be primarily known for its prodigious presence in the GSA dollar sales. About 600,000 pieces, or nearly half of the original mintage, were included! About 400,000 coins were sold to bidders submitting a bid of $32 or more. (All coins were sold at $32, even if the bidder was willing to pay more.) Slightly more than 200,000 coins were classified as "mixed," indicating that they did not meet minimum requirements for the uncirculated category. Because the coins were separated under very loose guidelines by inexperienced personnel, virtually all of them were later found, to the delight of the winning bidders, to be mint state as well.

It is safe to say that about ninety percent of all surviving 1882-CC's are in mint state. Therefore circulated coins, which enjoy strong demand, are priced inordinately near mint state value.

The surfaces of virtually all coins of this date from the GSA sale bear considerable bagmarks.

The price history of this issue is particularly interesting. The other two dates present in substantial numbers in the government sale — 1883-CC and 1884-CC — sold for the minimum bid set for all three dates (1882, 1883 and 1884), which was thirty dollars. This undoubtedly occurred because, as huge as the 1882-CC supply was, it was still 150,000 coins short of the number of 1883-CC's available, and 300,000 shy of the supply of 1884-CC's! Thus, because most bidders bid on one coin of each date, the 1882-CC's were the first of the three dates to be sold out.

Immediately following the distribution of the GSA coins, the trio of thirty-dollar-minimum coins equalized in value at around twenty dollars for an average example. With minor exceptions, the values remained the same for about five years; then the 1882-CC began pulling ahead. As it stands now, the 1882-CC enjoys about a twenty percent premium over the still equally valued 1883-CC and 1884-CC.

RARITY IN PROOFLIKE: Although a small percentage of the GSA hoard, a fair number of prooflikes emerged from the government vaults. They are readily available, but nonetheless command a premium of at least fifty percent above a frosty specimen of similar grade. Coins with deep mirror fields and frosty devices are seen with some frequency — certainly moreso than many less expensive dates.

RARITY IN SUPERB CONDITION: The 1882-CC is much rarer in superb condition than it is with prooflike surfaces. Paradoxically, most superb specimens are prooflike. The strike, surfaces and luster of 1882-CC's do not often prevent the MS (67) classification. Bagmarks are the primary detraction.

REDFIELD: No — the government had them all.

INVESTMENT POTENTIAL: Although widely distributed, the huge number of 1882-CC's sold in the GSA sales will always inhibit investors. Superb MS (67) frosty coins, sometimes priced at modest premiums, are worthy of consideration. If anything, the constant appearance of typical coins may reinforce collectors' appreciation of high quality specimens.

1883

Typical Mint State Example
MS (63), above average strike,
moderate bagmarks, frosty surfaces,
good luster.

GENERAL DISCUSSION: Mint state examples of the 1883 Morgan Dollar have been preserved in considerable quantities. A typical collection of primarily uncirculated coins will house an 1883 of at least MS (65) quality. Dollars of this date that grade less than MS (65) should carry little or no premium over common bulk mint state dollars. As a circulated dollar, 1883 is a common issue.

The majority of coins of this date are well struck, though a weakly struck example is certainly not unusual. Bagmarks are consistent both in their presence and in their density — they are neither typically light nor especially heavy. Dollars of this issue often exhibit satin-textured surfaces.

In terms of scarcity, value and the characteristics of the typical mint state example, 1883 dollars can be closely compared to the issue of 1882.

RARITY IN PROOFLIKE: The 1883 is scarce with fully prooflike surfaces. Semiprooflike examples are sometimes classified as prooflike in an attempt to realize the substantial premium that fully mirrored coins rightfully deserve. A semiprooflike coin may be worth as little as one-fifth the price of a real McCoy.

Specimens are occasionally available with excellent contrast between fields and devices. These coins invariably bring a price commensurate with their quality and desirability.

RARITY IN SUPERB CONDITION: The 1883 is legitimately scarce in superb condition, although tens of thousands of mint state examples exist. With patience, however, the collector can expect to find a selection of MS (67) pieces.

REDFIELD: No.

PROOFS: Proofs of this date are fairly typical, and as common as most dates. Inevitably, most were cleaned or slightly mishandled at some point in their history. Slight, but irreversible, damage to the fragile mirror surfaces resulted. Proof 1883 dollars are well struck and, more often than not, toned.

INVESTMENT POTENTIAL: The 1883 has no reason to perform in an inferior way when compared to the Morgan series as a whole. High quality, MS (67) or better coins should perform the best. As with any issue that is generally available in MS (65) grade, most collectors will desire the coin that is a cut above the norm.

1883-O

Typical Mint State Example
MS (63), average strike, moderate
bagmarks, frosty surfaces, good
luster.

GENERAL DISCUSSION: Moreso than any date from any mint that precedes it, the 1883-O runs the gamut from the worst possible to among the best possible in every important category of mint state coins. The strike can be shallow with no breast feathers, or it can be so sharp that the tiny, curled ends of every feather show. Bagmarks can densely cover the surfaces or be nearly totally absent. The surfaces may be frosty, deeply mirrored, or at any point in between. The luster may be dull, or it might be excellent.

Mint state coins are abundantly available. Uncirculated rolls are common. It is reasonable to assume that many bags of 1,000 mint state coins exist. Coins of this date are often used as common bulk mint state dollars. Circulated coins are also among the most common of the series.

Sales records of individual superb pieces are scant, because most auction houses are reluctant to offer such a common date as a single lot. Two noteworthy coins are the Miller plate coin, offered as part of the R.A. Donovan Sale (Steve Ivy Numismatic Auctions, April, 1978); it brought $265. The toned, dazzling prooflike coin in the C.T. Briggs Sale (SINAI, May, 1979) realized $340. That piece was quite likely originally in the estate of a famous singer who began his dollar collecting in the early 1960s when he was paid in bags of dollars as a publicity stunt for an engagement in Las Vegas. A number of 1883-O's in his estate possessed remarkably reflective surfaces that bore bands of rose and lavender toning.

Despite the number of coins available, and the many different dies used to strike them, no major collectible varieties of 1883-O dollars have been discovered.

RARITY IN PROOFLIKE: The 1883-O is one of the most common Morgans with prooflike surfaces. Superb, nearly mark free, deeply mirrored coins are nonetheless scarce.

RARITY IN SUPERB CONDITION: Although once frequently available, MS (67) examples are now very scarce. There are at least a half dozen dates less rare in MS (67) or better condition than is the 1883-O.

REDFIELD: Not beyond the extent to which coins of this date were present in the dozens of bags of common mint state dollars found as part of the Redfield estate.

PROOFS: Walter Breen states that twelve were struck. The noted numismatist states that these branch mint proofs might have been "Made for presentation to officials of some local celebration, possibly having to do with the cotton industry, though equally likely having to do with the establishment of Tulane University as the State University of Louisiana. The only one I have seen "carries its own credentials" like the 1879(O)."[2]

He goes on to state that the coin he verified appeared in a Harmer Rooke auction in November, 1969, and brought $1,600, a price that must have been considered very respec-

[2]Walter Breen, *Encyclopedia of United States and Colonial Proof Coins, 1722-1977* (F.C.I. Press, Albertson, New York, 1977) p.235.

table at that time, for the coin market as a whole was in the doldrums.[3]

Stack's offered a specimen as lot 807 of its H.R. Lee Sale in November, 1947. It was photographed and estimated at $12.50.

INVESTMENT POTENTIAL: Only the *creme de la creme* 1883-O dollar should be considered for investment purposes.

---

[3]Walter Breen, *Encyclopedia of United States and Colonial Proof Coins, 1722-1977* (F.C.I. Press, Albertson, New York, 1977) p.235.

1883-S

Typical Mint State Example
MS (63), sharp strike, moderate
bagmarks, semiprooflike surfaces,
excellent luster.

GENERAL DISCUSSION: The 1883-S Morgan is very scarce in mint state. Very lightly circulated coins, called "sliders," are abundant. Because these coins are not mint state, although they are often offered for sale as such, they were not considered when the authors enumerated the characteristics of the typical mint state example.

This issue marks an abrupt departure from the established consistency of the previous four years of San Francisco dollars. The 1879-1882-S coins are plentiful in mint state and relatively available in superb condition. Not so on either count for the 1883-S.

Partly because of an incorrect association with its San Francisco forerunners, and partly because of the overemphasis historically placed upon mintage figures as an indication of rarity, the 1883-S was one of the most underrated dates of the entire series for decades. Max Humbert, Chairman of Paramount International Coin Corporation, is always outspoken regarding the true rarity of a gem uncirculated 1883-S dollar. He was delighted to obtain the best examples of this issue from the Redfield collection.

The coins that appeared on the market as a result of the distribution of the Redfield collection acted as a catalyst for the price rise of the long dormant issue. Prior to the advent of Redfield (February, 1976), transactions involving true mint state coins were few and far between.

Possibly more than three-fourths of the present available supply of mint state 1883-S's can be traced to Redfield.

The availability of circulated examples is another indication of the coin's scarcity in uncirculated condition. Only coins that reach the almost uncirculated level command a significant premium. Such coins are plentiful; however, their value is understandable because many collectors may find the price of an uncirculated coin prohibitive but still desire to obtain the highest possible quality that they can afford.

The authors have seen bogus 1883-S's fabricated by adding an "S" mintmark to an 1883 Philadelphia coin. Because the general characteristics of a Philadelphia Morgan differ considerably from those of a San Francisco coin, a Morgan Dollar expert can quickly detect these spurious specimens. It is suggested that coins from this issue be purchased from reliable dealers, or that they be submitted to the American Numismatic Association Certification Service (ANACS) for verification of their authenticity.

RARITY IN PROOFLIKE: The prooflike 1883-S commands about a fifty percent premium over a frosty example of similar quality. This premium would be higher were not semiprooflike examples often sold as prooflikes. Several cameo prooflikes have been seen, the best of which was sold to a dealer for $850 at the suburban Washington D.C. show in February, 1979. That same coin is worth several times that amount today.

RARITY IN SUPERB CONDITION: This issue is rare in superb MS (67) condition. The authors are not aware of an MS (69) specimen; if one surfaced it would be met with overwhelming demand. Bagmarks prohibit all but a very few of the Redfield coins from reaching the superb level. The mint state coins that were avaiable prior to Redfield were as heavily bagmarked, if not moreso, than the hoarded coins.

REDFIELD: Paramount International Coin Corporation obtained several hundred fully struck, predominantly MS (65) examples from the Redfield estate.

INVESTMENT POTENTIAL: Despite the appearance of the Redfield coins, the 1883-S remains an important key date in the Morgan series. The new collectors created in the last decade by the GSA sales and by promotion of the Redfield estate far outnumber the "fresh" 1883-S's that have come onto the market. Although the date has shown some price spurts and drops in the past (most dates have), it has generally been underrated and is only lately realizing its potential. Typical mint state examples might have exhausted most of this potential, but solid MS (65) coins should continue to perform well. If an MS (67) example becomes available at a reasonable price, the astute investor should not hesitate to purchase it.

1883-CC

Typical Mint State Example
MS (63), above average strike,
moderate bagmarks, frosty surfaces,
good luster.

GENERAL DISCUSSION: About 750,000 pieces of 1883-CC Morgan Dollars were included in the General Services Administration's sales. This number represented an incredible sixty-two percent of the original mintage!

As with the other dates sold as part of the massive program, a limit of one to a customer was imposed. Many people successfully skirted the limit and bought more than one coin of a date by placing bids under the names of friends, neighbors, the family dog, etc. When the mailing list of successful Carson City dollar bidders was made available some four years after the initial sale, it was found that some addresses were listed as many as seventeen times! The distribution of such an immense number of dollars nevertheless might be considered quite thin, and a double blessing to the numismatic marketplace. Not only did the market value of the coins hold up surprisingly well, but many new collectors were also created.

Circulated examples of this issue are, understandably, scarcer than mint state coins. Collectors who are only interested in filling a space in their collections, or who desire a well-matched set of circulated coins, create a moderate demand that is sufficient to make the value of circulated pieces very near that of MS (60) coins. An almost uncirculated (AU) coin is valued at approximately seventy percent of the price of an MS (60) specimen. As a contrast, an AU 1883-S may be worth only twenty percent of the value of an uncirculated example.

Most examples of this issue are well struck. Bagmarks are ever-present, sometimes to a serious degree.

RARITY IN PROOFLIKE: Some deeply reflective prooflike examples were sold to lucky bidders in the GSA sales. Many of these prooflike coins are attractive cameos. However, bagmarks often mar the fragile surfaces. Overall, the 1883-CC is only moderately scarce in prooflike, and one can easily be purchased for a moderate premium over a frosty coin.

RARITY IN SUPERB CONDITION: A random sampling of the three Carson City issues present in the largest quantities (1882, 1883 and 1884) in the GSA sales may indicate that the 1883 is slightly more common than the other two in superb MS (67) or better condition. Bagmarks are the usual deterrent to a classification above the MS (65) level.

REDFIELD: No.

PROOFS: Breen reports one unverified example.

INVESTMENT POTENTIAL: This date has some obvious drawbacks. The huge quantity sold by the government will no doubt weigh heavily on investors' minds. One would expect this issue to perform in a sub-par fashion relative to the Morgan series as a whole.

1884

Typical Mint State Example
MS (63), above average strike,
moderate bagmarks, frosty surfaces,
good luster.

GENERAL DISCUSSION: The 1884 is the scarcest mint state Morgan Dollar of the 1880s from the Philadelphia Mint.

Because today's market is much broader than it has ever been in the past, prices are undergoing a long overdue realignment. Some of the gross disparities that have persisted for decades are being corrected by the burgeoning demand and shrinking supply of mint state quality Morgan Dollars. Although inconsistencies still exist, and may always do so to some extent, values are a much more accurate indicator of rarity today than they were a decade, or even only a few years, ago. One of the best examples of this progress is the advance of the price of the 1884 ahead of its Philadelphia counterparts of the same decade of issue. Experienced Morgan enthusiasts have long believed that such a surge was inevitable for this underrated issue.

We do not mean to imply that mint state examples are rare, or even particularly scarce. They are merely scarcer than some traditionally similarly priced issues. MS (63) or inferior uncirculated coins should command only a modest premium over common bulk mint state dollars. Circulated coins are generally regarded as common.

The dollars of 1884 are usually well struck. Considerable bagmarking is evident on the majority of coins.

RARITY IN PROOFLIKE: This issue is very scarce in prooflike condition. The considerable premium demanded for true prooflikes would be even higher if many semiprooflikes were not offered as prooflike. A superb cameo prooflike would no doubt require a record price when and if it were offered. Even brilliant prooflikes with no contrast between fields and devices are rarely encountered.

RARITY IN SUPERB CONDITION: A few superb examples, mostly with attractive toning, have been offered at public auction. MS (67) or better coins are in frequent demand.

REDFIELD: No.

PROOFS: Proofs are fairly typical in quality and rarity. Most have been hairlined or impaired in some minor way. Like many earlier proof Morgans, many were spent during the unstable economic periods our country underwent in the late 1800s, notably the Panic of 1893. Because proofs were sold on an individual basis at a ten percent premium above face value, many families gladly sacrificed a dime to obtain a dollar's worth of spending power. Once such proofs were spent, they had little occasion to be retrieved from circulation, and most were worn into oblivion.

INVESTMENT POTENTIAL: Although this issue has undergone some long overdue price adjustments, there may be considerable room left at the top. Once an issue such as the 1884 breaks away from a group of dates that it has long been equated to, there might be little price resistance. As the premium for a date increases, so does the necessity for strict grading. Solid MS (65) or better examples only are recommended. MS (67) coins or cameo prooflikes are vastly underrated.

1884-O

Typical Mint State Example
MS (63), average strike, moderate
bagmarks, frosty surfaces, good
luster.

GENERAL DISCUSSION: The 1884-O is one of the most abundant of all Morgan Dollars in mint state condition.

The difference in mintages of this issue and the 1884 Philadelphia underscores the unreliability of mintage figures as a true indicator of relative scarcity of Morgan Dollars. Although fifty percent more dollars dated 1884 were produced in Philadelphia than in New Orleans, there is no comparison in the frequency of appearance of uncirculated coins.

Rolls of twenty mint state coins are as common as most single mint state pieces. Only exceptional mint state or fully prooflike examples are collected as single coins. Circulated coins are also very common.

The strike of this issue ranges from weak to sharp, albeit most specimens have visible breast feathers on the eagle. Bagmarks can be dense or nearly absent.

Collectors have mildly accepted varieties with a doubled mintmark and with a filled mintmark.

The Wayne Miller plate coin, a superb cameo, brought $450 after spirited bidding on the floor of Steve Ivy Numismatic Auction's R.A. Donovan Sale (April, 1978). The same company, in May, 1979, offered a coin described as:

> Superb! A cameo prooflike with beauty that transfixes the viewer's
> attention. The pure mirror surfaces are not far from perfection. The
> creamy white devices are incredibly smooth and free of injury. When
> one considers the many hundreds of thousands of common date
> Silver Dollars in existence, and contemplates that only a few hands-
> ful can compare to the quality of this piece presently offered, the
> high-sounding price it is sure to bring seems quite justified.

The price of $400 that was realized for the coin described above should amply indicate that *any* Morgan Dollar, regardless of its overall frequency of appearance in mint state condition, is a significant rarity if it rests at the threshold of perfection.

RARITY IN PROOFLIKE: While this is surely one of the most common of all Morgans with reflective surfaces, sharply struck, superb specimens with prooflike properties are somewhat scarce.

RARITY IN SUPERB CONDITION: The 1884-O is among the most common Morgans in superb MS (67) condition. MS (67) coins can be frequently plucked from original rolls or bags at a modest premium.

REDFIELD: No.

INVESTMENT POTENTIAL: Any promise that this issue holds is restricted to superb MS (67) or better quality. Because superb, cameo prooflike examples are among the most inexpensive of the series, they may prove to be a good buy at today's levels.

1884-S

Typical Mint State Example
MS (63), above average strike, light
bagmarks, frosty surfaces, good
luster.

GENERAL DISCUSSION: This issue is very rare in mint state condition. Lightly rubbed coins ("sliders") abound. These almost uncirculated coins were not considered when the characteristics of the typical mint state example were listed.

Because of their relatively great value in mint state, high grade circulated examples command a considerable premium. Coins which grade less than extremely fine carry only a very slight premium.

One can only theorize why so few of this production were saved in mint condition. Melting and attrition are the two obvious explanations, but the relative contribution of each factor to the coin's rarity, and the reasons for their great influence upon coins of this particular date are not known.

Collections of dollars that were assembled in the 1930s, 1940s and 1950s, decades during which gems of virtually every issue were available, are more likely to include superb specimens of any other date, with the possible exception of 1901. Although composite auction records would no doubt rank many dates rarer in mint state than the 1884-S, most of the coins of this issue labeled "uncirculated" in those days were most likely not. Six mint state specimens were listed for sale in an important auction sale in the early 1970s, but not one was actually better than AU (55).

Most mint state specimens are well struck, with sharp breast feathers on the eagle. Some, however, show some weakness in that area. The authors have seen few mint state coins that have been very heavily bagmarked. This fact may indicate that 1884-S was one issue that was not stored in bag quantities, or at least, that the bags that were saved were all melted. Most of the mint state coins that survive today are probably due to the efforts of early collectors.

The nicest 1884-S to appear on the market in the 1970s was a fabulous piece with immaculate surfaces and abundant, shimmering luster. This sharply struck jewel made its debut at the February, 1979, Long Beach Convention. Our friend Nick Buzolich, a West Coast dealer, owned the coin at that time. News of the exciting coin quickly spread to the dealers and collectors attending the well known show. When the authors saw Nick, we asked him to describe the coin; he said that it looked like "an 1880-S that's worth $75," then a substantial sum. When we examined the coin a short time later, his evaluation was substantiated completely. If one ignored the date, the coin could be mistaken for a superb 1880-S or similar date. The strike, luster and surfaces were of quality unaccustomed to this issue.

The coin had been purchased about four months earlier from a coin dealer who was well known to Nick. That dealer had purchased the 1884-S, with some other dollars, from a collector who had owned the piece for about three years.

Not long after the Long Beach show, a major midwestern dealer procured the coin on customer approval. The customer not only approved, but was also probably in awe of the quality of this fabulous coin. The price he had to pay was $17,000, then a record price for a specimen of this issue.

To the authors' knowledge, the coin discussed above is the finest known 1884-S. There is a cameo prooflike firmly nestled in an advanced collection in the Midwest. Because of the virtual impossibility of locating a true gem, many MS (63), MS (60) and even AU (58) coins are sold as MS (65) or better examples. The resulting, inordinate number of offerings has undoubtedly contributed to the perennial underrating of this issue in gem mint state condition.

Although not a match for the Long beach coin, the best 1884-S ever offered at public auction sale may well have been a fully struck, frosty specimen with light golden toning that was sold as part of New England Rare Coin Auctions' Commonwealth Sale (July, 1977). That piece currently resides in an outstanding collection of dollars somewhere in the Northwest. If sold at public auction today, it would no doubt bring multiples of the $3,400 that the authors of this book paid for it from the New England sale. However, at the time, that was a lot of money even for a nice 1884-S. Many silver dollar dealers and advanced collectors with sufficient means had an opportunity to acquire the coin, but didn't. They have probably learned by now that the only thing rarer than a gem 1884-S is the opportunity to buy one.

Steve Ivy Rare Coin Company offered a superb toned example in the summer of 1981 at a fixed price of $22,500.

The authors have seen some counterfeit 1884-S's created by adding an "S" mintmark to an 1884 Philadelphia coin. These forgeries have ranged from crude to very deceptive. If the unscrupulous perpetrator is knowledgeable about the dollar series, it is possible for him to use an "S" mintmark from another coin that matches the characteristics of the mint letter on a genuine 1884-S. If he is a patient crook, he can also position the lifted mintmark in a manner that imitates the position of the mintmark on the genuine articles. Examination of the mintmark and comparison with a known genuine coin are helpful in detecting counterfeits, but by no means are such steps a surety of authenticity.

No forger, however, can give a Philadelphia dollar the basic characteristic of a San Francisco dollar. An experienced dealer, one who has handled thousands upon thousands of Morgans from each of the mints, can usually tell from what mint a dollar was issued by glancing at the obverse. One helpful hint: Many 1884 Philadelphia coins have a die break extending from the first numeral of the date to the base of Miss Liberty's bust near its point. Others may also have another break from the neck to the first star; still others may have a dash under the second eight of the date. A genuine 1884-S will have none of these checkpoints. The absence of the checkpoints, however, does not guarantee that the piece is genuine.

While bogus 1884-S's are not around in alarming numbers, it is nonetheless suggested that coins from this issue be purchased from reliable dealers, or that they be submitted to the American Numismatic Association Certification Service (ANACS) for verification of their authenticity.

RARITY IN PROOFLIKE: Of the scant mint state population of this issue, probably fewer than a dozen pieces have prooflike surfaces. At least three currently can be located; the presence of prooflike surfaces on a number of lightly circulated coins suggests the possibility of more. Few prooflikes have any cameo contrast, but one example is purported to reside in an advanced collection in the Northeast. If and when it appears, a gem prooflike, 1884-S will be a momentous numismatic occasion.

RARITY IN SUPERB CONDITION: An honest MS (60) 1884-S dollar is rare, and superb specimens are nearly unknown. The Long Beach specimen discussed previously is by far the best seen. If some outstanding coins have been "in the woodwork" for decades, perhaps the record price paid for that coin will bring them out. It's our guess that an even higher price would not produce the appearance of any heretofore unknown examples of the desirable 1884-S.

REDFIELD: No. Despite frequent rumors, and the logical inclusion of this date in Mr. Redfield's accumulation, there were no 1884-S's in any phase of Redfield, and none are anticipated.

INVESTMENT POTENTIAL: Compared to the number of people who wish to complete a collection of mint state Morgan Dollars, the supply of coins of this issue is miniscule. Although price resistance at the five-figure level must be considered, the number of collectors and investors (keep in mind the rising number of investor groups that are adding coins to their portfolios) who can afford mint state examples is increasing. This is one of the few issues in which investment in even MS (60) is recommended. The investor must be absolutely sure that he is purchasing a mint state coin and not a "slider."

1884-CC

Typical Mint State Example
MS (63), above average strike,
moderate bagmarks, frosty surfaces,
good luster.

GENERAL DISCUSSION: Of the 1,136,000 1884-CC dollars minted, more than 950,000 were part of the vast U.S. Treasury holdings of silver dollars that were eventually offered through the General Services Administration's sales beginning in 1972. Initially about half of the 1884-CC dollars were sold; most of those were awarded to bidders willing to pay at least the thirty dollar minimum bid set by GSA. About 100,000 coins, judged to be in less than uncirculated condition, were sold to participants who bid fifteen dollars each. These coins also proved to be in mint state condition; most merely exhibited some natural toning.

While costly to implement (the GSA reportedly operated on a ten million dollar budget), the strategy utilized by the GSA must be praised as successful. Established collectors could not have made a minor dent into the huge number of coins that the government had for sale. By exposing millions of Americans to the coins through mailing promotions and Post Office displays, the GSA created its own market. In the process, thousands of new collectors were introduced to the interesting and historic Morgan Dollar series.

Because this issue is understandably scarce in circulated condition, such coins bring a relatively high percentage of the price of mint state pieces. Similarly, MS (60) coins are very near in value to MS (63), and MS (63) to MS (65). Not until the superb MS (67) level is reached do the priced differentials increase significantly.

Like all of the Carson City dollars in the GSA sales, the 1884-CC's were stored in bags of one thousand coins from their year of mintage to the time they were removed and sealed in plastic holders in 1972. Consequently, bagmarks are a formidable obstacle to locating MS (65) or better specimens.

RARITY IN PROOFLIKE: Although the 1884-CC is the most common of all Carson City dates included in the GSA sales, it has demanded a greater premium with prooflike surfaces than the similarly priced 1882-CC and 1883-CC. This difference in premium values for prooflike specimens is due primarily to the pre-GSA population of prooflikes. In actuality, the 1884-CC is no rarer than its two Carson City predecessors with mirror surfaces. "Father Time" is already in the process of equalizing the prices of prooflike pieces to coincide with their true scarcity.

Some prooflikes, often highly contrasted cameos, were struck from reverse dies which were rusted or worn. Although not weakly struck, coins from such dies lack full detail on the eagle's breast and wings.

RARITY IN SUPERB CONDITION: Considering its relatively wide distribution, the 1884-CC occurs less frequently in superb MS (67) or better condition than might be supposed. It is nonetheless, in terms of absolute numbers, one of the most common Carson City dollars in superb condition.

REDFIELD: No.

PROOFS: Breen reports one verified example; not listed in any mintage records. He does not mention an 1884-CC offered as "brilliant proof" in the H.R. Lee Sale (Stack's 1947); they are probably two different coins. The proof status of the Lee coin cannot be verified. It was estimated at only $12.50 (an 1884 Philly proof which preceded it in the same sale was estimated at $10), and accompanied in the sale by two more otherwise unheard of branch mint proofs — an 1885-CC and an 1895-O. See discussion under 1891-CC "Proofs."

INVESTMENT POTENTIAL: The immense number of coins in the GSA sales will always seriously retard any desire by investors to purchase coins of this date. Superb MS (67) or better coins that can be cherry picked at modest premiums should perform in at least an average fashion. The preponderance of average, MS (60) or MS (63) coins may accentuate appreciation of the scarcity of superior examples.

1885

Typical Mint State Example
MS (65), above average strike,
moderate to light bagmarks, frosty
surfaces, good luster.

GENERAL DISCUSSION: This issue ranks as one of the most common Morgan Dollars in mint state condition. In circulated grades as well, the 1885 carries no premium value.

The average quality is high; the strike is usually full, and bagmarks are less bothersome than usual. The surfaces are typically fully frosty, though they may be fully prooflike. Most collections contain a specimen of at least MS (65) quality. MS (67) coins are readily available. Coins that fall below the quality level of the typical mint state example are valuable only as common bulk mint state dollars. The price of such dollars tends to fluctuate more in accordance with the price of silver bullion than in accordance with numismatic market pressures.

Superb, prooflike examples are swapped with some frequency. When the authors cataloged the William C. Kerr Sale in February, 1979, a note to the readers of that catalog introduced a particularly nice example of an 1885 dollar:

> Many collectors and investors now realize that in no other series of U.S. coins is the ratio of surviving truly superb coins to the total mint state population so small. The following lot is a good example. We are confident that less than one-tenth of one percent of all the surviving mint state 1885 Morgan Dollars are as nice!

Those comments are applicable to any common date Morgan. By the way, the lot brought $170, about eight times as much as the value of a typical representative of this issue at that time.

RARITY IN PROOFLIKE: Although very desirable and popular, nice prooflike examples of this issue are readily available. Some of the prooflikes exhibit a curious lack of detail on the eagle's breast; these coins are usually otherwise superb. The authors can recall seeing solid rolls of 1885 dollars, mostly superb, with deep mirror surfaces.

RARITY IN SUPERB CONDITION: The 1885 is among the most frequently encountered Morgans in superb MS (67) or superior condition. Coins of superb quality can still be found as parts of original rolls or bags. Nearly perfect, deeply reflective and/or spectacularly toned examples can command substantial premiums.

REDFIELD: No.

PROOFS: Proofs of this date are always well struck and sometimes exhibit a pleasant cameo effect. Most exhibit some faint hairline scratches.

INVESTMENT POTENTIAL: Any potential that this date possesses is restricted to superb MS (67) or better quality. While this is not to say that MS (65) or less coins will not go up in value — quite the contrary will likely be the case — the authors merely feel that coins of the highest quality obtainable and affordable will perform in the best manner.

1885-O

Typical Mint State Example
MS (63), average strike, moderate
bagmarks, frosty surfaces, good
luster.

GENERAL DISCUSSION: Coins of this issue are readily available in all grades from well circulated to superb MS (67).

Although all characteristics may vary greatly from coin to coin, the typical example generally adheres to the above description. Coins handled on an individual basis by dealers, or those coins collected by Morgan enthusiasts, will almost invariably be of better quality. The tens of thousands of common bulk mint state 1885-O's that exist are rarely traded on an individual basis.

If a collection houses a specimen of this issue that is inferior to MS (67) quality, the owner should consider upgrading while superb examples are still easy to locate.

RARITY IN PROOFLIKE: Although available in prooflike, this date is among the most frequently misadvertised issues; many so-called prooflikes actually only have a tendency toward reflective surfaces, and should be accurately called "semiprooflike."

Specimens with totally reflective, deep mirror surfaces are genuinely scarce.

RARITY IN SUPERB CONDITION: Auction records for superb specimens are scant. This is due more to the reluctance to offer 1885-O's on an individual basis than it is due to rarity of superb quality coins. Superb coins are frequently traded at coin shows or sold through the mail by major silver dollar dealers.

REDFIELD: No.

INVESTMENT POTENTIAL: Superb quality at a modest premium is a definite attraction that this and other common Morgans hold for the investor at the present time. Coins of less than MS (65) quality should be left for the silver speculator.

1885-S

Typical Mint State Example
MS (63), average strike, moderate to
heavy bagmarks, frosty surfaces,
good luster.

GENERAL DISCUSSION: For a coin that is quite scarce in mint state condition, this issue comes in a wide variety of appearances. Some 1885-S's are so weakly struck that no breast feathers on the eagle show, and others exhibit feathers on which the curled tips are in sharp evidence. The surfaces can vary from frosty to mirror. In fact, some of the deepest mirrors on any Morgan can be found on coins of this date and mint. One consistent characteristic that most of this issue possess is bagmarks, which can sometimes literally efface the surfaces of an 1885-S dollar.

In extremely fine or almost uncirculated condition, an 1885-S dollar commands a significant premium over common date dollars. In circulated grades of lower quality, however, this issue is only slightly more valuable than a common date.

This has long been an underrated issue. The conspicuous lack of 1885-S's in the Redfield Hoard did much to draw attention to the true scarcity of this issue. This date was the least expensive San Francisco Morgan Dollar not present in that famous estate. Although the most immediate and apparent reaction of silver dollar values to the Redfield Hoard was the promotion and immediate rise in price of the primary dates distributed on phase one. A delayed, secondary reaction was the upward adjustment of prices of some coins that became undervalued relative to the Redfield dates. One such date was 1885-S. Although a considerable rise in price has been enjoyed by this date in the last three years, it is still not priced in strict proportion to many other issues that are more common, yet more expensive, in comparable quality.

In the fall of 1977 Steve Ivy Rare Coin Company purchased seventeen original rolls of mint state 1885-S dollars. Most of these coins were sharply struck; without the addition of these coins to the market, the typical mint state example encountered today would have had to be termed "weak strike." These 340 coins were evenly and widely distributed, mostly on a single-coin, retail basis.

Steve Ivy Numismatic Auctions sold a fabulous roll of 1885-S's during three sales beginning with the R.A. Donovan Sale (April, 1978). Mr. Donovan selected the coins from original bags searched decades ago. They were very carefully chosen, because he had to pay an impressive premium — two dollars each! All of the coins were fully struck, and most were prooflike. Mr. Donovan placed the coins he bought in paper rolls, and some spectacular toning was gradually imparted to the surfaces of the end coins. The prices for the pieces ranged from $280 to $600.

RARITY IN PROOFLIKE: The 1885-S is very scarce in prooflike. One-sided prooflikes are often encountered. These one-sided examples usually have extremely deep mirrors on the reverse only. Occasionally, superb cameo prooflikes become available, and generally command prices in the four-figure area.

RARITY IN SUPERB CONDITION: Bagmarks prohibit the classification of many examples of this issue in the superb category. When MS (67) or better examples are found, they may be frosty or cameo prooflikes.

REDFIELD: Despite the logical inclusion of this issue in the Redfield Estate, no significant quantities were reported. It is possible that the seventeen rolls mentioned in the general discussion section were of Redfield provenance.

INVESTMENT POTENTIAL: Despite significant price advances in the recent past, much potential remains for gem MS (65) or better specimens. Relative to other more expensive issues, the 1885-S remains an underrated coin.

1885-CC

Typical Mint State Example
MS (63), above average strike,
moderate to heavy bagmarks, frosty
surfaces, good luster.

GENERAL DISCUSSION: Nearly two-thirds of the original mintage of this issue were discovered in sealed bags in the U.S. Treasury in Washington, D.C. in the early 1960s. They were offered as part of the great Carson City dollar sales commencing in 1972.

The appearance of the GSA coins greatly decreased the quality of the average mint state 1885-CC. Prior to the government sales, an uncirculated coin of this issue would usually meet or surpass the minimum requirements for MS (65). But the government coins were heavily bagmarked from their storage and frequent travel in bags of 1,000 coins. Although usually well struck, the typical 1885-CC is now only MS (63).

Perhaps as much as ninety-five percent of all 1885-CC's known are in mint state. Therefore, the scant supply of circulated coins is always in demand by price conscious collectors. In fact, in the early 1960s, the price of circulated coins enjoyed virtual parity with that of uncirculated coins!

Auction records for this ever-popular date are plentiful. One of the earliest indicators of the surge in demand for elite quality Morgans was the $280 realized for a beautifully toned, prooflike 1885-CC in Steve Ivy Numismatic Auction's Brazos Sale in October, 1977.

RARITY IN PROOFLIKE: This issue is not difficult to locate with reflective surfaces. Prooflikes are often beautiful cameos with a refreshingly small number of bagmarks. Most such specimens were already in collectors' hands before the GSA sales. The number of nice prooflikes in the CC auctions was relatively small.

RARITY IN SUPERB CONDITION: Some superb rolls of 1885-CC dollars exist. For example, a fantastic roll of twenty MS (67) or better cameo prooflikes was offered at a 1977 Los Angeles convention for $5,000, with no takers. Auction records for superb coins of this date are plentiful, but such lots invariably command a premium of double or even triple that of a typical mint state example. Dollars of this issue often have beautiful, natural toning.

REDFIELD: A small quantity, believed to approximate one bag of 1,000 coins, was in the Redfield estate. These coins were quickly distributed, among the first dates to be completely sold.

PROOFS: The only mention of a branch mint proof that our research uncovered was lot 813 of the H.R. Lee Sale (Stack's, November, 1947). Its true proof status is doubtful, since the term "proof" in those days was often used as a grade rather than a reference to a method of manufacture. Because superb prooflikes of this date exist, it is likely that one may have been called a proof during that period of numismatic history. See also the discussion of "Proofs" under 1891-CC.

INVESTMENT POTENTIAL: Although the mintage figure is a deceptive indicator of rarity, it has helped to maintain the price of this issue despite the spectre of 150,000 coins overhanging the market. The influence of this factor should decrease in the future. However, the popularity of the Carson City dollars in general and promotion by the General Services Administration may offset that decrease and enable this issue to perform in an average, but not better, fashion.

1886

Typical Mint State Example
MS (65), sharp strike, moderate to
light bagmarks, frosty surfaces,
excellent luster.

GENERAL DISCUSSION: This date ranks as one of the most abundant of all Morgan Dollars in mint state condition. MS (63) examples are often valued only as common bulk mint state dollars. Circulated coins are, of course, of no premium value. Original bags of mint state coins still exist.

Although virtually all 1886 Philadelphia dollars are well struck, about twenty percent or so exhibit some distortion of detail due to abnormal metal flow during the actual striking process. This type of metal flow, unseen on coins dated before 1886, may have been a result of a different stock of silver used to produce the metal blanks, or planchets, on which the dies were impressed.

Most collectors find coins which exhibit this metal flow, which may cause a rippling effect on the coin's surfaces, less desirable than those which do not.

Some of the highest quality Morgans to be offered on an individual basis have been coins of this issue. Records of both private and auction sales have exceeded $200.

RARITY IN PROOFLIKE: Although the typical mint state example of this issue has frosty surfaces, there are plenty of prooflikes to meet the present demand. These prooflikes seldom offer any marked contrast between the fields and devices, however, and are much scarcer with a cameo tendency than either the 1885 or 1887, two dates with similar populations.

RARITY IN SUPERB CONDITION: Superb MS (67) quality is not as elusive for this issue as it is for nearly all others. An occasional MS (69) surfaces, and is always met with great demand.

REDFIELD: No.

PROOFS: Most proof examples have been cleaned or abused in some manner. They are well struck, and are typical in rarity and quality for a proof Morgan Dollar.

INVESTMENT POTENTIAL: As with other extremely common dates, the 1886 possesses significant investment potential only in MS (67) or better condition. A superb prooflike example or an MS (69) coin may prove to be a bargain at today's levels. Although MS (65) or inferior coins may indeed rise in value, that increase will be due to silver bullion price pressures and not from numismatic causes. However, if silver bullion prices fall, coins of numismatic quality are likely to continue an unabated rise in value.

1886-O

Typical Mint State Example
MS (60), weak strike, moderate
bagmarks, frosty surfaces, poor to
good luster.

GENERAL DISCUSSION: This issue marks a radical departure from the pattern set by the New Orleans Mint's previous three years of Morgan Dollars. The 1883-O, 1884-O and 1885-O are three of the most common of all Morgans in mint state condition; the uncirculated 1886-O is among the top fifteen rarest. In circulated grades, however, the 1886-O commands little premium unless it is in strong extremely fine or better condition.

There are few, if any, other Morgans with such a drastic difference in rarity between MS (60) and MS (65) specimens. The 1886-O is frequently found in choice almost uncirculated condition; some coins that appear initially to be gem quality mint state specimens are, upon proper examination, nice AU coins with a bit of rub on the high points.

The collector or investor who wishes to locate an 1886-O with a full strike, minimal bagmarks and good luster faces a formidable challenge. One or more of these characteristics are usually lacking on mint state coins of this particular date and mint. Heartbreakingly often, a coin practically void of bagmarks will be very flatly struck, or a fully struck specimen may have poor, unattractive luster. A coin with even one major characteristic short of gem quality cannot be called MS (65) and command a gem's price.

When purchasing an 1886-O, the buyer should be confident in either his ability to discern the fine points of grading Morgan Dollars, or have faith in his dealer's ability to do so and his honesty in stating the coin's true grade.

The authors have seen a few spurious specimens — made by adding an ''O'' mintmark to an 1886 Philadelphia dollar — particularly as the price of gem quality 1886-O's has risen drastically in the last few years. They are quickly and easily distinguishable due to the basic characteristics that differ between dollars of the New Orleans Mint and dollars of the Philadelphia Mint. If one is suspicious of an 1886-O dollar, it is recommended that he send it to the ANACS for a certificate of authenticity. When buying an 1886-O, it is advisable that the coin already be accompanied by ANACS papers, or that one know he is buying it from a reliable and knowledgeable source.

Wayne Miller owns a fantastic, cameo prooflike specimen that is conceded to be the finest known by anyone who has seen it. Several superb (or so-called superb) specimens have been offered at auction sales in the last few years, but no records are established for confirmed MS (67) specimens. A nice MS (65) coin with prooflike surfaces brought $2,100 in February, 1979, at the William C. Kerr Sale (Steve Ivy Numismatic Auctions). That same piece would no doubt be in even greater demand today.

RARITY IN PROOFLIKE: The 1886-O is unquestionably among the rarest of the entire series with fully prooflike surfaces. Semiprooflike coins are scarce, and are more often than not sold as *bona fide* prooflikes when they come upon the marketplace. The few prooflikes that the authors have seen were not particularly attractive, with poor strike and luster being their main drawbacks.

RARITY IN SUPERB CONDITION: This issue is also extremely rare in superb condition, although primarily because of the reluctance of their owners to let them go. A decade or so ago, a truly superb 1886-O could be found by the patient dollar enthusiast. Most older dealers can recollect seeing multiple gem specimens, or even rolls that contained several superb coins. Whether those coins that are vaguely recalled would pass inspection at today's standards is doubtful in most cases. Nonetheless, the 1886-O, while rare in superb condition, does exist as such.

REDFIELD: No.

INVESTMENT POTENTIAL: In any level of mint state condition, an 1886-O that is fairly graded and priced should prove to be a good investment. As MS (65) or better specimens become even more difficult to locate, many collectors would prefer a weakly struck coin with virtually no bagmarks to one that may be sharp, but which has unsightly nicks and abrasions. When purchasing a mint state 1886-O for investment purposes, the most important thing to establish is that the piece is indeed in uncirculated condition. Although this is crucial in any rare coin purchase, it is especially vital in the case of this issue. The prospective buyer should keep in mind, also, the tremendous difference in value between an MS (60) and an MS (65) coin.

1886-S

Typical Mint State Example
MS (63), sharp strike, moderate to
heavy bagmarks, semiprooflike
surfaces, excellent luster.

GENERAL DISCUSSION: As the description of the typical mint state example indicates, bagmarks are often a problem on coins of this issue. The excellent luster and semiprooflike surfaces that are also typical characteristics exaggerate the seriousness of the inevitable signs of contact with other coins.

A high percentage of all 1886-S's are in mint state condition. The relatively scarce circulated examples command a significant premium. Primarily because of the Redfield Hoard, mint state examples of this production are readily available. MS (60) quality predominates, however, and coins of that quality are much more common than those that reach the MS (65) level.

The typical 1886-S is very sharply struck, but coins that lack full breast feathers appear occasionally.

Like other Morgan dollars in this price range, superb MS (67) or better examples do not command the same percentage premium as do less expensive issues. Fewer collectors and investors are able to pursue coins priced near or above the four figure level.

RARITY IN PROOFLIKE: If all examples of this issue that were offered as prooflike were just that, the 1886-S might be called rather plentiful with prooflike surfaces. Such is not the case, however. Many so-called prooflikes are merely semiprooflike coins, and therefore typical for this particular date and mint. Coins with fully reflective fields are scarce. Prooflikes usually have dazzling luster and good mirrors, but offer little contrast between fields and devices.

Many prooflike specimens exhibit a patch of parallel die striations surrounding the date.

RARITY IN SUPERB CONDITION: Because of a serious bagmarking problem, superb MS (67) or better quality coins of this issue are very seldom available. A few superb, gorgeously toned examples have been offered in the last few years. These examples undoubtedly predated the appearance of the Redfield coins.

REDFIELD: Yes. Multiple bags were contained in the hoard. It is not known if any remain, but if they do, the chances are good that the number is insignificant. John Love, our good friend and a highly respected dollar expert, purchased and distributed the majority of the Redfield 1886-S's. Most of the mint state examples available on the market today probably originated from that source.

INVESTMENT POTENTIAL: Quality less than a solid MS (65) should not be considered for investment purposes. MS (67) coins, if available at a modest price, are reasonable candidates for above average performance. If an investor prefers prooflikes, he should make sure that the 1886-S's he buys have fully reflective surfaces.

1887

Typical Mint State Example
MS (65), sharp strike, moderate to
light bagmarks, frosty surfaces,
excellent luster.

GENERAL DISCUSSION: The typical mint state example of this issue closely resembles that of its immediate Philadelphia Mint predecessor, although the 1886 probably is a bit nicer in overall average quality. This is the third Philly issue in a row that is considered among the most common dates of the entire series. Original rolls are common and entire original bags are not unusual. Circulated pieces are, needless to say, valued only a common bulk circulated dollars. Mint state pieces of MS (63) quality or less are valued only as common bulk mint state dollars.

A variety with the date "1887" over a faint "1886" is known. The evidence of the overdate is very light, and a glass is necessary for positive verification. The difficulty in discerning the overdate explains why it was not discovered until the early 1970s. The earliest record of a sale of one of these overdates was as lot number 878 of Lester Merkin's public auction sale of October 6 and 7, 1972. That coin, described as "Brill. Unc., prooflike," realized $550. At least several hundred overdates have been discovered since, and they are valued at less than half of the price which the first one brought. Because of the fascinating nature that overdates of any series hold for collectors, this variety, which is now listed in the *Guide Book of United States Coins*, will probably continue to meet with mild acceptance.

A splendidly toned, prooflike specimen brought $405 at Steve Ivy Numismatic Auction's Kerr Sale (February, 1979), a harbinger of the quality craze that persists in today's market.

RARITY IN PROOFLIKE: The 1887 issue is relatively common with prooflike surfaces, although a larger number of semiprooflike coins are erroneously dubbed "prooflike."

RARITY IN SUPERB CONDITION: Because of its large population of mint state coins, 1887 is an issue with good representation in the superb MS (67) and better quality levels.

REDFIELD: No.

PROOFS: Proofs of 1887 are slightly scarcer as a date, but do not command a premium price. Most examples have been lightly cleaned or mishandled in some manner. Some of the nicest proofs of this date are preserved as parts of original proof sets, and can be spectacularly toned. Proofs can be slightly weakly struck.

INVESTMENT POTENTIAL: Potential for above average future price appreciation lies only with superb MS (67) or better coins. Quality less than that will be readily available to collectors for many decades.

1887-O

Typical Mint State Example
MS (63), average strike, moderate
bagmarks, frosty surfaces, good
luster.

GENERAL DISCUSSION: This issue comes in a range of mint state qualities that is as broad as possible. The strike may range from pathetically weak to very bold. Bagmarks are almost always present, but superb examples virtually free of them entirely are offered with surprising frequency. Basically, though, this issue is very common in MS (60) condition, readily available in MS (63) condition, very scarce in strict MS (65) condition, and highly uncommon in superb MS (67) or better condition. In circulated grades, this issue commands little or no premium.

Several groups of rolls, probably resulting from original bags being broken, appeared in the 1970s. Consequently, the 1887-O has undergone considerable price promotion. High quality, MS (65) or better coins deserve the new prices, but typical mint state examples are overpriced at prices near the gem level.

A quantity slightly fewer than 1,000 pieces was sold at the 1977 American Numismatic Association convention in Atlanta. About one-fourth of these coins were of a variety known as the 1887 over 1886-O overdate (also written 1887-O, 7/6). The cause and appearance of this overdate is similar to that discussed in conjunction with the 1887 Philadelphia issue. They are similar in value, although auction records show significantly fewer appearances for the New Orleans Mint issue.

Most of the overdates at the Atlanta ANA were sold to First Coinvestors Incorporated of New York. They, in turn, distributed the coins on an individual retail basis.

RARITY IN PROOFLIKE: Although a highly regarded and popular date with prooflike surfaces, the number available at most major conventions attended by the important dollar dealers across the country leads one to believe that this issue may be slightly overrated in prooflike. Most prooflike examples are of an average strike, with moderate to light bagmarks.

RARITY IN SUPERB CONDITION: Most superb examples, those that reach or exceed the MS (67) level, are prooflike. Rarely does a frosty and superb 1887-O become available.

REDFIELD: No.

PROOFS: A branch mint proof example reportedly resides in a prominent Texas collection.

INVESTMENT POTENTIAL: Despite recent price increases, fully struck, solid MS (65) examples may still have good potential. Heavily to moderately bagmarked coins, readily obtainable, should not be valued near the price of true gems.

1887-S

Typical Mint State Example
MS (60), average strike, heavy
bagmarks, frosty or semiprooflike
surfaces, good luster.

GENERAL DISCUSSION: Primarily due to its presence in the Redfield Hoard, this issue is readily available in mint state condition. However, the great majority of mint state specimens are no better than MS (60) quality because of serious bagmarks. Circulated examples in less than extremely fine condition command little or no premium over common bulk dollars.

Coins of this issue often come with rims (the raised portion of the fields on the circumference of the coin) that are slightly wider than normal. The coins often have a concave appearance. This issue is one of the most consistently heavily bagmarked of the entire series.

Because of the poor quality of the Redfield coins, sales of the 1887-S's from that great accumulation have been slow. Collectors and investors have refused to settle for less than MS (65) quality.

No overdate variety, such as has been discovered on the Philadelphia and New Orleans Mint coins of this year, has been reported for the San Francisco Mint issues.

The Briggs Sale (Steve Ivy Numismatic Auctions, May, 1979) specimen is the best to have been offered at public auction sale in recent years. Within the description of that coin was an apt appraisal of the population of mint state 1887-S's: "The ratio of superb specimens extant to the total number of mint state coins surviving today is very low..." That atypical specimen realized $345 at a time when an MS (60) coin was worth sixty dollars.

RARITY IN PROOFLIKE: Prooflike surfaces are common on 1887-S dollars, but, unfortunately, such surfaces usually occur at the rate of one prooflike surface per coin. These one-sided prooflikes carry little or no premium over frosty coins unless the obverse is a superb cameo. Specimens with mirror surfaces on both sides are by no means rare, but they are definitely uncommon, especially if the fields and devices are not peppered with bagmarks. Truly prooflike 1887-S's have mirror fields that are one hundred percent, or very nearly so, reflective.

RARITY IN SUPERB CONDITION: Because of a severe bagmarking problem that plagues coins of this issue, superb specimens are very rare. The authors searched several bags from the Redfield Hoard, and not one coin reached the MS (67) level. Relative to the total number of mint state coins that are available, a superb 1887-S is one of the toughest dates of the entire series.

REDFIELD: Yes. The Redfield Hoard contained multiple bags of 1887-S's, the vast majority of which were heavily bagmarked. On the average, the quality of this date was among the worst of any in the Redfield holdings.

INVESTMENT POTENTIAL: Quality means everything when it comes to investing in coins of this issue. MS (60) coins may be one of the least desirable of all Morgan investments; superb MS (67) or better coins may be one of the most desirable.

1888

Typical Mint State Example
MS (63), average strike, moderate
bagmarks, frosty surfaces, good
luster.

GENERAL DISCUSSION: Although scarcer in mint state than the 1885, 1886 or 1887 Philadelphia Mint issues, the 1888 is not as scarce as the 1880-1884 productions from the same mint. Coins of MS (60) quality should be valued only as common bulk mint state dollars. MS (63) examples command a small premium; MS (65) condition brings a price about double that of the most common dates in mint state. Circulated dollars of this date are considered common.

This issue possesses the dubious distinction of being the most poorly struck date of the 1880s from the Philly Mint. The eagle's breast very often lacks any trace of breast feathers; the corresponding area on the obverse, i.e., the hair above Ms. Liberty's ear, is also weak on such specimens. Bagmarks are less a problem, but frequently prevent a fully struck coin from reaching the MS (65) level.

Auction records for individual coins are scant because most houses are reluctant to place relatively inexpensive coins in individual lots. Coins of quality sufficient to admit them to individual lot status are rare. The Stanford Sale (July, 1977) specimen, a superb prooflike, realized a then healthy $120. The coin that noted silver dollar authority Wayne Miller used to photograph in his book *An Analysis of Morgan and Peace Dollars* realized $800 in the Briggs Sale (May, 1979). That example was also a superb prooflike.

RARITY IN PROOFLIKE: The 1888 is scarce with prooflike surfaces. Coins of this date which have mirror fields are usually well struck. They only rarely exhibit any cameo effect. Prooflike, MS (65) specimens may bring a premium between five and ten times that of a frosty coin in equal condition.

RARITY IN SUPERB CONDITION: This issue is a sleeper in superb condition. It is much rarer in MS (67) or better quality than many more expensive coins of the series. While superior quality specimens are occasionally available on today's maket, there are few to go around to meet the demand of an always increasing number of fastidious collectors.

REDFIELD: No.

PROOFS: Proofs of this date seem to appear at a slightly less frequent rate than most other dates in the 1880s. Most coins offered on an individual basis have been hairlined to some degree by imprudent cleaning, albeit probably long ago when proof Morgans were worth only a few dollars. Some of the finest specimens that survive are parts of original proof sets, in which the silver coins often exhibit beautiful toning. A proof 1888 Morgan Dollar will not necessarily be fully struck, although the vast majority are.

INVESTMENT POTENTIAL: In MS (65) condition, this issue may be somewhat undervalued relative to other similarly priced dates in the series. In MS (67) or better condition, this date is greatly unappreciated. Original rolls still exist; if they can be cherry picked of their superb coins at a modest premium, the lucky buyer will own an excellent investment.

1888-O

Typical Mint State Example
MS (63), average strike, moderate
bagmarks, frosty surfaces, good
luster.

GENERAL DISCUSSION: Although an improvement over the issues from the New Orleans Mint of 1886 and 1887, this issue still experienced inadequate striking on about one-third of the production. Sharply struck coins are available to collectors; flatly struck coins of MS (63) or inferior quality are valued only slightly above common bulk mint state dollars. Circulated coins are common.

The 1888-O has been a favorite whipping boy of price promoters who artificially force the value of a certain issue up by bidding high prices that they rarely honor. These promoters may have a quantity of the date of which they are boosting the price; when the price reaches the desired level, they begin selling their holdings.

The price of MS (65) coins bearing this date and mintmark underwent a tremendous increase in the first six months of 1979. The *Coin Dealer Newsletter* (the greysheet) of January 12, 1979, listed the bid price for MS (65) 1888-O's at $28. The bid for the same quality coins in the June 15, 1979, issue was $120!

Now, the authors of this book are not ones to argue against the venerable law of supply and demand; however, we must question the credibility of such a high price for a coin long considered a common date in mint state condition. It certainly compares, in terms of scarcity of MS (65) pieces, more equally to common or slightly better dates than it does to other dollars priced in the one hundred dollar range. The authors have seen multiple original bags; rolls of twenty pieces, many of them of MS (65) quality, are available by the dozen at many major coin shows. Steve Ivy Rare Coin Company purchased three choice rolls, containing many prooflikes, at three consecutive conventions in 1979. At the Texas Numismatic Association convention of 1979, a group of 110 superb, semiprooflike pieces were offered at a little over one hundred dollars each.

Generally speaking, the rarity of this issue in mint state condition is overrated in MS (65) or less quality. The average quality of mint state examples is better than it is widely believed to be.

An interesting and popular variety of 1888-O dollars is the VAM 4, which Van Allen and Mallis call the "doubled head." But the variety is popularly known as "hot lips," for the doubling is most prominent on Miss Liberty's chin and lips. All examples of this variety seen by the authors have been well worn and/or weakly struck. A mint state example would bring a possibly shocking price.

RARITY IN PROOFLIKE: This issue is genuinely scarce in prooflike, although the recent increase in price for the issue has ferreted out quite a few nice specimens from hiding. When located, a prooflike 1888-O is usually fully struck with nice mirror surfaces. Contrast between devices and fields, if present at all, is normally mild.

RARITY IN SUPERB CONDITION: Fully struck, virtually mark free examples are very scarce and deserve the often high prices they bring. Most superb examples have prooflike or semiprooflike surfaces.

REDFIELD: No.

INVESTMENT POTENTIAL: Perhaps because of promotion, or perhaps partly because this date is sandwiched between much rarer New Orleans issues of 1886-1887 and 1889-1897, this date seems overrated in MS (65) or less condition. Therefore, for investment purposes, one may be wise to restrict purchases to MS (67) or better quality. Regardless of the performance of lesser quality coins in the future, superb pieces should do better.

1888-S

Typical Mint State Example
MS (63), average strike, moderate
bagmarks, semiprooflike surfaces,
good luster.

GENERAL DISCUSSION: A randomly chosen mint state 1888-S may be atrocious in overall appearance, or it may be quite attractive. If it is the former, this is probably because of a weak strike, peculiar luster and surfaces caused by severe polishing of the dies from which the coin emerged. If it is the latter, it will likely be fully struck with minimal bagmarks, and may have semiprooflike or totally reflective surfaces.

Examples with one superb side of MS (67) or better quality may be only MS (60) on the opposite side. Such disappointing specimens must be graded according to their worst side.

This issue is scarce in circulated grades, and non-mint state coins command a sizable premium, even if well worn.

In all grades, the 1888-S closely parallels the 1886-S. In the average quality of mint state coins, the two issues are also similar; the 1886-S is far superior in the strike category, while the typical 1888-S is slightly less bagmarked. San Francisco coins of 1886 vintage were not produced with the aforementioned evidence of extreme polishing of the dies. The similarity of the two issues is also supported by the quality and apparent quantity present of each date in the Redfield Hoard.

RARITY IN PROOFLIKE: This issue is scarce with truly prooflike surfaces. Many semiprooflikes are erroneously sold as prooflikes. The die polishing mentioned in the general discussion is often found on specimens with prooflike surfaces. Fortunately, the prooflike coins in the Redfield estate were, for the most part, superb specimens which lacked this detracting characteristic. A fully struck, MS (65) example with nice mirror surfaces can be confidently pedigreed to the Redfield accumulation.

One-sided prooflikes are often seen. Wayne Miller's plate coin was a one-sided prooflike.

RARITY IN SUPERB CONDITION: Most examples which reach the MS (67) level are prooflike or semiprooflike. Bagmarks and/or a poor strike prevent most frosty coins from reaching that classification. Virginia dealer Don Apte purchased a hand-picked, superb roll of prooflikes soon after the appearance of the Redfield coins. Coins of this quality have been almost completely absorbed by particular collectors and astute investors.

REDFIELD: The authors examined coins from two different bags included in the Redfield group. One bag contained primarily MS (60), unattractive coins; the other was replete with superb prooflikes! It is not known whether any 1888-S's remain undistributed, but no significant quantities heretofore unknown are anticipated.

INVESTMENT POTENTIAL: After a brief "breath-holding" period following the debut of the Redfield coins, this issue has risen steadily in value and met with unhesitating acceptance by investors and collectors. Since mint state coins of MS (60) or MS (63) quality are readily available, the wise investor would do well to seek out solid MS (65) or better examples for his portfolio.

1889

Typical Mint State Example
MS (63), average strike, moderate to
heavy bagmarks, frosty surfaces,
good luster.

GENERAL DISCUSSION: This issue is readily available in mint state condition. Original bags probably still exist; original rolls are relatively commonplace. However, this date is considerably scarcer than the most common issues of the 1880s — the 1885, 1886 and 1887. In less than MS (65) quality, mint state specimens are valued only as common bulk mint state dollars, and all circulated coins are considered common.

The recent advance in price of MS (65) coins of this issue is well deserved. For too long, this date was considered on a par with the most common of the series. This situation is an understandable one since, for many decades, knowledge of the Morgan series was limited to mintage figures and very little experience. After all, not many Americans could afford to collect a series with a face value of nearly one hundred dollars until the 1960s. In one sense, we have inflation to thank for the popularity of dollar collecting today.

But back to our point: it took many years of brisk market activity to verify the fact that, in MS (65) or better quality, the 1889 issue was not as common as the mintage would indicate. As activity continues and knowledge is further disseminated, the gap between the price of the 1889, and common dates, may widen even more.

Auction records for individual pieces are scant, since only superb specimens would be valuable enough to justify a separate listing in a major sale. Such specimens are by no means plentiful.

RARITY IN PROOFLIKE: This date is the rarest Philadelphia issue of the 1880s with prooflike surfaces. One-sided prooflikes are more often seen than are examples with reflective surfaces on each side. Most prooflikes that are located are rather drab in appearance. A vibrant specimen with mirror fields is rare, and when offered elicits much respect from experienced collectors.

RARITY IN SUPERB CONDITION: Like the 1888 issue from the same mint, the 1889 is a sleeper in superb MS (67) or superior quality. Like the 1887-S, it is very rare when judged from the ratio of superb examples extant to the total number of mint state specimens that survive. If bagmarks do not destroy the chances on an 1889 to reach the MS (67) level, a poor strike or inadequate luster likely will.

Collectors who casually await an opportunity to upgrade their MS (63) or marginal MS (65) example may be surprised at the duration of their vigil.

REDFIELD: Although not generally known to have been a part of the Redfield accumulation, several bags of 1889 were included. They were of typical quality for the issue. The authors recall seeing no superb nor prooflike pieces from the Redfield bags.

PROOFS: Proofs of this issue are fairly typical in terms of rarity and average quality. Most have been cleaned or mishandled in some fashion. Some exhibit a beautiful cameo effect, and virtually all seen have been fully struck. Some of the highest quality examples are preserved as parts of original proof sets, or have been relatively recently removed from such a set.

INVESTMENT POTENTIAL: As mentioned in the general description, the price of MS (65) or better quality coins of this issue is likely to increase at a faster pace than other near-common dates. Superb MS (67) quality has only begun to attract proper appreciation of its rarity.

1889-O

Typical Mint State Example
MS (60), weak strike, moderate
bagmarks, frosty surfaces, good
luster.

GENERAL DISCUSSION: The typical 1889-O dollar is poorly minted. Examples are apt to be very flatly struck. Those that are not frequently appear blurry and unattractive due to abnormal metal flow during the actual striking process.

Fortunately for today's collectors, a quantity, perhaps a few bags, of sharply struck specimens with normal metal flow were preserved. As the price of such specimens has risen, more have been seen on the numismatic market. In place of a weak strike, however, many sharp examples exhibit dense bagmarks. Coins with few marks and a superior strike deservingly receive much respect from knowledgeable dollar enthusiasts.

Except in almost uncirculated condition, non-mint state dollars of this issue are considered common.

When an exceptional specimen appears in an auction sale, it is invariably sought by many eager bidders. This issue has always been a very popular one, and one that has, on occasion, been hoarded and preyed upon by promoters. In any case, it has an interesting history of auction appearances.

The 1973 Florida United Numismatists (FUN) Convention Sale, conducted by RARCOA, featured the Bruce Todd collection of dollars. That sale marked the first occasion on which nationwide numismatic attention was focused on a single collection of Morgan Dollars. Included in the collection was an 1889-O described as an "Outstanding (prooflike) example of this difficult date with highly frosty devices." That coin realized the then impressive sum of $150. Keep in mind that a typical mint state example of an 1889-O was worth about fifteen dollars at that time. The Todd collection introduced a period of unprecedented popularity for the Morgan series. Four years later, another sale which also included a noteworthy 1889-O was to mark the upsurge of another era of "Morganmania."

The sale was the Stanford Sale (Steve Ivy Numismatic Auctions, July, 1977). The 1889-O contained therein was presented with the following description:

> Fully prooflike. Full hair above the ear, and each breast feather is sharp. Liberty's cheek is satiny and virtually free of any impairments. The fields are dazzling and incredibly mark-free, as the least bit of contact would leave a telltale sign on such fragile mirror surfaces.

That coin sold for $700 after spirited floor bidding. The ratio of this price to the forty dollars or so that a typical mint state coin was bringing at the time was even greater than the ten-to-one performance ratio brought by the Todd specimen. This increased ratio accurately reflected the main difference between the two eras: this time around, quality would mean proportionately more than it ever did before.

RARITY IN PROOFLIKE: The 1889-O is very scarce with prooflike surfaces. Since the typical mint state example is very low in quality, prooflike pieces with minimal abrasions and sharp strikes are precious. Some especially nice examples with considerable cameo contrast have appeared at auction sales and on the bourse floors of major numismatic gatherings.

RARITY IN SUPERB CONDITION: This issue is rare in superb MS (67) or better condition. Since the quality of the typical specimen is so low, the desire for exceptional specimens is especially high. Most coins that qualify as superb are prooflike as well; perhaps they were preserved by early collectors who were attracted to their reflective surfaces. Frosty coins of similar quality may have been thrown back into the bag.

REDFIELD: No.

INVESTMENT POTENTIAL: This issue has solidly established its popularity and its ability to withstand wholesale promotion. Sharply struck examples with few enough bagmarks to allow an MS (65) classification should seem attractive to investors. Since average quality specimens are in plentiful supply and enjoy only limited demand, they should be avoided.

1889-S

Typical Mint State Example
MS (63), sharp strike, moderate
bagmarks, semiprooflike surfaces,
excellent luster.

GENERAL DISCUSSION: The typical mint state example just misses the MS (65) level, due to frequent bagmarks. It is safe to say that the average mint state quality of this issue is superior to the San Francisco issues of 1885-1888. Like the 1886-S and 1888-S, this issue is relatively scarce in circulated grades. Even well worn coins command some premium value.

The San Francisco coiners must have learned a lesson about polishing the dies in 1888. None of the bothersome evidence of this practice can be seen on coins of this issue. The surfaces of an 1889-S are frequently semiprooflike, although frosty coins are nearly as frequently encountered.

An occasional specimen with gorgeous toning is seen. These coins no doubt were already in collectors' hands before the distribution of coins from the estate of LaVere Redfield.

RARITY IN PROOFLIKE: Like virtually any issue whose typical mint state example has semiprooflike surfaces, the true scarcity of the 1889-S in prooflike is underrated. Although such coins are by no means rare, they do deserve a higher premium than the nominal amount they now command. With mirror fields and frosted devices, this issue is becoming very difficult to locate.

RARITY IN SUPERB CONDITION: Although continually being removed from the market by quality conscious collectors and investors, MS (65) examples are available at the current time.

REDFIELD: Yes, the Redfield Hoard contained some number of bags of 1889-S's. Those seen were of typical mint state quality for the issue, or perhaps slightly better. Compared to most other Redfield dates, the 1889-S was one of the higher quality members of that fantastic group of coins.

INVESTMENT POTENTIAL: Examples with few bagmarks will be in the greatest demand in the future. Strike, luster and surfaces should pose no problem for the prospective purchaser. Typical MS (63) quality or less is readily available due to the Redfield coins. Superb MS (67) quality remains elusive.

1889-CC

Typical Mint State Example
MS (65), sharp strike, light
bagmarks, prooflike surfaces, good
luster.

GENERAL DISCUSSION: This issue qualifies as one of the key dates of the Morgan Dollar series. It is the rarest Morgan from the Carson City Mint.

Although this issue is rare in mint state condition, the typical 1889-CC that has never seen circulation is of high quality. The strike is sharp, enabling the eagle to display well defined breast feathers. The luster is almost always coruscant and pleasing. The surfaces are prooflike more often than not. The 1889-CC is the only Morgan Dollar issue of which over half of the surviving mint state examples have prooflike surfaces. Bagmarks are generally light.

The excellent condition of mint state 1889-CC's is due to two facts. First, the Carson City Mint obviously produced a fine product this year. After being closed nearly four years, the Mint resumed limited operations, coining a relatively small quantity of silver dollars and twenty dollar gold pieces. The small work load may have enabled closer quality control than was normally possible. Also, judging from the circumstances surrounding the mint's closing (which implied some dubious ethics on the part of highly placed Mint officials) the new superintendent may have felt that his product would be closely scrutinized.

Second, at an early point in the history of active American numismatics, the 1889-CC dollar was recognized as a scarce and potentially valuable coin. Consequently, many specimens were preserved that otherwise would have been spent to help alleviate a financial crisis. Not many families could afford to hold a collection of silver dollars through the Great Depression. The 1889-CC would have been one of the last coins to be parted with — an uncirculated example sold for about $10 in 1930.

Collecting United States coins by date and mintmark became more popular beginning in the late 1930s, a time during which thousands of bags of mint state dollars were yet unsearched for better dates. It is likely that, during this era, the eyecatching pieces with prooflike surfaces were retrieved from bags, and less attractive, bagmarked frosty coins were thrown back like a fish too small to keep. Thus, a preponderance of prooflikes exist today.

A basic axiom of the present numismatic scene is that the highest quality material is the first to be removed from the marketplace, and remains off of the market for the longest period of time. If this indeed is the case for 1889-CC dollars, and there is no reason to believe it is not, it is logical to assume that a high proportion of coins presently held in collections or investment portfolios are of MS (65) quality or better.

RARITY IN PROOFLIKE: Because of its overall rarity in mint state, this issue can be considered rare with prooflike surfaces. As a percentage of surviving mint state examples, however, this issue is one of the most common of the series with mirror surfaces. Slightly more than half of all uncirculated examples have prooflike surfaces.

RARITY IN SUPERB CONDITION: As may be implied from the characteristics of the typical mint state example, the average quality of this issue is high. The premium commanded by MS (67) or better specimens over MS (65) quality is relatively small.

REDFIELD: With the possible exception of a few circulated examples, no 1889-CC's were contained among the Redfield coins.

INVESTMENT POTENTIAL: The 1889-CC is a well established and highly respected rarity. Its potential for the future is limited only by its affordability. Specimens of virtually all grades are expected to increase in value at an equal or greater rate than the Morgan series as a whole.

1890

Typical Mint State Example
MS (60), average strike, heavy
bagmarks, frosty surfaces, poor
luster.

GENERAL DISCUSSION: This issue is readily available in mint state condition. However, most of the mint state examples encountered are only of MS (60) quality. In MS (65) or better grades, the 1890 is not to be confused with a common date.

This year ranks as one of the Philadelphia Mint's five worst efforts. The strike is often weak, and the surfaces are often unattractive due to abnormal metal flow. To make matters worse, bagmarks are usually present to a significant detracting degree.

Coins of MS (60) quality are valued only slightly above common bulk mint state dollars. Circulated dollars of this date command no premium.

Most auction records for individual specimens are for those with prooflike surfaces, which are very popular with collectors. Superb examples are very seldom offered, an indication of their scarcity.

RARITY IN PROOFLIKE: This issue is very scarce with reflective surfaces. Although the 1890-O receives more plaudits in prooflike, the Philly issue of this year is equally as rare. Specimens that are prooflike often exhibit numerous bagmarks, although they are generally well struck.

RARITY IN SUPERB CONDITION: Like the two Philadelphia issues immediately preceding it, the 1890 is extremely underrated in superb MS (67) or better condition. The experienced collector of the series knows how difficult it is to locate even a single specimen of this quality. Although original rolls are often available, thorough searching is not likely to uncover anything that would excite the Morgan connoisseur.

REDFIELD: A limited quantity of this issue was found as part of the Redfield dollars. They were, at best, of average quality.

PROOFS: Proofs of this year are noticeably scarcer than other dates. When found, however, they may be among the most attractive of the series, with a deep cameo effect. Unfortunately, many have been cleaned or mishandled in some way.

INVESTMENT POTENTIAL: In solid MS (65) or better quality, this issue should prove to be an above average investment. As the number of collectors grows and their quality consciousness heightens, the scarcity of this date in gem quality will be more widely recognized.

1890-O

Typical Mint State Example
MS (60), weak strike, moderate
bagmarks, frosty surfaces, good
luster.

GENERAL DISCUSSION: This issue is not difficult to locate in mint state condition. However, most mint state examples aren't worth finding — they are usually very weakly struck, and may have a bagmarking problem as well. Well struck coins are obtainable for those willing to pay the necessary premium.

MS (60) examples, although rather plentiful, command a premium of about double that of the most common dates in the same condition. On the other hand, MS (65) examples may bring a price ten times that for a common date! This great difference in price is an accurate indicator of the relative scarcity of this issue in gem MS (65) condition.

In circulated grades, the 1890-O commands little or no premium.

Auction records are scant, since few truly superb examples have appeared on the market in recent years. The usually higher priced 1889-O has been offered more frequently at public auction sales than the 1890-O.

The nicest example ever seen by the authors was a cameo prooflike sold at a coin show in New York in March, 1979. It was ushered into the private collection of a numismatic financier from Florida. The price he paid to obtain the piece was in excess of $700.

RARITY IN PROOFLIKE: Although highly touted as a rare issue in prooflike, the 1890-O has a record of appearances with reflective surfaces that belies this reputation. Prooflikes are often very attractive with considerable cameo tendency.

RARITY IN SUPERB CONDITION: Most superb examples of this issue are prooflike. A specimen of MS (67) or better quality with frosty surfaces and a minimum of bagmarks is rare. An unusually nice group of frosty coins was sold at several different coin shows in early 1979, bringing a price up to four hundred dollars each. Because of the preponderance of inferior specimens, superb coins enjoy a particularly brisk demand.

REDFIELD: No.

PROOFS: Little is known of the example that Breen mentions in his work on U.S. proof coins. He lists it as being a part of the DuPont collection.

INVESTMENT POTENTIAL: Typical mint state examples of this issue abound, and are not *apropos* to an astutely formed portfolio. Superb MS (67) specimens should be adequate performers. Frosty, well struck examples of MS (65) quality should not be overlooked.

1890-S

Typical Mint State Example
MS (65), sharp strike, moderate
bagmarks, semiprooflike surfaces,
excellent luster.

GENERAL DISCUSSION: This issue is relatively abundant on today's market in mint state condition. The appearance of the Redfield coins in 1976 markedly increased the number of uncirculated examples available.

Coins of this particular date and mint are almost always fully struck. The surfaces most often exhibit a vibrant, pleasing luster which is similar to that seen on the coins from the same mint produced in the 1879-1882 era. In fact, this year represents San Francisco's finest product in almost a decade. Because the majority of mint state examples that are extant today were stored for decades in bags of one thousand pieces, the inevitable contact marks resulting from abrasion from other coins are often a factor reducing the grade of an 1890-S.

Circulated examples are valued slightly more than the most common dates.

Before the Redfield Hoard was purchased and distributed, this issue was often touted as underrated. Perhaps the market absorbed the impact of the hoarded coins so well in part due to this.

RARITY IN PROOFLIKE: If all of the prooflike examples offered indeed had fully reflective surfaces, this issue might be considered common in prooflike; however, such is not the case. Most so-called prooflikes are merely typical, semiprooflike examples. Nice, genuinely prooflike coins are nonetheless available to the collector.

RARITY IN SUPERB CONDITION: Examples of this issue are relatively common in superb condition. Such coins may be either frosty or semiprooflike. Bagmarks are the primary deterrent to an MS (67) grade. For some reason, many superb examples are toned, such as one splendid specimen purchased by dealer Leroy Lenhardt for his son, David, at the Mid-Winter ANA Convention of 1982.

REDFIELD: The 1890-S is generally believed to have been one of the most numerous dates included in the LaVere Redfield estate. The exact number of bags acquired by the purchasers of the hoard has not been made known.

INVESTMENT POTENTIAL: Coins of this issue are more available in mint state condition than many more inexpensive dates. An adequate supply exists for generations of dollar collectors. It would be surprising if their performance as an investment outpaced or even equalled that of the Morgan series as a whole.

1890-CC

Typical Mint State Example
MS (63), sharp strike, moderate
bagmarks, frosty surfaces, good
luster.

GENERAL DISCUSSION: As Carson City Mint issues go, the 1890-CC is fairly typical in characteristics of the average mint state example. The strike is sharp on most of the coins available on the market today, and the luster is at least adequate. Mint state examples are generally obtainable with little difficulty. However, the collector who desires only MS (65) quality or better may have to examine several 1890-CC's before he finds one to his liking.

This issue may be the most common in circulated condition of any from the Carson City Mint. Well worn examples command a surprisingly small premium over the most common coins of the other mints. The premium accelerates as the grade of the coin increases, however, and specimens in extremely fine condition bring about triple the price of a common circulated dollar of the same grade.

Although not as abundant as the 1889-CC, this issue frequently is seen with prooflike surfaces. Most of the prooflike examples seen on the current scene probably came from the Redfield Hoard.

About four thousand mint state 1890-CC's were sold as part of the GSA sales commencing in 1972. Offered at a minimum bid of thirty dollars, the entire number was quickly sold out. The coins were awarded to bidders at $46 each. The coins were widely and evenly distributed.

One variety of 1890-CC dollar has a strip of extra metal extending downward from the left side of the eagle's tail. This "tailbar" variety has become very popular with collectors, no doubt due to its peculiar location and its ease of detection by the unaided eye. The 1890-CC is the only Morgan Dollar on which the "tailbar" appears.

RARITY IN PROOFLIKE: Due to the 1978 appearance of several hundred prooflike coins from the Redfield Hoard, the 1890-CC is frequently seen with prooflike surfaces. Once these coins are absorbed into the numismatic mainstream, however, one can expect prooflikes to become much scarcer.

RARITY IN SUPERB CONDITION: Dense bagmarking often prohibits an otherwise superb example from reaching the MS (67) level. Occasionally a beautifully toned example is seen; such a coin no doubts predates the appearance of the Redfield coins. The finest example ever witnessed by the authors was sold by Steve Ivy Rare Coin Company to a midwestern coin company in 1977.

REDFIELD: A relatively small quantity, perhaps one or two bags, of mint state 1890-CC's were included in Mr. Redfield's holdings. Several hundred of these coins were fully struck, prooflike examples.

INVESTMENT POTENTIAL: With the added dimension of demand from Carson City dollar collectors, the date possesses definite potential. The latest government sales contained none of this issue; since the campaign publicizing the sale was directed primarily to the allure of the Carson City Mint and the investment aspects of silver dollars, this issue will greatly benefit. Regardless of its future performance on an absolute dollars and cents basis, the 1890-CC should out-perform most of its Carson City counterparts.

1891

Typical Mint State Example
MS (60), weak strike, moderate to
heavy bagmarks, frosty surfaces,
poor luster.

GENERAL DISCUSSION: Beginning in 1888, the Philadelphia Mint began to relax its previously strict quality controls. The 1889 mintage was inferior to 1888; the 1890 likewise to 1889. In 1891 our first mint reached a new low in the quality of its silver dollar production.

Either from inadequate striking or abnormal metal flow, dollars of this issue are usually lacking complete details. The luster is often not pleasing, and bagmarks are a familiar sight. (The bagmarking problem cannot be attributed to the irresponsibility of the mint — the coins were indeed bagged into lots of a thousand at their point of production, but the contact marks were not irretrievably impressed upon their surfaces until they were later transported from city to city, from bank to bank, etc.)

This particular date is surprisingly easy to find in mint state condition. MS (60) examples abound in dealers' ads and at major coin shows. Finding an MS (65) example is another matter.

MS (60) and MS (65) examples were once, in the not too distant past, valued ridiculously close together. Increased knowledge and a heightened sense of quality consciousness on the part of today's collectors have rightfully increased the amount of this price difference.

Circulated examples command little or no premium over common dates.

At a time when the typical mint state example of an 1891 dollar was worth about sixty dollars, a brace of exceptional coins were offered at public auction sale. Steve Ivy Numismatic Auctions presented the William C. Kerr Sale in February, 1979. Lots 878 and 879 were 1891 dollars. The first was a beautifully toned, virtually mark-free example; the second, Wayne Miller's plate coin, was a superb, untoned specimen with semiprooflike surfaces.

The toned piece, after very spirited bidding, brought an impressive $925, a record price for the date by a considerable margin. The record proved to be short-lived, since Miller's coin was knocked down at an astounding $1,500.

RARITY IN PROOFLIKE: This issue is rarely seen with prooflike surfaces. Semiprooflike examples are scarce in their own right, and are often described as prooflike. The ratio of prooflike coins to the total number of surviving mint state examples is among the lowest of the entire series.

RARITY IN SUPERB CONDITION: Superb coins of MS (67) or better quality are quite rare. As the discussion of the auction records above indicated, such coins command great respect from knowledgeable and experienced collectors.

REDFIELD: A quantity of 1891 dollars was discovered to be part of the Redfield Hoard. Their quality was poor — the great majority were only MS (60).

PROOFS: Besides the usual cleaning and mishandling problems, proofs of this date may also be weakly struck. They are slightly scarcer than most other dates, but not sufficiently so to enable a premium price to be commanded.

INVESTMENT POTENTIAL: Mint State examples of this issue that are only of typical quality are very overrated — they are much more available than their three-figure price indicates. On the other hand, atypical specimens, i.e., those of solid MS (65) or better grade, are scarce and, even at the new higher levels, may have some upward mobility remaining.

1891-O

Typical Mint State Example
MS (60), weak strike, moderate
bagmarks, frosty surfaces, poor
luster.

GENERAL DISCUSSION: In terms of the typical mint state example, this issue ranks as one of the worst Morgans of them all. It may indeed be the most poorly struck issue of the entire series. Not only do many specimens lack even the faintest hint of a feather on the eagle's breast, but many are so weak that they appear to be concave in that area. If one is fortunate enough to find a well struck coin, chances are that it will be so bagmarked that no collector would want to add it to his set, thus explaining its availability. Virtually all superb, well struck specimens with minimal marks have been removed from the market by advanced collectors.

Average mint state examples are always available. In fact, the buyer of such an item can often bargain a seemingly attractive price. Circulated coins, unless one includes well struck and lustrous almost uncirculated examples, command no premium over the most common dates.

The Bruce Todd specimen (RARCOA, January, 1973) was a fully mirrored cameo prooflike. It brought a whopping $200 when a typical frosty coin of this issue was worth no more than ten dollars! This twenty-to-one ratio was repeated six years later when the William Kerr coin brought $2,200, then a record price for a coin of this date.

RARITY IN PROOFLIKE: This issue is extremely rare with prooflike surfaces. Most examples that qualify as prooflike are relatively unattractive, although some cameo examples are known. A genuinely prooflike example elicits profound respect from experienced collectors.

RARITY IN SUPERB CONDITION: This particular date and mint is exceedingly rare in superb condition. Most specimens which can be called better than MS (65) quality are prooflike — perhaps early collectors saved them because of their unusual and attractive surfaces. This issue is much rarer in fully struck, MS (67) condition than its New Orleans successor.

REDFIELD: No.

PROOFS: Breen says "two reported," one in the Dupont collection and one in the late Amon Carter's holdings.

INVESTMENT POTENTIAL: Similar to the Philadelphia issue bearing the same date, the 1891-O is underrated in high quality and overrated in typical quality. Since recent developments have drastically increased the value of an MS (65) or better specimen, investors must be sure that they are salting away a *bona fide* gem example of this date. Otherwise, the passing of decades still may not make their investment a wise one.

1891-S

Typical Mint State Example
MS (65), sharp strike, moderate
bagmarks, semiprooflike surfaces,
excellent luster.

GENERAL DISCUSSION: This issue is very similar to the 1890-S in every respect. The typical mint state example is of above average quality for the Morgan series. Weakly struck coins are seen a little more frequently than for the previous San Francisco Mint issue, as also are frosty rather than semiprooflike or fully reflective surfaces. The majority of coins have a full strike and some degree of prooflike surfaces, however.

Mint state examples are readily available, moreso than some more inexpensive dates. Circulated coins are considered common unless very close to uncirculated condition.

Most of the mint state examples available on today's market probably originated in the Redfield Hoard.

Of the several thousands of 1891-S's examined by the authors, one coin stands out in their memories. That piece is an exquisite MS (69) specimen offered as part of the Stanford Sale (Steve Ivy Numismatic Auctions, July, 1977) and described as "A true candidate for MS (70). Will surely bring a record bid." It surely did: $180. Thought to have been an enormous price at the time, the lucky owner of the coin would not doubt multiply his investment were he to reconsign the piece in today's quality-crazed market.

That coin and its price received much publicity, along with the 1889-O and other coins from the same sale. Whether the Stanford Sale coincided with the upturn in demand for superb dollars, or was partly responsible for that phenomenon is open to conjecture. In either case, that landmark sale will always be remembered as an early indication of the burgeoning demand for Morgan and Peace dollars in oustanding states of preservation.

RARITY IN PROOFLIKE: This issue is not particularly scarce in prooflike. With full mirror surfaces, it is considerably more common than the 1890-S. Prooflikes of this date usually have some degree of cameo contrast between the fields and devices. Most of the examples with reflective surfaces that are available to collectors today may have been marketed as part of the Redfield coins.

RARITY IN SUPERB CONDITION: Superb specimens of this issue occur more frequently than the typical Morgan. They are more common than superb examples of some less expensive dates. Any Morgan such as the MS (69) 1891-S from the Stanford Sale is a rarity in its own right, however.

REDFIELD: With the exception of the common S-mints from the 1879-1882 years, this issue, in the authors' opinions, seems to be one of the most plentiful of those included in the Redfield Hoard. This judgment is based on the relative frequency of appearance of dates from that source, and not on any direct knowledge of the precise contents of the Redfield Estate.

INVESTMENT POTENTIAL: There is no reason for typical 1891-S's to outperform the Morgan series as a whole in the future. As with all dates superb MS (67) or better specimens will be in the greatest demand in the future.

1891-CC

Typical Mint State Example
MS (63), above average strike,
moderate bagmarks, frosty surfaces,
good luster.

GENERAL DISCUSSION: The average quality of Carson City Mint silver dollars declined a bit in 1891. This date is the poorest in quality since the scarce 1879 issue from this historic Nevada mint. While above average for the Morgan series, the strike is fairly typical for a Carson City issue.

Mint state examples, though by no means abundant, are available on the current market. Coins of MS (65) or better quality are becoming more difficult to locate. Circulated examples are marginally scarcer than the 1890-CC and 1878-CC issues, and are most often seen in very fine or worse condition. Extremely fine or better coins command a significant premium over common dates.

About 5,500 mint state 1891-CC's were quickly sold from the GSA's holdings at a price of $42 each. While the price of both the 1890-CC and 1891-CC dollars has advanced in the years since the Great Carson City Dollar Sales, the 1891-CC has maintained a value of approximately ninety percent of the 1890-CC (the price of the GSA 1890-CC's was $46 each).

RARITY IN PROOFLIKE: The 1891-CC is deceptively difficult to locate with prooflike surfaces. This date is much scarcer than many more expensively priced items. When located, mirrored specimens are often sharply struck cameos. Unfortunately, the fragile surfaces magnify the damage done by the ever-present bagmarks. A prooflike with few contact marks should elicit much respect from knowledgeable collectors.

RARITY IN SUPERB CONDITION: The 1891-CC is also very scarce in superb MS (67) or superior condition. While usually well struck, even superb specimens often exhibit a somewhat indistinct look that may be due to overworked dies.

REDFIELD: A quantity, little affecting the market, was included in the Redfield estate.

PROOFS: Famed numismatist B. Max Mehl lists a brilliant proof in the Belden E. Roach Collection Sale of February, 1944. In those days, however, "proof" was regarded more as a grade rather than a method of striking. A particularly nice coin with prooflike surfaces was apt to be called "proof," "semi-proof," or even "about proof." This was the only dollar from the branch mints so designated by Mehl in this rather comprehensive catalog, so it would be unscholarly to assume that the coin had no chance of being a *bona fide* proof. It is untraceable today.

INVESTMENT POTENTIAL: The popularity of the Carson City dollars favors this issue's potential for future price appreciation. Since the GSA had no significant number of this date to offer, the new collectors created by the massive sale had to look to existing supplies to fill their needs for this date. Superb examples are vastly underrated at today's levels. He who locates an MS (67) specimen at a reasonable price has performed a numismatic investment gambit that may prove tough to match.

1892

Typical Mint State Example
MS (60), weak strike, moderate
bagmarks, frosty surfaces, poor to
good luster.

GENERAL DISCUSSION: The disappointing ineptitude of the Philadelphia Mint continued from the dismal 1891 production into 1892. It is possible, judging from the diversity of the quality of surviving mint state examples of this date and the high quality of the following year, that changes designed to improve the silver dollar were instituted late in the calendar year 1892. The majority of mint state 1892 dollars from the Philadelphia Mint resemble coins of 1891 vintage; these were likely produced early in the year, when the mint workers continued the methods, and possibly using some of the same reverse dies, employed during 1891. Other mint state dollars resemble coins of 1893 which, as will be discussed at the appropriate time, are of generally very high quality. It may be logically assumed that such coins were produced late in the production run of 1892 dollars.

The coins from the Redfield Hoard were of typical mint state quality. They probably constitute the majority of coins on the market today.

Unless in almost uncirculated condition, coins of this issue that have undergone any circulation are only slightly more valuable than the most common dates.

Although most superb examples of this date that exist are impounded in connoiseurs' collections, the rising prices of exceptionally well preserved Morgans have brought a few superior specimens beneath the auctioneer's gavel. The finest was a practically mark-free, semiprooflike example in the C.W. Henderson Sale (Steve Ivy Numismatic Auctions, January, 1978). That piece realized a now modest $650. In the same sale, an MS (65) prooflike example of the same date brought $660.

RARITY IN PROOFLIKE: The appearance of a small number of prooflike specimens in recent years should not deceive the dollar enthusiast into believing that this issue is anything but rare with fully reflective surfaces. Many so-called prooflikes are merely semiprooflike. Semiprooflike coins occur with an inordinately high frequency. Locating coins with true mirror surfaces however is another matter.

RARITY IN SUPERB CONDITION: This issue is very scarce in superb MS (67) or better grades. Most coins which qualify for this lofty level have semiprooflike surfaces, and were likely manufactured separately from the much more frequently encountered examples which exhibit the typical mint state characteristics for this issue.

REDFIELD: The unknown, though probably modest, quantity of 1892 Morgans to emerge from the Redfield saga typified the average mint state quality of this issue. No prooflike nor superb coins are known to have been part of Redfield's holdings.

PROOFS: Proofs of this year can be surprisingly weakly struck. Perhaps more attention was paid to the careful production of the proofs of the new dime, quarter and half designed by Charles Barber than to the Morgan Dollar. However, some of the nicest examples of Morgan proofs can be coins which bear the date 1892. The new designs for the minor coins were undoubtedly responsible for the preservation of a greater than average number of complete proof sets. Proof coins thus preserved, and Morgans are no exception, are generally of superior quality to those which have been handled individually over the decades.

An exquisitely and naturally toned Proof specimen appeared in the Roger M. Turner Sale (Steve Ivy Numismatic Auctions, November, 1978). That beautiful coin brought a pacesetting price of three thousand dollars. Proof Morgans of similar quality and rarity have since reached even higher levels.

INVESTMENT POTENTIAL: Typical mint state examples are rather abundant on today's market and should not be actively sought for investment purposes. Solid MS (65) examples may prove difficult to locate in the future. MS (67) or better quality is already a challenge to find, and will not become easier to acquire as the roster of dollar collectors continues to lengthen.

1892-O

Typical Mint State Example
MS (63), weak strike, light bagmarks,
frosty surfaces, good luster.

GENERAL DISCUSSION: The 1892-O is a notoriously weakly struck issue. A total lack of breast feathers and no hair detail above Miss Liberty's ear are typical traits of a mint state 1892-O dollar. Ironically, this issue is generally much less bagmarked than most. The authors have seen some coins that were virtually perfect as far as bagmarks were concerned, and left little to be desired in the luster department, but which lacked any detail at all on the high points.

At the present time, there are many more of these typically weakly struck coins available than there are buyers to absorb them. Circulated examples, unless near mint state, are common.

Much to the delight of frustrated collectors, a group of sharply struck coins, predominantly with full breast feathers, appeared through a Wisconsin dealer. The earliest point at which the authors examined any of these surprising coins was at the American Numismatic Association's first Mid-Winter Convention, in Colorado Springs during February, 1978. They were considerably bagmarked, but several were unmarred enough to enable an MS (65) classification. Some of the finest specimens, which could be described as MS (67), fully struck, were retained by the dealer who distributed the coins.

Most of the well struck examples on the market today probably originated in this group of coins.

RARITY IN PROOFLIKE: The 1892-O is one of the rarest coins of the entire series with prooflike surfaces. The authors have seen fewer than ten specimens in all; only two of these would reach the MS (65) level. The examples seen have all been unattractive and lacking significant cameo effect. It is doubtful that a truly attractive prooflike 1892-O exists.

RARITY IN SUPERB CONDITION: Specimens which qualify as superb from a bagmark standpoint are usually very weakly struck. Well struck specimens with minimal marks were virtually unknown before the appearance of the "mini-hoard" discussed above. As these coins are inexorably absorbed into collections, this issue will no doubt return to its position of being one of the most difficult of the series to obtain in superb condition.

REDFIELD: No.

PROOFS: Breen reports one unverified example in the Amon Carter collection.

INVESTMENT POTENTIAL: Weakly struck examples would most likely prove to be unwise investments, although they may rise in value with the Morgan series and inflation. Sharp specimens with as few bagmarks as possible, while they are available at all, should be seriously considered. As far as acquiring a sharp 1892-O is concerned, these *are* the good ol' days.

1892-S

Typical Mint State Example
MS (65), sharp strike, light
bagmarks, semiprooflike surfaces,
excellent luster.

GENERAL DISCUSSION: In mint state condition, this issue ranks as one of the greatest rarities of the Morgan series. As with some of the other rarer members of the series (e.g., 1884-S, 1893-S, and 1903-S), the 1892-S, when located in mint state condition, is usually a gem. In fact, some of the nicest Morgan dollars observed by this writer have been 1892-S's. This high ratio of superb pieces may be explained by the fact that virtually all 1892-S's were immediately released into circulation in the year of their minting. Bags of coins may have been transported from the mint in San Francisco to area banks, but no further. Thus, the coins that survived for collectors' pleasure today are refreshingly bagmark free. About half of the superb examples seen have been beautifully toned, always on both sides, indicating long-time storage in collections, rather than storage in paper rolls or canvas bags.

Several superb specimens of 1892-S's come to mind. The earliest recalled was a prooflike, near perfect gem, purchased by Max Humbert from the Coen-Messer Coin Co. in 1972. Mr. Humbert purchased a second outstanding gem, this one toned, on the floor of the 1977 American Numismatic Association Convention. Two gems, one brilliant semiprooflike and one toned, were featured in the Fairfield Collection (Bowers & Ruddy, October, 1977). They realized $13,500 and $14,500 respectively. In the summer of 1975, Paramount International Coin Corp. purchased a semiprooflike gem from Worldwide Coin Corp. of Atlanta, who had purchased the coin, along with such rarities as an 1831 silver proof set, from a midwestern collection. After the coin had been in their inventory for a while, it was sold into a prominent central Connecticut collection for approximately $20,000. There the coin resided for approximately a year and one-half. Dealer Jim Jelinski of Essex Numismatics then handled the coin, and sold it for an alleged $40,000 into a closely-held prominent collection.

In the December, 1981 ANA Building Fund Sale conducted by Steve Ivy Numismatic Auctions, a superb MS (67) 1892-S was offered. It was described as having a frosty obverse and a semiprooflike reverse. Dealer Charles Anastasio of Charles Coin Company purchased that magnificent specimen and immediately resold it to one of his better clients, a quality conscious collector from New Jersey.

Circulated 1892-S's in grades of Very Fine or less are quite easily locatable and are valued only slightly higher than the most commonly circulated Morgan dollars. Although not difficult to find in circulated grades above Very Fine, the dearness of this date in mint state condition begins to buoy the value of circulated coins as they approach the almost uncirculated level. Lustrous, almost uncirculated, coins can bring a four figure price.

Bogus 1892-S's made by adding a mintmark to an 1892 Philadelphia dollar are easily detected by qualified persons.

RARITY IN PROOFLIKE: Despite the fact that the typical mint state example bears semiprooflike surfaces, 1892-S's with fully reflective mirrors are extremely rare. When found, however, such examples are invariably sharply struck and quite pleasing.

RARITY IN SUPERB CONDITION: Incredible as it may seem, the 1892-S is probably the most common Morgan dollar in MS (67) or better condition as a percentage of the total mint state population. An MS (67) example is more often encountered than an honestly graded MS (60).

REDFIELD: No, as exciting as it would have been, no 1892-S's were among Mr. Redfield's holdings. Although the existence of some coins of this state was naturally suspected when the hoard was unleashed in February of 1976, such prophecies were never fulfilled.

INVESTMENT POTENTIAL: This date is firmly established as a major Morgan dollar rarity. Its investment potential will be limited only by the number of active collectors able to afford the significant investment that an 1892-S requires. Since superb examples are the rule rather than the exception, sub par examples should be avoided for investment purposes.

1892-CC

Typical Mint State Example
MS (63), above average strike,
moderate bagmarks, frosty surfaces,
excellent luster.

GENERAL DISCUSSION: The appearance of the Redfield dollars in 1976 altered the average quality of mint state examples of this issue available to collectors. Unlike the majority of uncirculated coins on the market prior to the dispersal of that historic numismatic legacy; the Redfield 1892-CC's were virtually all sharply struck. This writer vividly recalls the occasion when a sealed bag of 1892-CC's was opened in his presence; examination of the first handful of coins immediately indicated a great boon for silver dollar collectors.

Although many of the Redfield coins were considerably bagmarked, they were no worse than those to which collectors were accustomed. A surprising number of pieces were pleasantly void of dense contact marks. The pieces that Paramount International Coin Corporation received from the accumulation were notable for their overall quality.

Specimens from the Redfield estate are readily available, for a price. Time will undoubtedly serve to allow the worst quality to rise to the surface of the market, and cause the highest grade coins to be immobilized in collections or investment portfolios. Within the next decade, weakly struck coins, or sharply struck but bagmarked specimens will dominate the market.

An important point: the GSA held no 1892-CC's among the nearly three million Carson City dollars discovered in U.S. Treasury vaults.

Because of the value of mint state examples and the scarcity of circulated coins, this issue commands a sizable premium even in low grades.

One of the most memorable Morgan Dollars of any date was from the Bruce Todd collection. The catalog of the Todd Sale, conducted by RARCOA in January, 1973, highlighted this fantastic coin, describing it as ''easily mistakable for a true branch mint PROOF'' (sic). The then impressive price of $600 that the coin realized affirmed its remarkable condition.

RARITY IN PROOFLIKE: This issue is quite scarce with prooflike surfaces. Many semiprooflike examples, which are relatively commonplace, are offered as prooflike. Coins of this issue which have mirrored fields are usually well struck.

RARITY IN SUPERB CONDITION: The small percentage of Redfield coins that qualified as MS (67) or better have mostly disappeared from the market. Since very few superb coins were known in pre-Redfield days, the population of superior pieces remains well below the level that today's demand would support.

REDFIELD: Most of the mint state examples of this issue available on today's market emanated from the Redfield hoard. The number distributed was far short of that which would adversely affect the market. On the contrary, the appearance of the Redfield coins served to stimulate the market for this and practically all other Morgan dates. Whatever quantity the Redfield estate contained, it was miniscule when compared to the GSA holdings of other Carson City productions.

Although surprisingly high in average quality, many of the Redfield 1892-CC's exhibit a shiny scrape along the brow and cheek of Liberty on the obverse. This was caused by a coin counting machine. A hard rubber wheel drives the coins through the machine; those Redfield dollars which happened to pass under the wheel with the obverse up received the scrape. Those which passed through with the reverse side exposed to the wheel were not affected due to the geometry of the design — the high point of the reverse, the eagle's breast, did not touch the wheel. It is important to keep in mind that not all Redfield dollars were counted by such a machine and that, of those that were, only a portion were impaired.

PROOFS: Breen reports one unverified example, which is definitely not the Todd coin said to approach branch mint proof by RARCOA.

INVESTMENT POTENTIAL: Weakly struck and/or bagmarked specimens are readily available, at least for the time being. Even MS (63) specimens will eventually be absorbed by Carson City collectors, however. Solid MS (65) or better quality in this date should prove to be a viable investment.

1893

Typical Mint State Example
MS (65), average strike, light
bagmarks, frosty surfaces, excellent
luster.

GENERAL DISCUSSION: This year presents a refreshing change in the quality of the Philadelphia Mint's production of silver dollars. The typical mint state 1893 is far superior to the typical mint state coin of any of the preceding five years of our first mint's efforts. The only shortcoming of this issue is an occasional weak strike.

This issue is very scarce in circulated grades.

Because of its high average quality, its low mintage and its desirability for one-coin-of-each-year sets, 1893 has always been a very popular issue among collectors, investors and promoters. Only recently have nice mint state examples become difficult to locate.

Although of generally high quality, this issue has scant auction records in superb condition. The Ronald Keller specimen (Paramount, May, 1973) was listed as MS (70), and realized $285. The Fairfield Collection (Bowers and Ruddy, October, 1977) contained thirteen specimens, twelve of which were described as "choice" and only one as "gem."

RARITY IN PROOFLIKE: Prooflike examples are extremely rare. Semiprooflike coins are very scarce. Wayne Miller's rating of rarity-9 (the second rarest level) in prooflike is well deserved and may even be conservative. Most specimens with truly reflective fields seen by the authors have been in either almost uncirculated or MS (60) condition. An MS (65) or better specimen with prooflike surfaces would create quite a stir among dollar afficionados.

RARITY IN SUPERB CONDITION: As a ratio of superb examples to the total surviving mint state population, the 1893 is not particularly scarce; in fact, it probably ranks in the top fourth of the entire series. Most advanced collections contain a superior example of the 1893.

REDFIELD: A very modest number of this date was included in the Redfield estate. It is believed that a bag of 1893 dollars was sold from the estate before its sale in January, 1976. This may have occured approximately two years prior. Paramount International Coin Corporation acquired most of the coins of this date, and quickly sold them all.

PROOFS: Proofs of this issue are the most poorly struck of the series. It is very unusual to locate a proof example with full hair detail above the ear and full breast feathers on the eagle. Like other dates, many coins have been clean or mishandled.

INVESTMENT POTENTIAL: If you prefer to invest in a commodity with a proven successful track record, then 1893 Morgan Dollars are a definite candidate for inclusion in your portfolio. The popularity of this issue is well established, and they seem to be getting more difficult to locate in MS (65) or better condition. As a complete set of Morgans becomes prohibitively expensive, collecting only one coin of each date rather than one coin of each date *and* mint will likely become more popular. This issue is the only logical candidate for inclusion in such a set.

1893-O

Typical Mint State Example
MS (60), weak strike, moderate
bagmarks, frosty surfaces, good
luster.

GENERAL DISCUSSION: This issue is regarded as one of the most difficult of the series to obtain in mint state condition, particularly in MS (65) grade or better. A decade or so ago, while gem examples were difficult to locate, strictly uncirculated 1893-O's were much more available than they are today. The authors can recall selecting choice mint state examples from original rolls in 1972. A collection in Indiana contained several such rolls, which have long since been disassembled and sold as singles.

The typical mint state example of this scarce issue is weakly struck, but not so much so as other New Orleans issues from 1891 to 1896. Some very weak, but negligibly bagmarked, coins exist. They are strictly mint state but, like some 1892-O's, may exhibit the detail that a coin in very fine to extremely fine condition might normally show. Fully struck coins, or those nearly so, are very rare.

Circulated examples are scarce — high grade, extremely fine to almost uncirculated coins are very much in demand and hard to get, especially with any original mint luster remaining.

The owner of a strictly mint state 1893-O can be assured that he possesses a noteworthy coin. Those whose collections include an MS (65) example are even more fortunate. Superb MS (67) or better coins are indeed rarities; only two coins of this caliber have been handled by the authors.

The first was a superb prooflike coin whose only conceivable objectionable trait was a slight softness of strike. It was purchased from the now defunct El Paso Rare Coin Company at the Numismatic Association of Southern California's 1973 convention. It subsequently appeared in a Paramount sale, purchased therefrom for $775 by Maryland dealer Julian Leidman.

The second was a beautifully toned, well struck example that changed hands four times in three months before finding a home in an important midwestern collection in 1978. The last price at which the piece was sold was in the $4,500 range.

Added mintmarks are no problem for this issue, since a forger would not take the odds that are offered by altering an 1893 Philadelphia coin by adding a New Orleans mintmark — he would only be tripling the value if his job were perfect, which it never is. The more logical course would be to alter the date of an 1898-O, a common issue. Detection of this nefarious practice is easy by comparison with a known genuine 1893-O. The "3" of the date will be thicker and more rounded on the genuine example. Examination of the altered second "8" of the date of the 1898-O will reveal telltale tooling marks.

RARITY IN PROOFLIKE: This issue is very rare with fully prooflike surfaces. Semi-prooflike coins are occasionally encountered. Several coins with sparkling, near-prooflike reverses only are recalled.

RARITY IN SUPERB CONDITION: Relatively few specimens of this issue are believed to exist in superb MS (67) or better condition. There is ample reason to suspect that most of those which did survive in an exemplary state are imbedded firmly in fine collections. The proud owners of such pieces have refused to part with them, even in light of drastic price increases.

REDFIELD: No.

INVESTMENT POTENTIAL: As a key member of the series, this issue possesses
obvious investment potential. The most crucial factor in a successful investment is assurance
that a properly graded and fairly priced coin is acquired at the time of purchase. Well struck
examples of MS (63) or better quality will always be in great demand.

1893-S

Typical Mint State Example
MS (65), sharp strike, light
bagmarks, semiprooflike surfaces,
excellent luster.

GENERAL DISCUSSION: The 1893-S is the rarest and most valuable Morgan Dollar in both circulated and mint state grades. Its low mintage (100,000) and heavy circulation in the burgeoning commerce of America's West account for its scarcity today.

As the typical mint state characteristics indicate, when an 1893-S is found in mint state condition, it is usually a gem. In uncirculated grades, this issue is several times rarer than its immediate predecessor from the San Francisco mint. In circulated grades it is still quite scarce and is in great demand by collectors ambitious to complete a Morgan set yet reluctant to pay a solid five figure price for an uncirculated example.

The appearance of a gem 1893-S is always a momentous occasion among Morgan enthusiasts. Such appearances may occur only at the rate of a dozen or so per decade, including repeat offerings of the same coin.

"The finest known 1893-S" is a frequent topic of conversation among Morgan experts. While opinions vary on this subjective question, most respondents enumerate one of the following three specimens, each of which has appeared on the market at least once within the past ten years:

1.) *The George F. Mosher, Jr. Collection specimen.*
Obtained by Mr. Mosher from George Vogt of Colonial Coin Company in 1976 for $28,500.00. Colonial bought the coin from Norm Schultz, a venerable dealer who reportedly had three gem 1893-S's at the time.

2.) *The Love-Rettew-Kagin specimen.*
Presently in the collection of a New England collector who prefers anonymity. Described in Kagin's September, 1978, GENA sale as "Semi-Proof-like (sic) Gem Brilliant Uncirculated-65! Virtually fully struck up in all areas, all breast feathers showing. Full lustrous cartwheel effect over entire coin with shining satin surfaces." That lot sold to dealer Jim Jelinski of Essex Numismatic properties for $52,000.00 with Wayne Miller underbidding, then to a major Connecticut collection, then to Bruce Amspacher, at that time with Fred Sweeney Rare Coin Company, then to its present home for a price reportedly just over $100,000.00.

3.) *The Davies-Fairfield specimen.*
Present location unverified. Purchased by David Akers of Paramount International Coin Corporation in November, 1973 for $12,000.00, then sold to Fred Davies, one of Paramount's best customers, the following year. When Mr. Davies' collection was sold at the 1975 NASC auction by Paramount, his 1893-S was described as: "Unc-70. A superb GEM that is easily the finest that I have ever seen of this date. Very boldly struck both over the ear and on the eagle's breast. Beautiful light violet brown and golden toning around the edges...a few totally insignificant marks..."
It brought $35,000.00 from a wealthy Connecticut numismatist, who sold his holdings through Bowers and Ruddy's Fairfield Sale in October, 1977. At that time the same coin realized $29,000.00. Bowers and Ruddy's described by as "among the

top several finest known."

As many as a dozen other examples have appeared in the last ten years. Probably the most notable is the late Amon Carter, Jr.'s sold by Stack's in January, 1984. Steve Ivy Rare Coin Company sold a gem in 1978 to an Eastern collector; that coin is the only gem deeply toned specimen seen by the authors. Dealer Julian Leidman reports having two different coins; one, as of this writing, was in the hands of Texas dealer Bob Astrich. Brian Beardsley, of Gulf Coast Coin Brokers, kindly afforded the example pictured above. California dealer Mike Kliman reportedly offered a gem in June, 1983, for over $50,000.00.

This key issue is commonly forged, usually by adding an "S" mintmark to an 1893-P dollar. Other nefarious methods are altering an 1898-S to an 1893-S, or attaching an entire "S" reverse to an 1893 obverse.

Fortunately, several die characteristics make counterfeit detection relatively foolproof for an expert. Some lumps of extra metal can be seen in the base of the upright of the "R" of "LIBERTY" on the obverse. Also in "LIBERTY" there is a straight die scratch extending up and to the right from the left intersection of the crossbar and upright of the "T". A small bridge of metal connects the otherwise slightly separated ball and loop of the "9" in the date. None of these traits are found on 1893 Morgans from other mints.

RARITY IN PROOFLIKE: The 1893-S is unknown in mint state condition with uncontestably prooflike surfaces. While it is almost certain that some of the 100,000 minted were deep mirrors (some high grade circulated examples exhibit deep mirrors in the protected areas near letters or devices), none are traceable in unused condition today.

RARITY IN SUPERB CONDITION: As a ratio of superb examples to the total number of surviving mint state specimens, 1893-S is one of the most common of the series; in terms of absolute numbers, however, it is one of the rarest.

REDFIELD: No.

INVESTMENT POTENTIAL: One of the few Morgans with potential in any grade. As with any investment, assurance of equitable value at the time of purchase is most important. A coin in the range of a lustrous, problem free EF 45 to AU 55 seems prudent, as would an honest MS 63 with appealing color and surfaces. Locating either would be a considerable challenge.

1893-CC

Typical Mint State Example
MS (60), weak strike, moderate
bagmarks, frosty surfaces, excellent
luster.

GENERAL DISCUSSION: There are basically two groups of mint state 1893-CC dollars:

1. Pre-Redfield; i.e., those mint state examples which were already in collectors hands at the time the Redfield hoard came upon the market (February, 1976). The typical mint state characteristics for this group are described by the terms beneath the illustration above. The photo is undoubtedly of a coin not included in Redfield.

2. Redfield, i.e., those mint state examples which were included in the Redfield hoard. The typical mint state example from this group can be described as MS (63), sharp strike, moderate to heavy bagmarks, frosty or semiprooflike surfaces, good luster.

While the present market's population of mint state pieces of this date and mint is composed of approximately sixty percent of the Redfield coins and forty percent of the weakly struck pieces, it is nonetheless believed by the authors that a census of the total mint state population would reveal that the weakly struck coins are in the majority. In any case, the predictable trend of higher quality coins being taken off of the market and replaced by inferior specimens is already obvious. Eventually, 75% or more of the number of mint state coins available to collectors will be either weakly struck, pre-Redfield coins, or examples taken from the bottom of the Redfield barrel (figuratively speaking, of course — the coins were stored in canvas bags).

This basic principle of the numismatic market is parallel, both in a practical and a literal sense, to a fundamental law of economics called Gresham's Law, which is most often stated as "bad money drives out good money."

The weakly struck coins are extremely flat above the ear, exhibiting no breast feathers whatsoever. However, the luster is usually intense and attractive.

Many coins of this issue were struck from clashed dies, the evidence of which is most visible on the reverse. To the right of the eagle, between the wing and the wreath, can be seen a V-shaped, raised line pointing to the eagle. If this line is projected through the coin to the surface of the obverse, it will coincide with the juncture of Liberty's cap to her hair curls. When the dies clashed together due to the absence of a planchet between them, it was this portion of the obverse design that was impressed into the reverse die. Some coins exhibit a double V-shaped line, indicating that the dies clashed again later in the production run.

These clash marks do not detract from the grade nor value of the coins on which they appear.

Circulated specimens are scarce and in steady demand, especially if they are in extremely fine or better condition.

The Midwestern collection mentioned in the 1889-CC discussion also contained several superb 1893-CC's. The finest example seen by this writer was a superb prooflike example, once possibly believed to be a branch mint proof, owned by Harlan White of San Diego.

Although a valuable issue, altered or forged examples of the 1893-CC are never encountered. An attempt to create such a counterfeit could be made by altering the date of an

1890-CC or 1891-CC, but such an attempt would be foolhardy, since detection would be easy.

RARITY IN PROOFLIKE: Prooflikes are quite scarce. Many semiprooflike examples are often offered as fully prooflike. Specimens which have reflective surfaces are almost always weakly struck. A fully struck prooflike 1893-CC is extremely difficult to locate.

RARITY IN SUPERB CONDITION: The finest examples from the Redfield holdings reached the superb MS (67) level. An insufficient strike and/or excessive bagmarks prevent the vast majority of mint state examples of this issue from reaching the superb plateau.

REDFIELD: One of the most pleasant discoveries in the Redfield Hoard was a quantity of sharply struck 1893-CC's. In fact, all of the 1893-CC's that are definitely traceable to that Nevada estate have been exceptionally well struck for the date. The specimens vary rather widely in the bagmark category, with most coins that remain on today's market being either moderately or heavily marked. Also, many coins available today have not been purchased by collectors due to the bothersome scrape on Liberty's face resulting from passage through a coin counting machine.

PROOFS: A dozen proofs were struck, apparently for distribution at the ceremony marking the closing of this historic mint. The first specimen to be so identified and offered at public auction sale was a part of the Bruce Todd Sale (RARCOA, January, 1973). It was accompanied by a letter of authenticiation from Walter Breen, whose mentor, the late Wayte Raymond, originally reported the mintage. Another specimen appeared in the inventory of Manfra, Tordella and Brookes, a major New York dealer, in 1976. A third (second?) is in the Amon Carter collection. Breen lists a fourth as being in a private collection. The Todd coin reappeared in the July, 1979, Auction '79 Sale, conducted jointly by Stack's, RARCOA, Paramount and Superior. That piece, which had realized $18,000 in the 1973 RARCOA auction, brought $39,000.

INVESTMENT POTENTIAL: While relatively recent drastic price advances have occurred, the anticipated demand for this issue should outpace the available supply. The government had none in their holdings; but the sale and promotion of CC dollars can only enhance the appeal of this key Carson City product. Sharply struck coins, while available, should be strongly considered. They may be much more difficult to find in the future.

1894

Typical Mint State Example
MS (63), sharp strike, light
bagmarks, frosty surfaces, poor
luster.

GENERAL DISCUSSION: Very few mint state examples of this issue have survived. Even before the boom in dollar collecting, mint state examples were not easy to locate. This date has a history of being one of the keys of the series. Because of its overall scarcity in all grades, it gained its reputation before quality became as important as it is today.

This issue has an unusual combination of typical mint state characteristics. On the positive side of the coin (please pardon the expression), this issue is almost never seen weakly struck. On the negative side, it is almost always deficient in luster. While fully mint state, many examples merely do not emit that pizzazz that fully lustrous Morgans do.

Circulated examples are very scarce; behind the 1893-S, they are the most valuable of all regularly issued Morgans in circulated condition. Beware of circulated examples with a removed mintmark.

The finest known example of this rare date may well be the piece described in Paramount International Coin Corporation's Rare Coin List Number Seven (March, 1974):

> 1894 MS-70. Full prooflike surfaces. Choice uncirculated 1894's are very rare, but when they are available they are invariably frosty. Even with partially prooflike surfaces they are almost unheard of. This coin, however, has full prooflike surfaces that are as reflective as those seen on many early "S" mint Morgan Dollars . . .
> The surfaces, however, are not merely prooflike, they are also superbly clean and totally free of the usual bagmarks. All in all, this is a stunning coin and we doubt if its equal could be found anywhere. Many, many times rarer like this than in Proof.

The piece was priced at $2,000. In the same listing, a proof was tagged at $1,100. The coin ultimately was sold to a dealer at a convention for about $1,800. Its present whereabouts is unknown, but its value is open to conjecture.

RARITY IN PROOFLIKE: This issue is extremely rare in prooflike, both in terms of absolute numbers and in terms of the percentage of total surviving mint state examples. A few circulated coins with vestiges of prooflike surfaces have been seen, plus a couple of uncirculated coins with reflective surfaces. These coins exist in prooflike, but their appearance on the market is infrequent and quite noteworthy.

RARITY IN SUPERB CONDITION: This issue is also extremely rare in superb MS (67) or better condition; a frosty example of this quality is available more often than is one with prooflike surfaces. Many examples described as superb should only be called MS (65) due to insufficient luster.

REDFIELD: Although the previous five years and the following three years of Philadelphia dollars (excluding the 1895) were included in Redfield, no mint state 1894 coins are known to have been a part of that fabulous accumulation.

PROOFS: Because of the extreme rarity and desirability of mint state examples, proofs of this date are very important. Often, though he may prefer a superb business strike, a fastidious collector must settle for a nice proof. Thus, the price of a proof, which is not particularly rarer than other Morgans in proof, is buoyed by the value of mint state examples.

Proofs are generally very well struck, and can often be seem with spectacular toning. Many original proof sets have been disassembled so that the silver dollar could be transferred to a Morgan collection. This accounts for the high percentage of toned examples. The average quality of proofs of this date is slightly above that of most other dates.

INVESTMENT POTENTIAL: Many collectors who began sets of Morgans as a result of the intense GSA campaign and the Redfield promotions are just now reaching the point of needing the key issues. Also, additional numbers of investors desire coins in the price range of an uncirculated 1894 dollar to add to their portfolios. Thus, only positive results can be forecast for the demand for coins of this date. Proofs as well as mint state examples should always be the object of constant searching.

A superb mint state example will probably always maintain a value which is above that for a superb proof example.

1894-O

Typical Mint State Example
MS (60), weak strike, light to
moderate bagmarks, frosty surfaces,
good luster.

GENERAL DISCUSSION: Despite fantastic rises in MS (65) prices for this issue, no deluge of superb specimens has been unleashed upon the market. On the contrary, not a single MS (67) specimen, and very few of MS (65) quality, have changed hands in recent years. The simple explanation for this is the few coins of this quality which exist are firmly in the grasps of collectors who know a good thing when they see one.

Many who seek a gem example may have to settle for a typical mint state specimen. Those fortunate few who own sharply struck and minimally marked coins are reluctant to part with them.

Like the 1892-O, some examples that are very flatly struck are highly lustrous and nearly void of marks.

Circulated coins are common, indicating that most of the mintage which was not melted made its way into circulation. Only examples in the higher circulated grades, with some mint luster remaining, bring a significant premium.

No quantities of this date are known to exist as a group. No original, or assembled for that matter, rolls of coins are recalled by the authors, though there are no doubt some older dollar dealers who may remember them.

Forgeries have not been a problem to date, but that does not mean that one should not examine the date and mintmark carefully before purchasing a high grade specimen.

RARITY IN PROOFLIKE: This issue is extremely rare with prooflike surfaces. Some almost uncirculated and MS (60) coins with full mirror surfaces, or what remained of them, have been seen, but no coin of MS (65) or better quality with mirror surfaces has ever been examined by the authors. Judging from the number of lesser grade specimens seen, statistics would indicate that some MS (65) prooflikes may exist.

RARITY IN SUPERB CONDITION: The 1894-O is quite rare in superb condition. Seldom attributes necessary for MS (67) classification occur simultaneously on a coin of this date and mint. Although perhaps a hundred or more coins exist that are sufficiently bagmark-free to enable a superb grade, the strike is usually deficient. An unqualified MS (67) 1894-O is one of the most desirable issues of the entire Morgan series.

REDFIELD: No.

INVESTMENT POTENTIAL: Because of the tremendous rise in value in a relatively short period of time, it is difficult to gauge the prospects of this issue. However, the person considering an investment in this date should regard that price rise as a proper adjustment in values between this issue and others in the Morgan series. For too long, the 1894-O was drastically undervalued in MS (65) or better condition. When collectors progress to the point of needing an 1894-O in their collections, they will discover how difficult an MS (65) coin is to obtain. Many will purchase MS (60)s in the hope of later upgrading. With this in mind, the 1894-O is thus one of the few dates in the series which may have considerable potential even in MS (60). If an MS (65) or better coin is purchased, the buyer should be as sure as possible that it is accurately graded and priced with or only slightly ahead of the market.

1894-S

Typical Mint State Example
MS (65), sharp strike, moderate
bagmarks, frosty or semiprooflike
surfaces, excellent luster.

GENERAL DISCUSSION: Although scarce, this issue is generally more available in mint state than other mintmarked coins dated 1893, 1894 or 1895. It is comparable in availability in mint state to the 1893 Philadelphia.

Most mint state examples are quite sharply struck and have full, attractive luster.

Above very fine condition, circulated coins are scarce and command a significant premium. In almost uncirculated condition, the 1894-S is priced unusually high, approaching half the value of an MS (60) coin!

A perennially underrated issue, the 1894-S's true scarcity was attested to by its absence from the Redfield Hoard. Although this issue would have been a logical one to find in the estate, no mint state pieces that can definitely be pedigreed to the Redfield holdings are known to exist. Although the immediate and apparent reaction of silver dollar values to the Redfield Hoard was the promotion and immediate rise in price of the dates included, a delayed, secondary reaction was the upward adjustment of prices of some coins which became undervalued relative to the Redfield dates. The 1894-S is a conspicuous example of one of those dates.

A small but significant portion of the demand for mint state examples of this issue is its suitability for date sets, i.e., collections which include one coin of each year that Morgans were produced. Of course, the vast majority of collectors, wanting the highest quality possible for the money they have available to spend, choose the least expensive issue of each year to include in their date sets. Thus the 1894-S, being much less valuable in mint state condition than either the Philadelphia or New Orleans Mint issues bearing the same date, is in demand by virtually all date set collectors.

RARITY IN PROOFLIKE: The 1894-S is not particularly scarce with prooflike surfaces. Perhaps as much as fifteen percent of the mint state examples available on the current market are apt to have nice mirror fields. Prooflikes are usually sharp but may be plagued with bagmarks, which seem to be magnified in their severity by the fragile surfaces of a prooflike dollar.

RARITY IN SUPERB CONDITION: Since the quality of the typical mint state 1894-S is high, it is not surprising that superb examples are usually available for a price. This availability is no doubt a temporary condition. By no means, however, do the authors mean to imply that location of a superb MS (67) or better 1894-S is just a matter of money — more than a smidgen of patience may be required.

REDFIELD: Although the following six years of San Francisco Morgans have been verified as having been a part of the Redfield estate, not a single mint state 1894-S is definitely traceable to that source.

INVESTMENT POTENTIAL: Because of its broad basis of demand, the 1894-S is an issue that should fare as well or better than the Morgan series as a whole. Since MS (65) specimens are not too difficult to locate in relation to MS (63) or inferior specimens, MS (65) coins only should be considered for investment purposes.

1895

Typical Mint State Example
Proof (63), light hairlines, some
cameo contrast.

GENERAL DISCUSSION: We must suspend our format to discuss this issue, which has often been referred to as "the king of the Morgans."

In terms of total population of all grades, the 1895 is by far the rarest Morgan Dollar. Only 12,880 coins were struck, and all 12,000 business strikes (those minted with the intent of being placed into circulation) were condemned to the melting pot. The 880 proofs are the sole source for today's collectors. Of those, probably no more than five hundred are extant. Any reports of business strike that survived the melting pot are unconfirmed.

Circulated examples are very rare and in great demand.

The 1895 Morgan Dollar is no rarer than other dates of Morgan Dollars in proof. In fact, because of its extreme rarity as a member of the Morgan series, a high percentage of the proofs of this date were saved by the few collectors and dealers active in the early 1900s. Although it might be expected that the value of this issue would have prevented wholesale cleaning and impairment, such as is common among less expensive dates, a cross section of the coins available in recent years indicates otherwise. However, it is likely that the average quality of coins withheld from the current market is higher than those offered in the immediate past.

Auction records for 1895 proof Morgans are numerous. This valuable and highly publicized rarity is welcomed by any auction company, even those not customarily associated with offerings of Morgan Dollars.

Superb examples are too widespread and too frequent in past appearances, both in auction sales and in private sales, to properly pedigree.

The Robert Marks Collection Sale, Part II (American Auction Association, November, 1972) contained a pristine specimen. Beneath one of the most breathtaking photographs ever taken of a Morgan dollar, the coin offered in the sale was described as "one of the choicest 1895 Proof dollars in existence." The prophetic comments that accompanied the description of the coin told of how the upcoming government sales of dollars would influence silver dollar collecting. Prospective bidders were told that "the continued fame of the 1895 date seems assured." That piece realized a then impressive $6,250.

The finest example ever offered by the authors is presently in a prominent Dallas collection. Despite repeated offers of handsome profits, the proud owner refuses to part with his numismatic prize. It is a beautifully toned example, void of the hairlines so frequently seen on proof Morgans.

RARITY IN SUPERB CONDITION: For a proof Morgan dollar to qualify for the superb Proof (67) category, it must be void of hairlines or other impairments. Very few 1895 Morgans meet this qualification. An educated guess of the number of superb examples in existence would probably be in the 50-75 range by most experts.

REDFIELD: Although the twelve bags of business strike 1895 Morgans were not found in his Nevada estate, Mr. Redfield would no doubt have loved to have located and owned them.

INVESTMENT POTENTIAL: Strictly on a basis of supply and demand from collectors of the Morgan series, the 1895 is an overpriced issue. As many as one-fourth of the existing supply may be in the hands of those not primarily collectors of Morgans. Investors, collectors of rarities only and dealers comprise this group. However, there is no reason that the supplement to the pure demand for this issue will not continue, or perhaps increase, in the future. As inflation continues its inexorable spiral, and as coins simultaneously gain a more widespread acceptance as a serious and viable investment medium, the 1895 Morgan will be in solid demand. Like other investments, periodic peaks and valleys may occur in the value of this coin, although the general direction of its value seems pointed upward.

1895-O

Typical Mint State Example
MS (60), weak strike, light bagmarks,
frosty surfaces, good luster.

GENERAL DISCUSSION: The 1895-O is one of the rarest of all Morgan dollars in mint state condition. In terms of appearance of MS (65) or better specimens during the last three years, it ranks among the three least encountered issues, the 1893-S and 1901 being the other two.

Even typical mint state examples are almost never available on today's market. These weakly struck coins, while never common, were at one time occasionally seen, and, in fact, were quite difficult to sell. Many collectors who refused to purchase one of the typical MS (60) examples, and held out for a higher quality specimen, may have never located a suitable coin. The demand for high quality examples of this issue is intense. Even an MS (63) example, particularly if sharply struck, would create much excitement among advanced dollar collectors.

No quantities of this issue are held by any single collector, investor or dealer. The record price that a gem would fetch on today's market would surely have dissolved any such holding if it had existed.

Circulated coins, especially well struck and lustrous examples, have enjoyed increased demand since the true rarity of mint state coins has become common knowledge. These are, however, still available at the present time.

Precious few MS (65) or better coins of this issue are traceable. Paramount International Coin Corporation handled a few in the 1972-1976 years, after which time the dearth of mint state 1895-Os affected their stock, as well as that of all other dollar dealers. The most outstanding specimen that company offered during that time was described in their Rare Coin List Number Seven as "MS (65) obverse, MS (70) reverse." The coin was a dazzling prooflike specimen, whose reverse was likened to a proof in the description. There were practically no bagmarks at all on its surfaces. The only possible objection to its obverse were two planchet streaks, i.e., shallow marks that were already in the planchet before it was struck. Those marks account for the obverse qualifying as *only* MS (65). The piece was purchased at a formidable price for the market at the time; the subsequent retail price of $4,950, though a fraction of the value today, prevented the sale of the coin. In fact, it appeared in Paramount's inventory as late as their list Number Eleven in September, 1975. It was eventually included in a "superset" of Morgans assembled by Paramount and sold to a prominent New England collector, who, in late 1976, consigned the set to Essex Numismatic Properties. The coin was subsequently placed in a prominent Connecticut collection, the same one mentioned in conjunction with the Love-Rettew-Kagin 1893-S and several other outstanding Morgans.

One should keep in mind, throughout this and other discussions, that numerous transactions involving important silver dollars often take place in total anonymity. The dealer and collector, or, rarely, the two collectors involved in a transaction may wish to conduct their business on a private basis. Occassionally, a major Morgan rarity may be transferred from one collection to another, and not a ripple of publicity be associated with the deal. Eventually, however, some news of the event becomes a part of numismatic history. The very fact that all major rarities of this series are impossible to completely pedigree is part of their mystique.

One of the most beautiful 1895-O's ever examined by this writer was a part of an original mint set of 1895 coins from the New Orleans Mint. The set was sold as a whole in the December, 1973, sale of the Hergeden Collection. The sale was conducted in New York City by Schulman Coin and Mint. All of the coins were beautifully toned; the dollar, though not quite fully struck, was void of significant marks. The set remained intact until the summer of 1979, when the spiraling price of the dollar ended its existence as a set. As a set is was likely unique, and any true numismatist should lament its dispersal. By the way, the set realized three thousand dollars at the Herdegen Sale.

Another exciting example of this undeniably rare issue was seen at a California convention in February, 1979. A collector was proudly displaying his 1895-O to an appreciative audience of dollar dealers. The coin was not for sale, but that did not stop one zealous dealer from offering the owner $15,000 for the coin. The offer was ignored. The coin was superb save for a short scratch on the eagle's breast; its strike and luster left little to be desired.

A skillfully forged or counterfeit 1895-O has never been reported. However, the propsective purchaser should never underestimate the greediness of a crook.

RARITY IN PROOFLIKE: Needless to say, because of its extreme rarity in mint state, the 1895-O is excessively rare in prooflike. The number of prooflikes reported, plus the percentage of high grade circulated examples with vestiges of prooflike surfaces remaining, indicate that as a ratio of surviving mint state examples, the 1895-O is comparable in rarity to the 1894-O. Prooflike 1895-O's are usually sharply struck.

RARITY IN SUPERB CONDITION: In superb MS (67) or better condition, this issue is virtually unavailable on today's market. Far fewer superb examples have been offered in the past decade than superb 1892-S's or 1893-S's.

REDFIELD: No.

PROOFS: Lot 833 of the H.R. Lee Sale (Stack's, November, 1947) reads: "1895-O Absolute Brilliant Proof, much discussion has taken place between collector and dealer about branch mint proofs, there can be no question about this perfect specimen." See 1891-CC "Proofs" discussion for comments on the use of the term "proof" during this period of time.

INVESTMENT POTENTIAL: This issue is well on its way to being recognized as one of the major rarities of the Morgan series in mint state condition. Even MS (60) specimens will eventually be met with great eagerness on the part of serious dollar collectors. The primary limiting factor to this issue is its affordability. As coins become more popular with institutional investors, and become generally more acceptable as an investment medium, this factor should be easily surmounted.

Lustrous, well struck almost uncirculated examples appear underpriced relative to a strictly mint state specimen.

1895-S

Typical Mint State Example
MS (63), above average strike,
moderate bagmarks, frosty surfaces,
excellent luster.

GENERAL DISCUSSION: Although the most common of the three Morgans bearing the 1895 date, the San Francisco Mint product of this year is nonetheless a scarce and desirable issue. In circulated grades, the 1895-S is very much in demand, and is rarer than the 1895-O. In mint state condition, however, the 1895-O is several times rarer than the 1895-S.

Many of the examples of this issue on the market today are from the renowned Redfield Hoard. The typical mint state characteristics listed above apply to coins from this source.

Because of the distribution of the Redfield coins, the 1895-S has one of the most interesting and revealing price histories of any Morgan issue.

Initially, when dealers and collectors heard of the presence of some unknown number of 1895-S's in the newly discovered Nevada estate left by some eccentric millionaire, many of them predicted that the then current $1,500 price tag would be reduced to a mere fraction of that value. Those skeptics analogized the situation to the 1964 release of multiple bags of 1903-O dollars, which did indeed result in a drastic price reduction for that previously rare issue. However, the 1976 market was quite a different arena from that of more than a decade previous. More importantly, the number of coins involved was vastly different. Instead of thousands of coins flooding a market still in its infancy, such as was the case in 1964, the relatively few Redfield 1895-S's were greeted by the demand of an eager and mature group of modern collectors and investors.

If the dealers involved in the Redfield transactions had not been financially sound enough to hold the 1895-S's (and other issues) long enough to insure their widespread and even distribution, the reaction of the values of the dollars involved could have moved in a different direction. Confidence in the future of the dollar market, fueled largely by the results of the government's great sales of Carson City dollars, and fiscal strength of the distributors were two primary reasons for the positive reaction of the market toward Redfield. Many other factors were involved — creative promotion and marketing techniques were of paramount importance, as was the intertwined relationship of inflation and the increasing popularity of coins as investments to combat this evil. The causes and effects, actions and reactions to the great Redfield transactions would be a fascinating subject for an economic scientist to study.

The quality of the 1895-S Redfield dollars was remarkably homogeneous. The luster, strike and degree of bagmarking all seem to fall within a relatively narrow range on coins of this issue which are believed to have been a part of the estate. The public auction sale of the Roy Harte Collection (Bowers and Ruddy, November, 1977) contained fourteen uncirculated 1895-S's which were from the Fairfield Collection, the most valuable collection ever sold through public auction sales prior to that firm's disposal of the Johns Hopkins' University Garrett collection. Although the catalogers chose not to mention the Redfield estate in their description, it is highly likely that the pieces were indirectly procured from the Redfield estate. Supporting the homogeneity of condition of the Redfield 1895-S's is the catalogers statement that the fourteen pieces were "near-identical coins."

Several notable specimens in superb MS (67) or better quality have been offered at public or private sale over the last decade.

The Ronald Keller specimen (Paramount, May, 1973) was described as "Uncirculated 70. Full mirror surfaces, frosted devices. A perfect flawless specimen. In fact it appears equal to a branch mint proof." Whether or not the piece would live up to today's more rigorous requirements for MS (70) is not known, but this writer does recall the coin's eminent quality. The dealership of Coen and Messer in New York City sold the piece, accompanied by a magnificent 1892-S (see the discussion for that date), to Max Humbert of Paramount in 1972. It realized $4,500 in the Keller auction.

Two beautifully toned examples are among the finest known. The Herdegen Collection (Schulman, December, 1973) contained a superb (save for the half) mint set of 1895 San Francisco silver coins. The set, which contains a fully struck, virtually flawless dollar, is believed to remain intact today.

A second gorgeous specimen was sold privately to a prominent Southern collector in 1978 for about $4,500.

A superb cameo prooflike was examined at the 1979 Central States Numismatic Society's convention in Dearborn, Michigan. It traded hands for $6,000 before the show ended.

Although one of the more valuable issues of the series, the lack of a logical method to fabricate counterfeit coins of this date has prevented the appearance of any deceptive bogus specimens.

RARITY IN PROOFLIKE: Offerings of prooflike examples are often seen, but many of these coins are actually only semiprooflike. A healthy percentage of the Redfield 1895-S's were semiprooflike, but very few had fully reflective surfaces. Those that did were well struck, moderately marked and had little or no contrast between the fields and devices.

About a half dozen specimens are known which closely resemble proof coins; a couple of these have been called branch mint proofs. They have high rims and are meticulously well struck. The surfaces are reflective, though not quite so much so as on a Philadelphia proof Morgan.

RARITY IN SUPERB CONDITION: This issue is quite scarce in superb MS (67) or better condition, but not so much so as some other similarly priced members of the series. The patient collector can expect to find a suitable example, no matter how particular he is.

REDFIELD: From what the authors have seen on the open market, at least a few rolls of 1895-S's have appeared that originated in the Redfield estate. Paramount was the first company to offer coins of this issue that were identified as Redfield's. One pleasant surprise that this fabulous estate held for dollar collectors was the average high quality of this issue. The 1895-S's were the rarest and most valuable issue found in the Redfield Hoard.

PROOFS: Breen lists three specimens. One example, possibly one which Breen had already listed in his work on proof coins, was sold at a Kagin's sale in October, 1978. Other coins referred to as " presentation pieces" or "resembling a proof" are known.

INVESTMENT POTENTIAL: Since this issue survived the sale of the Redfield estate, fears about the market crashing for 1895-S's should be put to rest. One thing now working in this issue's favor is that enough coins are available so that meaningful transactions can take place. An increase in the supply of an actively demanded item, such as a key date Morgan Dollar, can actually drive the price upward. Typical mint state quality coins are not as advisable for investment purposes as are superior examples.

1896

Typical Mint State Example
MS (65), sharp strike, moderate
bagmarks, frosty surfaces, good
luster.

GENERAL DISCUSSION: Not since 1889 was the Morgan Dollar preserved in mint state in such great quantities as was this issue. After a seven year span of scarcer dates, 1896 marks one of the most abundant issues of the series up to that point in its history.

Coins of this issue, until mid-1978, were roughly equated with the most common of the series in terms of value. Promotion has been the primary reason for the recent price advance. In the past, even MS (65) examples were valued as common bulk mint state dollars; now, hoever, these coins are demanding premiums up to triple that of the least expensive mint state Morgans. While some premium may be justified, this ratio seems drastic in light of the large number of coins available.

Uncirculated rolls are common; original bags surely still are stored intact in various vaults around the country. Regardless of the price of MS (65) examples, MS (63) or inferior coins should be valued only as common bulk mint state dollars. Similarly, circulated coins should bring only the going market price for the most common Morgans in non-mint state grades.

Most collections which have received an adequate amount of attention contain an MS (67) example, or perhaps an attractive, prooflike coin. The average quality of mint state coins of this issue is high. The strike is almost always full. The surfaces are usually fully frosty or fully reflective, and only infrequently are seen between those two states. Bagmarks are not generally a major problem on specimens traded on an individual basis.

Quite a few auction records for superb examples have been recorded. No one coin stands out from the others except for the Wayne Miller plate coin, which brought $400 in Steve Ivy Numismatic Auction's R.A. Donovan Sale, Part II in July, 1978.

RARITY IN PROOFLIKE: This issue is relatively common with prooflike surfaces. Fully struck, pleasantly mark-free coins are available for a price. These examples usually have some cameo effect, but coins with a deep contrast between fields and devices are becoming scarcer by the month. Some of the most deeply mirrored Morgan dollars bear this date.

RARITY IN SUPERB CONDITION: Not many dates of Morgans are easier to find in superb MS (67) or better condition than the 1896. This is not to say that coins of this issue in superb condition are easy to locate at a moment's notice — the demand for quality Morgans has virtually eliminated the term "common" from reference to superb members of this noble series.

REDFIELD: A quantity of mint state examples of this date were in the Redfield Hoard of Morgan and Peace dollars. Compared to the mint state population already known at the time of their appearance, the number of 1896s involved was negligible.

PROOFS: Proofs of this and the following two years mark the high point, quality-wise, of proof Morgan Dollars. A strikingly bold contrast between fields and devices is the rule, rather than the exception. Other silver and gold coins manufactured in proof by the Philadelphia Mint during this year also display outstanding quality. Like other dates, however, the 1896 was also often cleaned or mishandled to some extent. Deeply mirrored, nearly mark-free examples have been offered as proofs to unknowledgeable collectors. This practice is much less common on today's sophisticated market than in the past.

INVESTMENT POTENTIAL: Moreso than for most dates, quality is the key to investing in coins of this issue. Examples of typical quality may prove to be overrated, at least in comparison to superb examples.

1896-O

Typical Mint State Example
MS (60), weak strike, moderate
bagmarks, frosty surfaces, poor
luster.

GENERAL DISCUSSION: One of the favorite words to describe this issue has been
"underrated." Whether or not this term is still applicable, since tremendous price increases
for gem examples have come to pass, is a matter of opinion. The coin's rarity in MS (65) or
better condition is fact. In such quality, the 1896-O is now considered a major Morgan rarity.

Even when mint state examples of this issue were one-tenth the price they are today,
scarcely an MS (65) coin could be located. A multiplication of value has produced only a scant
increase in the number of high quality 1896-O's seen on the market. It has, however, resulted
in a drastic increase in the number of overgraded coins of this date and mint. MS (60) examples with good arm's length eye appeal are prime candidates to be sold as MS (65)s at
"bargain" prices.

Comparing the rarity of a true MS (65) 1896-O to an MS (60) coin of the same date is practically meaningless. The difference in rarity, and consequently, in value, between those two
grades makes the pricing of an honest MS (63) example very difficult.

Deceptively lustrous, almost uncirculated examples are relatively abundant. These
"sliders" must sometimes be carefully examined before the slight rub which renders them
AU is detectable.

The rarity of this issue in prime mint state condition is further attested to by the scant
auction records for gem examples.

An alarmingly large number of spurious specimens have been seen. These coins, which
are fortunately easy to distinguish from the genuine article by dollar experts, are created by
adding an "O" mintmark to an 1896 Philadelphia dollar. Since the rim, reeding and general
appearance of a Philadelphia Mint dollar of this era are different from those of a New Orleans
Mint product, an expert can often tell whether or not an 1896-O is genuine just by looking at
the obverse. If in doubt, however, the prospective purchaser may be well advised to send the
coin to the American Numismatic Association Certification Service (ANACS) for verification.

RARITY IN PROOFLIKE: Prooflike examples of this issue may be considered among
the "rarest of the rare." Not only are mint state examples infrequently found, but prooflikes
constitute a very tiny percentage of that group. The few specimens that the authors have had
the privilege to examine have been almost unanimously unattractive. Some notable prooflike
collections have housed a semiprooflike example, or none at all.

RARITY IN SUPERB CONDITION: The 1896-O Morgan Dollar is almost unknown in
superb condition. If such specimens exist, they do so in collections built long ago by
discriminating owners. The appearance of a true MS (67) specimen would generate a powerful current of interest among serious collectors.

REDFIELD: No.

INVESTMENT POTENTIAL: True mint state examples, if accurately graded and fairly
priced, should be good performers regardless of their precise MS rating. Naturally, one would
expect the highest quality specimens to outdistance their lower grade counterparts.

1896-S

Typical Mint State Example
MS (63), average strike, moderate to
heavy bagmarks, frosty surfaces,
good luster.

GENERAL DISCUSSION: The majority of mint state examples of this issue on the market today probably came from the Redfield Hoard. Typical mint state coins are somewhat more frequent in appearance presently than they were in the years preceding Redfield's appearance.

Specimens which predate the release of the hoarded coins are often weakly struck, with only light bagmarking. Redfield coins are usually well struck, but may have serious bagmarks. These bagmarks are not particularly severe in their size, but tend to densely cover the coins' surfaces. The luster is generally frosty on the weakly struck coins, and somewhat semiprooflike on the sharply struck ones.

This issue is considered common in the lowest (good to fine) circulated grades. However, as examples approach the almost uncirculated level, the rarity and value increase dramatically. A lustrous, well-struck almost uncirculated coin with no major detractions may have a value of more than half of an MS (60) 1896-S. Because of the relatively high value of AU and MS (60) coins, the ratio between MS (60) and MS (65) specimens is lower than normal. In actuality, true MS (65) examples are many times rarer than MS (60) coins. In the future, collectors may see an expansion of the price differential between coins of these two grades.

Although not high in overall quality, the Redfield 1896-S's did provide a fresh supply of MS (65) coins for collectors and investors. The tendency for the best examples of Redfield to be taken off the market is already evident.

Be wary of coins with an added "S" mintmark. Since the Philadelphia issue bearing the 1896 date is very common, the valuable 1896-S is vulnerable to such alteration. Quite a few of these bogus specimens have been seen, some of which could be very deceptive to the average collector.

RARITY IN PROOFLIKE: The 1896-S is very scarce in prooflike. Only a few truly prooflike coins have been examined by the authors. The Redfield group apparently contained a very small number of prooflike examples. A cameo prooflike is of the utmost rarity.

RARITY IN SUPERB CONDITION: Bagmarks prevent an MS (67) classification for almost all coins of this issue which may otherwise be considered superb. As MS (65) coins are many times rarer than MS (60) coins, MS (67) specimens are many times rarer than MS (65)s. Some pre-Redfield coins may be nearly bagmark-free, but they also will be more than likely weakly struck.

REDFIELD: The unknown quantity of coins owned by Mr. Redfield was not enough to depress the market on this date; on the contrary, it was just enough to stimulate interest and enable widespread marketing of this key issue.

INVESTMENT POTENTIAL: Weakly struck and/or heavily bagmarked specimens should not be considered for investment purposes; the money spent for such coins would be more wisely applied for one nice MS (65). The potential for this issue, while positive, may not be quite as good as some others in a similar price range at the present time.

1897

Typical Mint State Example
MS (63), sharp strike, moderate to
heavy bagmarks, frosty surfaces,
good luster.

GENERAL DISCUSSION: Although readily available in mint state, the 1897 issue is quite scarce in MS (65) or better condition. Rolls of mint state coins from which the choicest examples have already been removed are relatively common. Original bags may still exist.

The true scarcity of gem examples of this issue has been camouflaged in the past by the overall availability of mint state coins and because the 1897 is sandwiched between the more common Philadelphia Mint issues of 1896 and 1898. Also, both these issues have a higher quality typical mint state example than does the 1897. In recent times, the price of an MS (65) example of this issue has skyrocketed, while typical examples have remained relatively stagnant. The performance of each category of coin is entirely deserved.

Circulated examples command virtually no premium over the most common dates. They are valued only as bulk circulated dollars.

The quality of the coins suspected to have come from the Redfield source coincides with the quality of mint state coins observed before Redfield liquidation occurred.

RARITY IN PROOFLIKE: This issue is moderately scarce in prooflike. A Kansas dealer sold several rolls of predominately MS (65) prooflikes in spring, 1979. Cameos are the exception rather than the rule.

RARITY IN SUPERB CONDITION: To be so abundant in typical mint state condition, this date is surprisingly difficult to locate in true MS (67). Many of the superb examples which have been seen are prooflike. In fact, a frosty piece which qualifies as MS (67) is almost as rare as a prooflike coin of equal quality.

REDFIELD: Some quantity, insignificant in size to the extant mint state population, of this issue was present in Mr. Redfield's holdings.

PROOFS: Although not of the overall high quality and excellent appearance of the 1896, proofs of this date are a cut above the average. Exciting cameo contrast is often seen. As with all dates of proof Morgans, many have been cleaned or mishandled in some fashion at some time in their history.

INVESTMENT POTENTIAL: High quality examples, though they have undergone dramatic price increases in the last few years, should still be attractive to investors. When a tremendous price increase fails to produce a significant flow of new material, the obvious conclusion is that such material simply does not exist. This may be the case with MS (67) or better coins of this issue.

1897-O

Typical Mint State Example
MS (60), average strike, moderate
bagmarks, frosty surfaces, poor
luster.

GENERAL DISCUSSION: This issue has often been compared to the New Orleans Mint dollar of the previous year. However, rarity of MS (65) examples is not comparable; the 1897-O, while definitely rare, is significantly more common than the 1896-O.

From its typical mint state characteristics, however, the two issues are similar. Except that 1897-O's are more sharply struck than 1896-O's, the descriptions of the typical mint state examples are identical.

Dramatic price increases for MS (65) coins failed to bring about a discernible increase in the number of MS (65) 1897-O's on the market. It did, however, increase the frequency of overgrading MS (60) or MS (63) examples so that they could be priced at higher levels. Lustrous, well-struck coins with just the slightest amount of wear are often called mint state. Paradoxically, the crime of misgrading an almost uncirculated coin as mint state is less serious, at least in terms of values, than calling an MS (60) example MS (65).

Circulated coins of this issue, unless in almost uncirculated condition, bring little or no premium above common dates.

This writer vividly recalls a nearly perfect, lightly toned and sharply struck example sold to a New England collector through dealer Bob Cohen at a New York coin show in 1974. Although Morgan Dollars were near a low point in the market cycle at the time, this superb example still sold for multiples of the then current "bid" price. It is reported that the coin still resides in the same collection (not surprising, since discriminating collectors who are for-tunate enough to procure such a prize are loathe to let it go) and that it is shown from time to time at area shows.

Another superb example, probably the finest to have been sold through a public auction sale, appeared in Steve Ivy Numismatic Auctions' Roger Turner Sale (November, 1978). The cataloger was obviously impressed:

Relative to what is generally available on today's market, this coin is without ques-tion the finest dollar in this date. After seeing hundreds of typical 1897-O's, it is breathtaking to discover that a coin of this caliber exists. The coin boldly ap-proaches MS (70). The impeccable surfaces show no significant marks. A light golden tone warmly blankets both obverse and reverse. The strike is nothing short of incredible; the breast feathers are pointed, the talons are complete, all of Liber-ty's curls are sharp. The experienced Morgan specialist will not be able to take his eyes off of this remarkable specimen. The new owner will no doubt have to pay a record price, but he may be secure in the knowledge that no one, regardless of his resources, can possess a superior coin.

The audience gasped at the then impressive $3,100 winning bid. Few in attendance believed that, less than a year later, a handsome profit would have been realized had the coin once again been offered for sale. The piece was purchased by California dealer David Hall and placed by him into a private collection.

RARITY IN PROOFLIKE: The 1897-O is extremely rare in prooflike. Although more common in mint state condition than its New Orleans Mint kin of 1893-1896, the 1897-O is of comparable rarity with prooflike surfaces. The appearance of a fully reflective, MS (65) or better example would be of major importance to advanced prooflike collectors.

RARITY IN SUPERB CONDITION: The 1897-O is rarely obtainable in superb MS (67) condition. Appearances of such coins are limited to once or twice a year; in the future, opportunities to acquire superb examples may virtually cease altogether.

REDFIELD: No.

INVESTMENT POTENTIAL: Mint state examples, if properly graded and fairly priced at the time of purchase, should prove to be above average investments. Contrary to popular belief, more than half of the surviving mint state examples are of at least average strike. Therefore, weakly struck coins should be avoided for investment purposes.

1897-S

Typical Mint State Example
MS (63), above average strike,
moderate to heavy bagmarks, frosty
surfaces, good luster.

GENERAL DISCUSSION: Mint state examples of this issue are readily available on today's market. The appearance of the Redfield coins added greatly to the supply of uncirculated coins which were already in dealers' or collectors' hands.

Coins of this issue may or may not be well struck. Mint state 1897-S's are often heavily bagmarked. The luster is always at least adequate.

Most collections contain at least an MS (65) example of this issue. If they do not, an upgrading is in order. Nominal expense and minimal patience are the only requirements to secure an MS (65) specimen.

Circulated coins enjoy no significant premium unless they are in nearly mint state condition.

RARITY IN PROOFLIKE: Coins of this date and mint are not particularly scarce with prooflike surfaces. Pleasant, cameo examples are seen with regularity.

RARITY IN SUPERB CONDITION: Most auctions which contain a comprehensive offering of Morgans are apt to offer a superb MS (67) or better 1897-S. MS (69) coins exist, and always command a huge premium when swapped.

REDFIELD: This issue, in the authors' judgement, which is based upon the available market supply of mint state pieces, was one of the most plentiful of the Redfield Hoard. The quantity present, while it did not depress the market for the date, did delay its price increase until most other members of the series had advanced significantly.

INVESTMENT POTENTIAL: At the present time, coins of this issue are more available in mint state than some less expensive issues. While they may indeed rise in value, mint state 1897-S's have good reason not to perform so well as the average Morgan Dollar over the next decade or so unless they are in at least MS (67) condition.

1898

Typical Mint State Example
MS (65), sharp strike, light to
moderate bagmarks, frosty surfaces,
excellent luster.

GENERAL DISCUSSION: This issue is slightly scarcer than the most common mint state Morgan Dollars. It commands a modest premium over common dates in all mint state conditions. Circulated examples command no premium.

The average mint state quality is high; the typical mint state example is very sharply struck and, for a change, is usually only lightly bagmarked. Weakly struck and/or bagmarked examples should be valued only slightly above common bulk mint state dollars.

Superb MS (67) or better coins appear occasionally at coin shows or in auction sales. Generally speaking, an example of this date must possess outstanding qualities for it to be offered on an individual basis in a major auction sale. An extraordinary piece appeared in the William C. Kerr Sale (Steve Ivy Numismatic Auctions, February, 1979) described by the following paragraph:

> Superb! A brilliant prooflike example with as much cameo effect as we've seen for this date. Mirror fields rippling with luster. No mentionable bagmarks whatsoever. This coin traces its pedigree to Wayne Miller who used it to illustrate this particular date in his classic work *An Analysis of Morgan and Peace Dollars.*

The coin's eminence and pedigree enabled it to bring a rather incredible (at the time) $650.

RARITY IN PROOFLIKE: The 1898 is moderately scarce with prooflike surfaces. Cameo examples comprise a smaller than average percentage of the total number of mint state prooflike examples extant.

RARITY IN SUPERB CONDITION: Since the average mint state quality of this issue is high, and a sizeable number of uncirculated coins were saved in roll and bag quantities, superb examples are not too difficult to locate.

REDFIELD: A relatively small quantity of mint state 1898 Morgans is believed to have been among the coins sold from the Redfield accumulation.

PROOFS: Proofs of this year are among the most beautiful Morgan dollars produced. Breathtaking contrast between deep gray, mirror fields and bright white devices can be seen on some examples. Hairlines are consistently present. The authors recall seeing a photograph from a RARCOA catalog of the early 1970s of an 1898 proof that was so remarkably contrasted that it looked enameled. That piece brought about $600 at a time when typical proofs were worth less than half that amount. That coin would be worth several thousand dollars today.

INVESTMENT POTENTIAL: Since typical mint state examples are in adequate supply on today's market, superb examples may perform much better.

1898-O

Typical Mint State Example
MS (65), above average strike,
moderate bagmarks, frosty surfaces,
excellent luster.

GENERAL DISCUSSION: Huge quanitites of mint state 1898-O's were released as part of the thousands of bags of dollars that the U.S. Treasury held until 1964. Prior to that time, the 1898-O was ranked as the third rarest Morgan dollar in mint state! Now, it is one of the most common. It enjoys only a slight premium over such dates as 1883-1885-O's and 1885-1887 Philadelphia Mint coins.

While rare, circulated examples command no premium over common dates due to the abundance of mint state examples. The owner of a circulated 1898-O can make an unusual claim: the coin was worth more twenty years ago than it is today.

Dollars of this issue are well struck more often than not. Since virtually all mint state examples on today's market came from the Treasury bags, which were transported frequently during their history, bagmarking is a consistent problem. A nice MS (65) specimen is easy and inexpensive to find. A collection need not go without an MS (67) coin if the owner is willing to expend a little extra money and patience to locate one.

Auction records are scant, since most mint state examples are not valuable enough to justify individual listings. Most such offerings are for prooflikes.

RARITY IN PROOFLIKE: This issue is relatively common with prooflike surfaces, although the offering of semiprooflikes has tended to overstate the availability of 1898-O's in true prooflike state.

RARITY IN SUPERB CONDITION: The 1898-O is not a difficult issue to locate in superb MS (67) or better condition. Specimens of this supreme quality, whether prooflike or frosty, bring substantial premiums. Pleasantly toned examples are available from time to time.

REDFIELD: No.

PROOFS: Although a half dollar is known in proof from the New Orleans Mint in 1898, there are no such reports nor records of a silver dollar so struck.

INVESTMENT POTENTIAL: The fact that average mint state examples were once worth $300 has no bearing on the future of this issue. Any investment potential that exists for this date lies with superb examples.

1898-S

Typical Mint State Example
MS (63), average strike, moderate
bagmarks, frosty or semiprooflike
surfaces, excellent luster.

GENERAL DISCUSSION: This issue, though it has undergone significant price increases in recent times, is readily available on today's market. This availability is no doubt due to the Redfield Hoard. As dispersal of coins in the Redfield group widens, gem examples will undoubtedly become more difficult to find. Inferior Redfield coins, those with dense bagmarks, will most likely always be available for a price. When shopping for a typical mint state example, for whatever reason, it is the buyer, not the seller, who is in the driver's seat of that transaction.

Circulated examples are valued as common dates in grades of very fine or less; extremely fine examples bring a modest premium, and those in almost uncirculated condition are considered scarce.

Some of the Redfield coins had fully prooflike surfaces, but most were semiprooflike. Some of the highest quality coins of the entire hoard were a few superb, brilliant prooflike 1898-S's. The Redfield coins of this issue differed from those available prior to their debut in that they were more prooflike and were more sharply struck.

One coin that is most definitely pre-Redfield was a fantastic MS (69) example that is one of the finest Morgans the authors have ever had the privilege of handling. It was described in the Roger M. Turner Sale (November, 1978) as "A virtual MS (70). A nearly imperceptible distance away from perfection. Light golden toning. Unimprovable!" The happy winning bidder paid $1,000 for his prize.

Although none have been seen or reported, spurious examples may appear. The recent increase in value for the San Francisco Mint issue of 1898 and the low price of the Philadelphia Mint issue may prove irresistible to some nefarious ne'er-do-well.

RARITY IN PROOFLIKE: One of the pleasant surprises which the Redfield holdings provided for collectors was a number of prooflike 1898-S's. The prooflikes of this date from that source were generally well struck with nice reflective surfaces and no contrast between fields and devices. Bagmarking ranged from light to heavy. The finest of these coins are very attractive, and among the best that Mr. Redfield owned.

RARITY IN SUPERB CONDITION: For a coin in this price range, superb MS (67) examples appear with surprising frequency. However, they nonetheless command a substantial premium. If a superb example has prooflike surfaces, chances are that it came from the Redfield Hoard. The authors have seen some Redfield specimens with reverses that could be called MS (70). These specimens have all but disappeared from the marketplace.

REDFIELD: It is certain that a quantity of mint state 1898-S's were included in the hoard. Most of the pieces were well struck, and many were semiprooflike or prooflike.

INVESTMENT POTENTIAL: Coins of typical mint state quality or worse are not recommended for investment purposes. Portfolios should include only MS (65) or superior coins of this issue. Even though there is a wide difference in the price of an MS (60) and an MS (65), do not be duped into believing that the MS (60)s will close the gap in the future. The market is firmly committed to quality.

1899

Typical Mint State Example
MS (65), above average strike,
moderate bagmarks, frosty surfaces,
good luster.

GENERAL DISCUSSION: This has always been an extremely popular date with collectors and investors, no doubt largely due to the low mintage. As we have pointed out before, the mintage figures for Morgan dollars are a poor guide with which to estimate their rarity in mint state. The 1899 Philadelphia Mint dollar is one of the best examples to substantiate this claim. At whatever price level this issue has occupied in the past, a collector or investor has not had any difficulty in locating as many mint state examples as he wished to purchase.

Apparently, most of the mintage was preserved in mint state condition, since circulated examples are seldom seen. They command a premium that is a relatively large one for such an inexpensive coin.

Quality is seldom a problem. In fact, it is more unusual to see an MS (60) example of this issue than to see an MS (65) example. Original rolls still exist, and bag quantities are constantly rumored. Chances are that most bags have been broken by now, although the possibility of the survival of several is certainly plausible.

Auctions containing Morgan Dollars are replete with offerings of coins of this issue. Many of the coins have been superb and/or prooflike. It is quite unusual to locate a toned specimen, since the vast majority of mint state examples have been stored in rolls or bags over the years. The protection that other coins give prevents the natural toning process, unless a coin is the end piece in a roll; in which case, a one-sided toning takes place.

One of the most impressive prices realized for an 1899 Morgan is the $175 that the Bruce Todd (RARCOA, January, 1973) specimen brought. In 1973 that was quite a sum of money to pay for a coin that cataloged for thirty dollars.

This issue includes many specimens whose surfaces and strikes are very similar to those of a proof. No doubt, in previous decades, unwitting collectors and dealers bought and sold prooflike business strikes as proofs. Such occurrences are not continued to this date, but it is certainly more pronounced and occurs with greater frequency than other issues. For example, the Todd coin was described as "as close to being a Proof as they come." A specimen in the Briggs Sale (not the toned one mentioned above) was "...so deeply mirrored that an honest difference of opinion concerning its business strike versus proof status may occur from time to time."

Although much needs to be learned, modern, knowledgeable collectors and dealers will have little difficulty in determining whether or not a coin of this issue is a business strike or a proof.

RARITY IN PROOFLIKE: Coins of this issue are not difficult to locate with prooflike surfaces, although they bring a premium of about double a frosty piece, using MS (65) examples for comparison. Prooflikes are always well struck and usually fairly free of marks. Specimens with surfaces as deeply reflective as a proof's are occasionally seen, and bring an additional premium to that of normal prooflikes.

RARITY IN SUPERB CONDITION: Most superb examples seen of this issue have been prooflike. While a great many MS (65) examples exist, frosty coins of the MS (67) or better category are scarce. However, the patient collector can count on obtaining one for a modest price.

REDFIELD: Although Philadelphia Mint issues of the previous three years were found in the Redfield Hoard, no 1899 Morgans are known to have been included.

PROOFS: Proofs are moderately scarcer than some other so-called common dates. This year marks a departure from the mint's outstanding workmanship on proofs of 1896-98, with the cameo contrast of those years ceasing in 1899. Some of the finest examples of this year are preserved as parts of original proof sets, perhaps saved in a greater than usual number to commemorate the final year of the 1800's.

INVESTMENT POTENTIAL: Many analysts have considered this issue overpriced at every level it has occupied in the last fifteen years. But despite their warnings, investors and collectors keep buying, and prices continue to rise. It has been a favorite pastime of promoters to create false markets and then allow prices to readjust. Thus, though pointed in a generally upward direction, the price graph of this date resembles a roller coaster. Even though it may yet prove to be a successful investment, the 1899 is too available in MS (65) condition to be heartily recommended.

1899-O

Typical Mint State Example
MS (65), above average strike,
moderate bagmarks, frosty surfaces,
excellent luster.

GENERAL DISCUSSION: This issue enjoys a very high overall quality. The luster on 1899-O's is, generally, equal to or better than all other Morgan dates. A nice, fully struck MS (65) specimen with only light bagmarks is not difficult to locate.

Many mint state 1899-O's are undobutedly from the bags released from the great Treasury hoards in 1963-64. Before that time, this date commanded a significant premium above that of common dates in uncirculated condition.

In circulated grades, this issue is valued at no more than the most common issues.

Some of the finest Morgans extant are 1899-O's. The authors witnessed one example, touted as perfect (and a quick examination with a 5x glass did not reveal evidence to the contrary) sell for $900.00 at a coin show in the spring of 1983.

RARITY IN PROOFLIKE: Semiprooflike specimens are often stretched to prooflike status. While scarce, deep mirror examples appear regularly. The problem is locating a reflective example without heavy bagmarking. Prooflikes are usually well struck; seldom is there significant cameo contrast between fields and devices.

RARITY IN SUPERB CONDITION: This issue clearly ranks as one of the most common in superb MS (67) or better condition. Luster can be abundant on select pieces, affording instant eye appeal. The most common deterrents to superb levels are bagmarks and, less frequently, strike.

REDFIELD: No.

INVESTMENT POTENTIAL: Possibilities here are limited to solid MS (65) or better coins. Coins with noticeable problems, a weak strike or deficient luster should not be considered.

1899-S

Typical Mint State Example
MS (65), sharp strike, moderate
bagmarks, frosty surfaces, good
luster.

GENERAL DISCUSSION: The San Francisco Mint Morgan Dollar of 1899 is a scarce and valuable issue in mint state. After the appearance of the Redfield Hoard, which contained a quantity of mint state specimens, a temporary increase in the availability of uncirculated coins was experienced by the growing market. The demand outpaced the supply, and the price of coins of this issue steadily rose.

The average quality of mint state 1899-S's is high. The strike and luster are usually unobjectionable, as are the number of bagmarks. The majority of examples are very pleasant in overall appearance. As time goes on, the nicest coins will disappear from the market and be replaced by lesser quality.

Auction records for superb examples are relatively frequent. Interestingly, the premiums garnered by these MS (67) examples have been very modest. Perhaps because of the high overall quality, collectors are less inclined to pay a substantial amount extra for a little more quality in this particular issue's case. Also, price resistance plays an important role. Many more collectors are willing and able to pay $200 for a superb dollar that might sell for $20 in typical condition than $1,000 for a superb cartwheel that is a $100 coin in typical condition.

Circulated examples in extremely fine or better condition are considered scarce and bring a healthy premium. In lesser grades, the premium is slight.

Although a valuable issue in mint state, altered examples have not been reported, nor are they likely to be.

RARITY IN PROOFLIKE: Prooflike examples are quite scarce, but as a percentage of the total surviving mint state population, they are not as rare as many other similarly priced issues. The serious collector need not jump at the first example offered to him; others will surely come along. Mirrored examples are usually attractive and void of serious bagmarking. There is usually no contrast between fields and devices. A cameo prooflike is rare, and would bring a much greater price than a brilliant prooflike.

RARITY IN SUPERB CONDITION: The average mint state quality of this issue is quite high; therefore, superb examples occur with some frequency. When sold, they command a surprisingly modest premium over typical mint state examples.

REDFIELD: A considerable number of 1899-S's were included in the Redfield estate.

INVESTMENT POTENTIAL: The superb examples that are currently available for a modest premium may be the best investments that this issue has to offer. They will inevitably be replaced on the market by inferior specimens.

1900

Typical Mint State Example
MS (63), above average strike,
moderate bagmarks, frosty surfaces,
good luster.

GENERAL DISCUSSION: With the exceptions of the 1885-1887 and 1921 issues, this year is the most common Philadelphia Mint Morgan in mint state condition. Preserved in bag quantities, mint state examples of typical or lesser mint state quality are valued only as common bulk mint state dollars. Because most of the surviving population is not seen as individual coins, it may appear that the typical mint state example should be graded MS (65) rather than our assigned MS (63). However, while MS (65) may indeed be the typical grade of the 1900 Morgan encountered on the open market, all mint state examples, including those buried in bags with 999 other coins, are considered when assigning the typical mint state grade. Eventually, most of these coins will appear on the market individually.

Circulated coins are grouped with the most common of the series.

Commencing in 1900, a refined reverse was used on some dollars. The new reverse changed the overall appearance of the Morgan. In their diligent and invaluable research, Van Allen and Mallis pinpoint the changes, and enumerate the dates on which these occur:

A new minor design type reverse ... was used on some 1900 P, S, 1901 P, S O, and 1902 O, and on all 1902 P, S, 1903, and 1904. This ... reverse had a larger space between the edge of the eagle's left wing and the eagle's neck, a larger center space in the I of IN, and larger stars.

This new reverse design had an additional effect that is more difficult to describe than those that can be physically measured. It may be most aptly described by focusing attention on the eagle's breast feathers, which often appear blurry and indistinct on coins on which the new reverse was employed. These coins are fully struck — a stronger pressure from the dies would not have created sharper breast feathers nor other details of the coins. Many coins of the dates on which this new reverse was used have been mistakenly termed as "weakly struck" when, in actuality, they are not. On the more valuable issues, such as 1903-S or 1904-S, which we will discuss later, this can be a very important point.

On dates on which both the former and new reverse designs were employed, such as the presently considered 1900, the new reverse type is considered less desirable than the previous one. Any difference in value between the two types is due overwhelmingly to the difference in quality, and not to the fact that different reverse types were used.

RARITY IN PROOFLIKE: This issue is scarce with truly reflective surfaces. Many prooflikes exhibit dense die striations, or very thin, curved lines in the fields of the coin. These striations may appear to be hairlines at first glance, but close examination will reveal otherwise. Striations will end abruptly at the base of a letter or device; a hairline will usually cease a millimeter or so away from the base.

A cameo example is quite unusual, and commands a significant premium above that of normal prooflikes.

RARITY IN SUPERB CONDITION: This issue is both abundant in total mint state population and high in typical mint state quality of pieces traded on an individual basis.

Therefore, superb examples appear with greater regularity than most issues.

REDFIELD: No.

PROOFS: One might think that an inordinate number of proofs might have been produced and saved to commemorate the initial year of the 1900s, but only a slightly higher than average number were made. They are neither rarer nor more common than most Morgan proofs. Many have been carelessly handled or cleaned. Proofs of this year invariably have no contrast between fields and devices.

INVESTMENT POTENTIAL: Superb MS (67) or better examples will be in demand in the future by both date and type collectors. Coins of lesser quality should always be in plentiful supply.

1900-O

Typical Mint State Example
MS (63), average strike, moderate
bagmarks, frosty surfaces, good
luster.

GENERAL DISCUSSION: At least dozens of bags, perhaps hundreds, of this issue were distributed in 1962-1964 when the Treasury liquidated most of its holdings.

The strike on 1900-O's can vary considerably. Some specimens may exhibit weak breast feathers, while others may show the curled tips of those feathers plainly. Bagmarks on coins that are swapped on an individual basis are usually not serious. However, on coins still stored in bags of common bulk mint state dollars, they can be heavy.

Circulated examples are valued as common dates only.

RARITY IN PROOFLIKE: This issue is moderately scarce with fully prooflike surfaces. Specimens with fully reflective surfaces constitute a very small percentage of the total mint state population. Die striations, similar to those seen on the Philadelphia prooflikes of the same date, are often encountered. Coins with the striations should not be considered inferior to those which do not have them, but, since many confuse the striations with hairlines, striated examples bring less. Prooflike examples are almost always fully struck.

RARITY IN SUPERB CONDITION: Superb examples can occasionally be selected from original rolls. Because the total mint state population is relatively large, and the average mint state quality of individual pieces traded between collectors and dealers is high, a 1900-O in superb MS (67) condition is not among the most difficult Morgans to locate at the present time.

REDFIELD: No.

INVESTMENT POTENTIAL: Any potential that this issue possesses lies with superb MS (67) or better coins.

1900-O over CC

Typical Mint State Example
MS (63), average strike, light to
moderate bagmarks, frosty surfaces,
good luster.

GENERAL DISCUSSION: This interesting and popular Morgan Dollar variety was discovered in the early 1960s. The mintmark area shows clear evidence of a "CC" beneath the "O." This evidence is bolder on some varieties than on others; the varieties with the sharpest overmintmark are the most popular among collectors. Other overmintmark varieties exist in the series, such as the 1882-O over S, but they are not accepted as widely as is this issue.

The Carson City Mint ceased production of all coinage in 1893. However, it was to remain legally a mint, with the capability to produce coins should the need arise, until 1899.[4] Therefore, it is not unreasonable that some reverse dies bearing Carson City's mintmark were prepared during the time the mint's existence was in limbo. When the Secretary of the Treasury officially designated the Carson City facility as an Assay Office, and the coin presses were dismantled, the existing dies with "CC" mintmarks destined for Nevada were re-punched with an "O" and sent to Louisiana instead.

Van Allen and Mallis list six different varieties of the 1900-O over CC. Most collectors seek just one example to represent this interesting variety.

The typical mint state quality of the issue closely approximates that of the regular 1900-O. Most of the examples probably came from the Treasury bags distributed in the early 1960s. This would explain the variety's late discovery date.

Circulated examples are moderately scarce, and demand a small premium. Most collectors, in an effort to procure an example that adequately displays the overmintmark, prefer to add a mint state coin to their sets if possible.

RARITY IN PROOFLIKE: This issue is extremely scarce with prooflike surfaces. An occasional semiprooflike example is encountered, but hardly ever does one have the opportunity to examine a piece with truly reflective surfaces.

RARITY IN SUPERB CONDITION: About the same ratio of 1900-O over CC's exists in superb MS (67) condition as 1900-O's, relative to their respective total mint state populations. At the current time, superb examples of this variety command a surprisingly modest premium.

REDFIELD: No.

INVESTMENT POTENTIAL: The popularity of this variety can only increase in the future. It has been listed in the Guidebook since the mid-1960s, and has become an integral part of the Morgan series in most collectors' minds. MS (65) or better examples with clear evidence of the overmintmark will be in the highest demand.

---

[4]Howard Hickson, *Mint Mark: "CC"* (The Nevada State Museum in Carson City, 1972) p.73.

1900-S

Typical Mint State Example
MS (63), average strike, moderate
bagmarks, frosty surfaces, good
luster.

GENERAL DISCUSSION: The most significant fact about 1900-S dollars is their presence in the Redfield Hoard. As of this writing, mint state examples believed to have been part of that hoard are still readily available. This issue seems to be among the most abundant, at least compared to other Redfield dates in the same price range.

The Redfield coins roughly matched the typical pre-Redfield 1900-S in terms of typical mint state characteristics. The Redfield coins were slightly more sharply struck, and were more often found to have semiprooflike surfaces. Some of the Redfield coins were, inevitably, heavily bagmarked. However, some of the most superior quality coins from that remarkable accumulation were some fully prooflike, nearly mark-free, sharply struck 1900-S's.

Circulated examples of this issue do not command a significant premium unless in extremely fine or almost uncirculated condition.

The few superb examples to reach major auction sales have brought prices of a relatively modest premium above that of MS (65) examples.

RARITY IN PROOFLIKE: The Redfield coins refueled the supply of prooflike examples. However, time and the eager demand of prooflike collectors and investors will inevitably decrease the number of such coins available. Prooflikes of this issue are generally sharply struck and highly attractive if they lack dense bagmarks. Many of the coins from the Redfield holdings were only lightly marked, and represent some of the highest quality present in the nearly half-million coins stashed by that eccentric Nevadan.

RARITY IN SUPERB CONDITION: Superb 1900-S's are sometimes available for a relatively modest premium. Such specimens are divided about 60-40 percent into frosty and prooflike categories.

REDFIELD: Present market conditions indicate that a large quantity of this date was included in the Redfield Hoard. Decreasing average quality of available examples are signs that the finest specimens are being retained by collectors or investors.

INVESTMENT POTENTIAL: The abundance of this issue in the Redfield Hoard can work to the advantage of the investor. At present, superb examples, some with exquisite prooflike surfaces, are available for a modest premium. Once these coins are acquired by quality conscious collectors, they will likely return to the market infrequently, and then be met with greater enthusiasm than they generate today.

1901

Typical Mint State Example
MS (60), weak strike, moderate
bagmarks, frosty surfaces, poor
luster.

GENERAL DISCUSSION: The 1901 Morgan Dollar is now recognized as one of the most challenging members of the entire series to locate in mint state condition. Only in the present generation of dollar collectors has the knowledge of this coin's true rarity become widely known.

True MS (60) examples, apparently offered frequently, are in reality scarce. All too often, a so-called MS (60) is nothing more than a lustrous almost uncirculated coin. These "sliders" can be treacherous, with the slight rub on the high points visible only in good light, with the coin tilted at just the right angle. The surfaces and luster of mint state 1901 dollars are so poor that detection of rubbing is often difficult.

MS (63) coins that meet every criterion of that grade are rare. A collector who owns a strict MS (63) example has reason to be proud.

Compounding the challenge of locating a pleasing mint state example of this issue is the often abnormal metal flow, usually most visible on the reverse of 1901 dollars. This effect, which causes the surfaces to have a curious, rippling appearance, is more pronounced on the coins of this issue than on any other Morgan. This effect, by the way, is the same as that which was first discussed in connection with the 1886, and several dates thereafter.

Most of the mint state coins available either exhibit the abnormal metal flow, or may bear unsightly bagmarks. Bagmarks are almost never numerous on coins of this date, but they are apt to be singularly severe. This may indicate the production was released almost in its entirety into circulation; few bags, if any, were preserved. The consistency with which specimens with heavy abrasions appear is not coincidental; the ones without them have long been retained by collectors familiar with their rarity.

Also supporting the theory that practically all of the production was placed into circulation is the preponderance of circulated examples. Even almost uncirculated coins are easy to find. The lack of enough mint state examples to go around maintains the price of those coins near uncirculated condition.

Although the high value of mint state examples would logically produce some attempts to produce bogus coins by removal of the mintmark from a 1901-O, very few such attempts have been reported, and these have been quite crude. The characteristics of the New Orleans Mint and Philadelphia Mint issues of this year are easily differentiated; detection of an altered coin is easy for the experienced dollar dealer.

Very few noteworthy coins of this issue have appeared at public auction. The few true mint state examples that have been offered were, for the most part, typical in quality. The Ronald Keller specimen was graded MS (65) to MS (70) in Paramount's May, 1973, Greater New York Sale: it was one of the few non-prooflikes in Dr. Keller's collection. That piece is untraceable today.

Kansas dealer Joe Flynn owned an outstanding specimen seen as part of a set that he assembled.

Without a doubt, the most famous 1901 Morgan Dollar is the prooflike specimen first sold at public auction in RARCOA's landmark 1973 FUN Sale, featuring the Bruce Todd collection of dollars. This coin is mentioned in Wayne Miller's work as "the only (prooflike) specimen to appear in the past several years."

It is indeed a rare Morgan Dollar that can be completely pedigreed from the present back to the time it first fell into a numismatist's possession. Unlike early type coins, Large Cents or most Nineteenth Century United States coins, which were popular with early collectors, Morgan Dollars were not widely collected until the early 1960s, and hardly at all as late as the 1940s. With the help of several of the owners of this Morgan rarity, the authors have been able to trace the complete pedigree of the Bruce Todd 1901 dollar:

1. In the late 1960s, a banker in Kalispell, Montana, extracted an unusually reflective example of a 1901 dollar from a bag of mixed dollars which had occupied his bank's vaults for an indeterminate length of time.

2. He sold the coin to Dean Tavenner, a coin and book dealer from Deer Lodge, Montana, for $110. The banker had sold Mr. Tavenner some "keeper" dollars on prior occasions.

3. Dean Tavenner sold the piece to a good customer of his who was interested in assembling a set of Morgan Dollars which had reflective fields and minimal bagmarks. He was even willing to pay premium prices for coins he needed that met his standards. The few people in the nation pursuing similar goals referred to the dollars they sought as "prooflikes." The customer's name was Bruce Todd; he paid about $250 for his prize.

4. Mr. Todd consigned his virtually complete set of Morgans to RARCOA for their January, 1973, Florida United Numismatists' Auction Sale. Wayne Miller, a dollar specialist who would soon become a full-time dealer, purchased the piece for $360.

5. Bruce Amspacher, on behalf of Steve Ivy Rare Coin Company, purchased the 1901 prooflike from Wayne Miller.

6. Ron Howard, on behalf of Paramount International Coin Corporation, purchased the coin from Steve Ivy for $800 in the early months of 1975.

7. California dealer Steve Deeds bought the Todd 1901 from the 1975 Grand Central Auction Sale conducted by Paramount.

8. Mr. Deeds sold the coin to collector Earl Green.

9. Mr. Green consigned the now-famous coin to Steve Ivy Numismatic Auctions. It appeared as lot 1043 of the Stanford Sale, which was replete with exceptional Morgans. A young dealer named David Hall, who was partial to nice Morgans, bought the trophy for $3,700.

10. Mr. Hall sold the coin to dealer Mike DeFalco for a reported $5,000.

11. For the second time, Bruce Amspacher handled the coin. This time, on behalf of Fred Sweeney Rare Coin Company, he placed the piece in a collection in the Midwest, where it remains as this book goes to press. The last selling price was near the five figure level.

The Todd 1901 is clearly identifiable by its unique prooflike surfaces, and by a mark above Miss Liberty's ear. This mark has been described by various owners and catalogers in a variety of ways: RARCOA merely mentioned a "couple of light marks on head;" in the Stanford Sale the mark was termed "an unobtrusive scratch;" Miller tactfully proclaims it to be "a long, deep laceration." Those who wish to add to the glossary of descriptions can examine the photos in the Todd and Stanford Sale catalogs.

The only other prooflike specimen seen by the authors is a coin held by a prominent Illinois collector. This piece, while superior to the Todd specimen in terms of marks and strike, did not have surfaces of equal desirability. The preference that an individual might express in favor of one or the other of the two coins is strictly subjective.

A scarce and interesting variety is known as the "shifted eagle." It is also referred to as the "doubled eagle" variety. In either case, it is VAM 3. Van Allen and Mallis elaborate upon its description and cause:

> Eagle has been shifted to twelve o'clock so that the lower part of the eagle's wings, tail feathers, olive branch and leaves, arrow shafts and arrowheads, and eagle's lower beak are strongly doubled. Letters OD and W are doubled below and within the motto IN GOD WE TRUST. The doubling was caused by a misalignment between the hub and die in one of the early blows.

This variety commands a significant premium from collectors who wish to obtain an example for their collections.

RARITY IN PROOFLIKE: The foregoing discussion should amply convey the rarity of this issue in prooflike condition. As RARCOA put it when they sold the Todd specimen, it is "probably the most difficult to obtain piece in the set (with prooflike surfaces)."

RARITY IN SUPERB CONDITION: In the authors' opinion, the 1901 is the rarest Morgan Dollar in superb MS (67) condition. It is perhaps unknown in that grade, unless the previously mentioned example once owned by Joe Flynn meets today's strict standards for description at that elite level.

REDFIELD: No.

PROOFS: Due to the prohibitive rarity of mint state examples in appealing quality, many collectors have resorted to proof coins to fill the void in mint state collections. Thus, the value of proofs is totally unrelated to the number of proofs available; it is more akin to the value of typical mint state examples. Many of the nicer proof coins are more or less permanently impounded in collections; most of those seen on the market in the last few years have been obviously cleaned, impaired, or circulated. Proofs of this date have a slightly doubled reverse.

INVESTMENT POTENTIAL: An MS (65) example will always create much excitement when it is sold. An MS (63) coin, if strictly graded, will become a highly respected Morgan rarity. Although a natural part of the coin, the abnormal metal flow discussed earlier will always be a detriment to the value and desirability of a mint state 1901. For investment purposes, pieces with this should be avoided as much as possible. On few Morgans is accurate grading so important as on mint state examples of the 1901.

1901-O

Typical Mint State Example
MS (63), average strike, moderate
bagmarks, frosty surfaces, good
luster.

GENERAL DISCUSSION: Of the seven New Orleans issues (1898-1904) that were held in multiple bag quantities by the U.S. Treasury and distributed in 1962-1964, the 1901-O is clearly the second scarcest in mint state condition on today's market. In terms of typical mint state quality, it is the worst of the seven issues.

While scarcer than common dates, this issue is readily available in mint state. Gem MS (65) examples may be harder to obtain than might be expected by the beginner. Many 1901-O's are weakly struck; others may bear too many bagmarks for an MS (65) classification.

In circulated grades, the 1901-O is scarce, but the relatively low value of the most inferior MS (60) examples keeps the price of such circulated coins essentially at the common level.

The price record for a coin of this particular date and mint is $900, which the Wayne Miller plate coin brought in Steve Ivy Numismatic Auctions' C.T. Briggs Sale in May, 1979. It was a nearly mark-free, prooflike example.

RARITY IN PROOFLIKE: For an issue so readily available in mint state condition, the 1901-O is very scarce with prooflike surfaces. When encountered, however, prooflike 1901-O's are usually well struck and pleasing, albeit they most often lack any cameo contrast between fields and devices.

RARITY IN SUPERB CONDITION: It is difficult to locate a 1901-O with all the requirements of a strict MS (67) grade. Patience and a price about double that of an MS (65) coin may reward the searcher with a superb example of this issue.

REDFIELD: No.

INVESTMENT POTENTIAL: For strict, sharply struck MS (65) or better examples, the future looks bright for this issue. Recent price increases have been well deserved; expect the differential between typical and superb coins to widen in the future.

1901-S

Typical Mint State Example
MS (63), weak strike, moderate
bagmarks, frosty surfaces, good
luster.

GENERAL DISCUSSION: There have been no significant quantities of 1901-S Morgans released upon the market in the last two decades. The Redfield Hoard, although it contained bags of earlier and later San Francisco coins, did not contain any of this issue. Coupled with the many obstacles that coins of this issue face in achieving the MS (65) level, this accounts for the sparsity of the MS (65) population on today's market.

Coins of this issue are often seen with parallel lines that pass through the high points of either the obverse or reverse designs. Advertisers and catalogers often call these lines "die striations." They are not die striations, which are tiny hairline scratches incused in the die when the die is cleaned or polished. The lines present on many 1901-S's (and some other S-mint coins of the same era) are "roller marks." These raised, parallel lines occurred when the strips of silver from which the planchets were punched were being rolled down to the proper thickness. As the long strips passed between the huge rollers, they were subjected to tremendous pressure. On one or more of the rollers, some narrow ridges of uneven metal must have been present. When the strips of silver passed between these particular rollers, the ridges on the rollers were pressed into the surface of the silver strips, causing the "roller marks." Planchets were then cut from the silver strips, and of course, the roller marks remained. When the marks were deep enough, or when striking pressure was not sufficient, they were not completely eliminated when the planchets were struck as coins. Thus they remained on some coins when they left the dies.

On sharply struck 1901-S's, which are the exception rather than the rule, the roller marks are usually not visible. On average or weakly struck coins, they are present on almost half of the mint state examples seen.

Circulated coins are scarce, and command at least a modest premium if they are in very fine or better condition.

Superb examples have been very rare as far as public auction appearances go. In fact, in the eight auctions that Steve Ivy Numismatic Auctions conducted between July, 1977, and May, 1979, in which superb examples of Morgan Dollars abounded, only one superb 1901-S was offered.

The finest known 1901-S is a possibly unique cameo prooflike sold to a Northeastern collector in 1978.

RARITY IN PROOFLIKE: The 1901-S is extremely difficult to locate with prooflike surfaces. No other coin of comparable rarity in all mint state condition, with the exception of 1904, is so dear in prooflike. Most prooflike examples of this issue are very weakly struck. A specimen with reflective surfaces and a strong strike is avidly sought by many collectors.

RARITY IN SUPERB CONDITION: Multiple reasons — strike, roller marks, bagmarks, etc. — make the location of a superb MS (67) or better 1901-S a formidable task. Some issues are both more expensive than the 1901-S in superb condition and more common.

REDFIELD: No.

INVESTMENT POTENTIAL: Coin show scuttlebutt has often mentioned the possibility of the coming of the Redfield 1901-S's, but time has given no truth to the rumors. Recent increases in value for gem examples are more than justified, and may reflect only a fraction of this issue's potential. The investor should avoid weakly struck and/or roller-marked coins; while the latter shortcoming technically does not affect the coin's grade, it invariably decreases its desirability to collectors.

1902

Typical Mint State Example
MS (63), above average strike,
moderate bagmarks, frosty surfaces,
good luster.

GENERAL DISCUSSION: This issue is moderately scarce on today's market in mint state condition. Occasionally, a roll of twenty uncirculated pieces is seen; no bag quantities have been recently rumored.

A slightly revised reverse (see the discussion under 1900) requires that collectors exercise a degree of understanding and tolerance for this issue. Although a 1902 Morgan might be as fully struck as it is possible for it to be, the breast feathers on the eagle may appear indistinct. A sharp 1902 dollar (or any other issue which employs the revised reverse) may appear weakly struck to the novice. It is not possible to demand from this issue the same standards of strike that apply to earlier dates.

Lustrous, nearly uncirculated coins of this date are often seen, and may be offered as mint state by a dealer who is either inexperienced or unscrupulous.

RARITY IN PROOFLIKE: The 1902 is not as rare in prooflike as either its price or reputation would indicate. The authors have seen several different rolls of twenty coins with reflective surfaces. However, many prooflikes of this issue are unattractive — die polishing, similar to that found on prooflikes of 1888-S, often makes the surfaces somewhat gray and blurred. Cameos are virtually nonexistent.

RARITY IN SUPERB CONDITION: Superb, nearly mark-free specimens are available on surprisingly frequent occasions. This may not always be the case, as collectors become even more desirous of higher quality.

REDFIELD: No.

PROOFS: Proofs of this date are usually unattractive, with no contrast at all between fields and devices. In common with other dates of Morgan proofs, many have been hairlined by cleaning.

INVESTMENT POTENTIAL: Most of the potential, at least in the short term sense, of this issue may have been exhausted by the recent steep price increases. In the long run, this issue, if purchased in gem MS (65) or better condition, should perform as well as the Morgan Series on the average.

1902-O

Typical Mint State Example
MS (63), above average strike,
moderate to heavy bagmarks, frosty
surfaces, good luster.

GENERAL DISCUSSION: This is yet another of the New Orleans issues that was so heavily distributed from the U.S. Treasury's holdings of vast quantities of dollars. Prior to that distribution, the 1902-O was considered a semi-key member of the Morgan series. Now, the issue is one of the most common in terms of the total mint state specimens available. Original bags obtained from the Treasury are no doubt still held intact by some investors.

This issue is found somewhat more heavily bagmarked than the other New Orleans Mint dollars from the Treasury group. Mint state examples are usually well struck, although exceptions to this general rule abound, especially in rolls that have been "cherry picked" of the nicer pieces.

Circulated coins, while seldom seen, command no premium above common bulk dollars because of the easy availability collectors and investors have to mint state specimens. Mint state examples of MS (63) or inferior quality should be valued only as common bulk mint state dollars.

RARITY IN PROOFLIKE: Despite frequent offerings of prooflike specimens, this issue is scarce with truly reflective surfaces. Many of the coins so advertised are semiprooflike examples, which are not difficult to locate. With deep mirror fields, the 1902-O is an underrated issue. Cameo contrast between the fields and devices is hardly ever seen on prooflikes of this date and mint.

RARITY IN SUPERB CONDITION: This issue is surprisingly difficult to locate in true MS (67) or better condition. Although hundreds of thousands of mint state examples have survived, the relatively few superb coins have, for the most part, already been tucked away into collections. Some remain for the time being, and can be procured if the person who seeks one will be patient and can afford to pay two to three times what an MS (65) would cost.

REDFIELD: No.

INVESTMENT POTENTIAL: Superb MS (67) or better quality is always desirable for investment purposes, regardless of what date of Morgan one is considering. For this date, though, such quality is especially recommended. As a percentage of the total surviving mint state population, superb 1902-O's are one of the scarcest Morgans.

1902-S

Typical Mint State Example
MS (60), weak strike, heavy
bagmarks, frosty surfaces, good
luster.

GENERAL DISCUSSION: Many of the mint state examples of this scarce Morgan available on today's market emanated from the fabulous Redfield Hoard. The quality of the Redfield 1902-S's generally coincides with that of the previously known mint state coins of this issue, with two exceptions: the Redfield 1902-S's were more sharply struck, and a higher percentage of them lacked the roller marks so common on coins of this issue.

The typical 1902-S is among the poorest quality of all Morgan issues. Roller marks are more often encountered on coins of this particular date and mint than they are on any other. The strike is often poor, and bagmarks are almost invariably dense. Although they were nothing to write home about, the Redfield 1902-S's improved the average quality of the mint state 1902-S population.

Circulated examples are quite scarce, and demand a healthy premium. Even specimens in only good condition are worth double the price of a common date.

Several superb specimens of this issue have been offered at public auction over the last few years. As with other dates of Morgans in the same price range, the premium for superb quality is not equal to the premium paid for similar condition in more common issues.

RARITY IN PROOFLIKE: This is an extremely scarce and underrated issue in prooflike. The Redfield hoard contained not one verifiable prooflike example. Those offered as prooflikes are often only semiprooflike. When a true prooflike is found, it is usually weakly struck. Fully struck examples with fully reflective fields are rare.

RARITY IN SUPERB CONDITION: Although superb examples bring a relatively modest premium, they are truly scarce items. Most of the superb coins found on today's market were already in collectors' hands before the appearance of the Redfield coins.

REDFIELD: In the authors' opinions, a substantial quantity of 1902-S dollars was included in the Redfield Hoard. This quantity was not enough to materially depress the market, nor even prevent the price of this issue from rising with virtually all other dates of Morgan Dollars.

INVESTMENT POTENTIAL: With the added supply of MS (60) coins from the Redfield source, typical mint state examples of this issue should be in adequate supply for generations to come. However, there may be a decided shortage of superb and prooflike examples in the future. If investment in this issue is considered, solid MS (65) quality or better is recommended.

1903

Typical Mint State Example
MS (65), sharp strike, light
bagmarks, semiprooflike surfaces,
excellent luster.

GENERAL DISCUSSION: Except for a few temporary shortages in the last decade or so, the 1903 Morgan has always been readily available in mint state condition. Rolls, while now scarce, once existed in quantity.

This issue possesses one of the highest average Mint State qualities of any Morgan. MS (60) examples are rarer than MS (65)s, a statement that can be made for very few issues. No collection need be without a superb MS (67) specimen. Besides the existence of some highly lustrous, almost uncirculated examples that are liable to be offered as mint state, the buyer need have little concern over getting advertised quality on this issue.

Circulated examples command a very modest premium over common dates, except for almost uncirculated coins, which may bring about double the price of a common coin in the same condition.

Superb examples are frequently offered at public auction and, because there is little price resistance at their level, they bring substantially above what their rarity should dictate.

RARITY IN PROOFLIKE: The 1903 is very scarce with fully prooflike surfaces. However, semiprooflike coins abound; in fact, the typical mint state characteristics of this date include semiprooflike surfaces. Therefore, the value and scarcity of true prooflikes is understated by the frequent offering of semiprooflikes and prooflikes. Even when a specimen with mirror surfaces is found, it is often of the unattractive gray brilliant type. Deep, smooth and fully reflective surfaces are hard to find on a 1903 dollar.

RARITY IN SUPERB CONDITION: This issue is one of the easiest of all Morgans to locate in MS (67) or better condition. MS (69)s exist, and are much in demand by type collectors as well as date enthusiasts.

REDFIELD: No.

PROOFS: Proofs of this date are not normally particularly attractive, since there is no contrast between the fields and devices. Many have been impaired to some degree by injudicious cleaning or mishandling.

INVESTMENT POTENTIAL: A minor factor to consider is the date's suitability for a one-coin-from-each-date set. A more important factor is its overall high quality. Superb MS (67) coins are available, and should not carry a huge premium at this time. There is no reason to settle for less when assembling a well-devised investment portfolio of silver dollars.

1903-O

Typical Mint State Example
MS (65), above average strike, light
bagmarks, semiprooflike surfaces,
excellent luster.

GENERAL DISCUSSION: Many bags of 1903-O dollars were released by the U.S. Treasury in 1962 through 1964. Prior to that time, this issue was regarded as one of the key issues of the series. In the 1962 edition of the *Guidebook of United States Coins*, only the 1895 Morgan surpassed the valuation of the 1903-O! After the release of the Treasury coins, its price plummeted to a fraction of its former value.

Since this issue is often traded, the price has fluctuated over the years since the Treasury distribution, but has moved in a steadily upward fashion. The 1903-O has been a favorite of promoters, and is likely to be heavily manipulated at various times in the future. There are no doubt many caches of multi-roll quantities still intact that were put away shortly after they were sold by the government.

The average mint state quality of this issue is very high. Most 1903-O's are well struck and have pleasing surfaces and luster. The primary factor in determining grade is the degree of bagmarks present.

Circulated specimens are, understandably, very scarce, and bring an unusually high percentage of the price of a mint state coin. The owner of a circulated 1903-O knows that he possesses a coin that was once unaffordable to the vast majority of Morgan collectors. As testimony to this, witness lot number 1587 of the Belden E. Roach Sale (B. Max Mehl, February, 1944). That 1903-O dollar was described as "Strictly very good but very rare. Rarest dollar of this mint. Catalogs $50 in uncirculated." It realized $15.75, slightly less than the $17.50 which an 1895 proof brought in the same sale!

Current price records for superb examples have approached the seven hundred dollar level; not a restoration to the former glory for this date, but a respectable recovery from their dip to less than thirty dollars immediately after the Treasury distribution of dollars in the 1960s.

RARITY IN PROOFLIKE: The abundance of semiprooflike examples of this issue has tended to hold down the value of truly prooflike coins, which are scarce. A fully reflective example does not command much premium when encountered; however, this may not be the case in the future.

RARITY IN SUPERB CONDITION: Coins of this issue are usually not too difficult to locate in superb condition. When found, such pieces command only a modest premium on today's market.

REDFIELD: No.

INVESTMENT POTENTIAL: This issue has been seeking its proper price in relation to the rest of the Morgan Dollar series since its precipitous plunge after the Treasury distribution of 1962-1964. Since mint state examples seem to be readily available at the new, higher levels, perhaps much of the potential this date possesses has already transpired. No parallels between this issue and the coins distributed in the Redfield Hoard should be drawn; the quantity of 1903-O's distributed would dwarf the quantity of any single date present in Redfield.

1903-S

Typical Mint State Example
MS (65), sharp strike, light
bagmarks, frosty surfaces, excellent
luster.

GENERAL DISCUSSION: While undeniably a scarce issue in mint state, the 1903-S has always been surprisingly available to collectors, especially when one considers the high price of mint state examples. At no point in the dollar market's history of the past two decades has there been anyone in serious pursuit of an MS (65) example of this issue who has not been able to locate one within a reasonable period of time. It is, frankly, difficult to understand how this issue became so highly priced.

The 1903-S may well have the highest average mint state quality of the entire Morgan series. MS (65) examples account for almost half of the mint state coins seen on the market. A group of about a dozen toned, mostly MS (67) coins appeared at the 1977 Numismatic Association of Southern California (NASC) Convention. Their quality epitomized the entire issue — they were sharply struck with minimal marks, and quite attractive in appearance.

One of the most beautiful Morgans of any date handled by the authors was a 1903-S purchased at a coin show in Harrisburg, Pennsylvania, in October, 1978. This blazing specimen had gorgeous peripheral toning and an incredible amount of mint luster. As the demand for superb Morgans increased, so did the value of this coin. From an original purchase price of $3,200, it was reported to have been sold, after passing through another dealer's hands, at a price near $6,000.

At about the same time (November, 1978), one of the few prooflike examples of this date to be offered at public auction appeared in Steve Ivy Numismatic Auction's Roger Turner Sale, and was described as:

> Superb! Prooflike. Fully brilliant, reflective surfaces. The only prooflike example of this rare date we have offered for sale, and one of precious few we can recall seeing or hearing about. Well struck and virtually mark free... Miller assigns the date his highest prooflike rarity rating, and states that 'The 1903-S is excessively rare in prooflike condition... A Gem prooflike specimen would deservedly bring a record price.' This is a very attractive and rare coin, and it may well garner the record price to which Mr. Miller alludes.

The piece brought $3,800 which was, at the time, a record price.

RARITY IN PROOFLIKE: The foregoing discussion should dramatize the rarity of this issue with prooflike surfaces. To amplify the point, consider the fact that the fabulous Bruce Todd collection (RARCOA, January 1973) contained a frosty, rather than prooflike, specimen. Mr. Todd strove to obtain high quality prooflikes if they were available. The Keller collection (Paramount, May, 1973), which was replete with rare prooflikes, also contained a frosty 1903-S.

RARITY IN SUPERB CONDITION: As a percentage of the total mint state population, superb 1903-S's occur with at least an equal frequency to any other Morgan issue. MS (69) examples exist; both the Todd and Keller specimens mentioned in the above paragraph were

graded MS (70). In many advanced collections, one of the nicest dollars in the set is the
1903-S.

REDFIELD: No.

INVESTMENT POTENTIAL: Although this issue may indeed increase in price in the
future, some adjustments are in order to correctly position its value in respect to some other
Morgan key and semi-key dates. This process can already be seen taking place. For instance,
the rare O-Mint coins of the 1893-1897 years are rapidly, and deservedly, overtaking the
1903-S in terms of MS (65) prices. The 1904-S should be much more closely valued to its San
Francisco Mint predecessor than it is. If investment in this date is desired, the purchaser
should seek no less than MS (67) quality, and should not pay a large premium over MS (65)
prices to obtain it.

1904

Typical Mint State Example
MS (60), average strike, moderate
bagmarks, frosty surfaces, poor
luster.

GENERAL DISCUSSION: This issue is deceptively scarce in mint state. An abundance of specimens that would be mint state were it not for a very slight rub on the high points have confused the market in the past. Now, with stricter grading standards and an increase in the knowledge and ability of the collectors and dealers doing the grading, the true scarcity of the 1904 issue has come to light. The resultant price increases are not surprising.

The vast majority of mint state examples are only MS (60) quality. A pleasing coin of this issue is difficult to find, since luster, strike or bagmarks, or some combination of the three, can render some otherwise collectible examples undesirable. A friend of ours who was confident in the future of dollars wanted to invest some capital in selected dates of Morgans at the 1977 American Numismatic Association's convention in Atlanta. High on his preferred list was the 1904. We agreed with his selection, and urged him to buy all of the MS (65) examples he could find at the show, at which over two hundred major dealers held bourse tables. He did buy all of the MS (65) examples he could find — both of them. He paid about seventy dollars each for the coins, and naturally declined our offer of a modest but quick profit. That was in August, 1977; in December, 1978, he sold us one of his seventy dollar 1904 Morgans for $375! As of this writing, that piece has quadrupled in value.

Although the market history of the 1904 discussed above is a special case, it does accurately indicate how both an increase in demand for high quality Morgans *and* the increase in knowledge of true scarcity of certain issues can combine to enable individual issues to attain their proper price levels. The dollar market has by no means undergone the last of these adjustments.

Circulated examples of this date are given little respect, and are usually left with common bulk circulated dollars unless of strict extremely fine or better quality.

Superb examples at auction create serious interest from collectors. Once the potential buyer is satisfied with the quality of a superb 1904 Morgan, he is quite willing to pay a handsome price to obtain it for his collection. The $1,100 fetched by a sharp, toned MS (67) in the C.T. Briggs Sale (Steve Ivy Numismatic Auctions, May, 1979) may have been considerably less than the buyer was willing to pay.

A superb prooflike example of this date brought an awesome $5,500 at an early 1979 convention. Although an impressive price to pay for a 1904 Morgan, the owner has the security of knowing that no amount of money would necessarily be able to procure a finer specimen.

RARITY IN PROOFLIKE: The 1904 ranks as one of the most challenging Morgans to locate with prooflike surfaces. The authors have never seen an example with deeply reflective mirror surfaces. The few true prooflikes that have been available on the market in the last decade have been relatively unattractive, with no contrast between fields and devices. Semiprooflike coins are scarce; when they come upon the market, they are almost invariably offered as prooflikes. The serious prooflike collector may be faced with a dilemma concerning the 1904 issue; either include a semiprooflike coin, or leave that spot in his collection blank.

RARITY IN SUPERB CONDITION: This issue is rarely seen in superb MS (67) condition. It is probably nonexistent in MS (69) grade. Recent dramatic price increases have failed to produce a noticeable increase in the number of superb coins on the market. Thus, the superb 1904 Morgan has passed the truest test of rarity to which a coin can be subjected.

REDFIELD: No.

PROOFS: Proofs of this issue are moderately scarcer than most other dates. Decades ago, they were regarded as rare, and brought premiums of about double that of "common" dates. There is usually no contrast whatsoever between fields and devices. Many examples have been cleaned at one time, leaving telltale hairlines on the surfaces.

INVESTMENT POTENTIAL: Despite recent dramatic price increases, this issue should nonetheless perform in at least an average fashion in the future. Accurate grading at the time of purchase is critical. A fully struck coin (which, for a 1904, will not exhibit the detail of an 1881-S, for instance) which will grade at least MS (65) should be sought. Strict MS (63) examples, if reasonably priced, may also prove to be good investments.

1904-O

Typical Mint State Example
MS (63), average strike, moderate
bagmarks, frosty surfaces, good
luster.

GENERAL DISCUSSION: This issue is a prime candidate for the most common Morgan Dollar in mint state condition. Hundreds of original bags were released from Treasury vaults in the great 1962-1964 liquidation of the government's dollar holdings. At least one hoard in excess of one hundred bags of mint state coins is still known to exist. Rolls of mint state coins are seen in multiple quantities at every coin show of even modest size.

Because of the huge number of pieces available, the individual pieces that are traded between collectors and dealers are of generally high quality, probably averaging MS (65). But when the hundreds of thousands of mint state examples that are traded or stored in rolls or bags are taken into consideration, the average mint state quality is considerably reduced.

Coins of MS (63) quality or worse are considered common bulk mint state dollars. Circulated coins, while scarce, naturally do not command any premium over common dates.

Like the 1898-O and the 1903-O, the 1904-O was considered a key Morgan before the Treasury released its bags.

RARITY IN PROOFLIKE: The 1904-O is one of the most common of all Morgans with prooflike surfaces. Prooflikes are often very attractive, with deep mirror fields being the rule. This issue is the only Morgan made in the Twentieth Century that is readily available with prooflike surfaces.

RARITY IN SUPERB CONDITION: Because of the abundance of mint state specimens, a rather large number of superb pieces are available. As a percentage of the total surviving mint state population, however, the 1904-O is as respectable as many other, more expensive issues.

REDFIELD: No.

INVESTMENT POTENTIAL: Any potential that this issue possesses in a numismatic sense, as opposed to bullion related speculation, lies in superb MS (67) or better quality. The premium required to obtain such quality is quite small today, and may drastically increase in the future.

1904-S

Typical Mint State Example
MS (63), average strike, moderate
bagmarks, frosty surfaces, good
luster.

GENERAL DISCUSSION: For the second straight year, the San Francisco Mint produced a Morgan Dollar that would eventually be coveted by collectors. While this issue may be more common in all mint state grades than the 1903-S, it is scarcer in MS (65) and better grades.

No significant quantities of 1904-S dollars have ever been unleashed upon the market. Apparently, no groups in excess of single rolls were preserved. Despite the presence of most San Francisco Morgans in the Redfield Hoard, no 1904-S's were included. At several different times during the current active market for dollars, it has been very difficult to locate even a single MS (65) example of this scarce issue. Knowledgeable dealers, collectors and investors were not surprised when the price of high quality examples of this date began rapidly escalating in the latter part of 1978. Adjustment of the value of the 1904-S in relation to other Morgan issues had been long overdue, and may not have completed its course as of this writing.

Circulated examples are scarce above very fine condition. As the grade approaches almost uncirculated, the premium accelerates progressively.

Aution records for superb examples are sparse. It is interesting to note that Steve Ivy Numismatic Auctions did not offer a single superb example in all of its auctions from the Stanford Sale in July, 1977, to the Henry Hermann Sale in July, 1979. In those two years, auctions presented by that company became well known for fine selections of Morgan Dollars. A dozen MS (65) 1904-S's were offered in the Ivy sales, but not one met MS (67) standards, not even Wayne Miller's plate coin, which sold for $2,800 in the Briggs Sale in May, 1979.

Surely the finest 1904-S sold at public sale was the incredible specimen sold as part of the Fairfield Collection (Bowers and Ruddy, October, 1977). In that encyclopedic catalog, the coin was described as:

Gem uncirculated with full prooflike surfaces. Beautiful multi-colored iridescent toning. Acquired as a branch mint Proof. Possibly struck as a presentation piece. Undoubtedly the finest known example of this scarce San Francisco Mint issue.

That unusual piece brought a record-shattering $3,200. As a point of reference, an MS (65) example sold in the Brazos Sale, conducted by Steve Ivy Numismatic Auctions in the same month as the Fairfield Sale, for $630.

Another memorable example, a toned, frosty piece, was sold in an obscure Florida auction in spring, 1978. It was eventually sold to an Eastern collector who has assembled an outstanding Morgan set.

RARITY IN PROOFLIKE: Besides the Fairfield specimen described above, only three other auction records can be found for prooflike examples. One of those lots (Roger M. Turner Sale, Steve Ivy Numismatic Auctions, November, 1978) references a prooflike example sold at the 1978 ANA for $2,750. The Turner coin brought $3,100. Needless to say, prooflike examples are rare and command much respect when offered. However, of the dozen dates to which dollar expert Wayne Miller assigns his highest prooflike rarity rating, the 1904-S is one of the least rare.

RARITY IN SUPERB CONDITION: The 1904-S Morgan is quite rare in superb MS (67) condition, much moreso than the 1903-S. Bagmarks and/or an insufficient strike often prevent superb classifications on coins of this issue.

REDFIELD: No.

PROOFS: The reference to a branch mint proof of this date cited in the general discussion above is the only such reference discovered. There are no official records of branch mint proofs, and Breen, despite his exhaustive research on U.S. proof coins, does not mention the possibility of one.

INVESTMENT POTENTIAL: This issue must rank as one of the most historically underrated Morgans. Price adjustments are currently underway. The inexorable law of supply and demand will determine this issue's ultimate ranking among the Morgan keys, but it will surely be a few notches up from its earlier position. Solid MS (65) or better 1904-S's should perform in an above average fashion with respect to the Morgan series as a whole.

1921

Typical Mint State Example
MS (60), average strike, moderate to
heavy bagmarks, frosty surfaces,
good luster.

GENERAL DISCUSSION: After a seventeen year hiatus from dollar production, the Philadelphia and San Francisco Mints resumed Morgan Dollar minting in 1921, spewing forth an unprecedented number of cartwheels then were joined by the Denver Mint. Under the Pittman Act of 1918, more than 270,000,000 silver dollars had been melted; nearly one-third of that number would be restored by the mints in 1921 alone.

The Philadelphia Mint turned almost all of its attention to the production of silver dollars. There were more silver dollars minted than there were cents; of the nearly fifty million silver coins produced by the Philadelphia Mint in 1921, more than fourty-four million were dollars.

This issue is so abundant in mint state condition that it enjoys a market of its own. It is valued between twenty and thirty percent less than the most common Morgan dates of the 1878-1904 era. Circulated examples are similarly proportioned.

Although the average mint state quality of examples traded between dealers and collectors is considerably higher than that enumerated above, the vast quantities still stored in bags and rolls reduce the grade of the typical mint state example.

Superb coins are another story. To the casual observer, the prices that some superb examples of this issue have brought are amazing in light of the abundance of mint state coins. To the experienced collector, the large mint state population merely underscores the coin's scarcity in superb condition. This phenomenon may be more adequately described from the C.T. Briggs Sale catalog, in which a 1921 Morgan was said to be:

> Superb! This stunning coin has a combination of qualities unheard of for this date.
> The color, luster, strike and surfaces are all impeccable. What an unappreciated
> rarity! The novice may think the winning bid is ludicrous, but the initiated
> Morgan collector will consider it justified.

With mint state 1921 Morgans available for fifteen dollars each, the Briggs example brought $370 after spirited bidding.

While $370 may sound like a record price, it is not even close. The Wayne Miller plate coin, a superb, frosty example, brought an incredible $900 at the Roger Turner Sale in November, 1978.

The design was modified for both the obverse and reverse for the revitalized Morgan Dollar. Coins bearing the date 1921 can be easily distinguished from previous issues, disregarding the obvious difference in the date. On the obverse, Liberty's hairlines are different, with the area immediately above the ear somewhat flatter. Other details and lettering are slightly modified. From a general appearance standpoint, the contours are not as rounded as before, and the coin gives a flatter impression. On the reverse, the eagle's breast was flattened and minor modifications were made in the details and lettering.

RARITY IN PROOFLIKE: This issue is moderately scarce with prooflike surfaces. Prooflikes, when found, are usually only of MS (60) or MS (63) quality, and may bear some heavy bagmarks. They are usually well struck.

RARITY IN SUPERB CONDITION: Superb examples are very scarce. Particularly attractive specimens may bring high prices at public or private sale. Most examples that have broken the one hundred dollar level have had some degree of toning. Superb pieces are almost always frosty, and seldom prooflike.

REDFIELD: No.

PROOFS: Some controversy and confusion has always surrounded the proof Morgan Dollars bearing the date 1921. This need not be the case. Proofs of this year may be placed in two categories:

1. Regular issue proofs. Also known as Chapman proofs. Breen reports that twelve were struck. Proofs of this type should have all the earmarks of a proof Morgan of any previous year, plus the following characteristics, defined by RARCOA in the catalog of the Todd Collection: A recut "T" in "UNITED," and a die break, very light, around the stars on the left obverse.

2. Zerbe proofs. Sometimes referred to as "Zerbe striking" or "presentation piece." According to Breen, "The story has been told that Farran Zerbe had these proofs made . . . as a kind of consolation for his not being able to get the Peace Dollars into the public's hands during the calendar year 1921." Zerbe was a prominent numismatist of his day, and enthusiastically promoted the production of the Peace Dollar. The Zerbe proofs possess many of the normal characteristics of a Morgan proof of previous years. They are further identifiable by a slight, although detectable with a magnifying glass, die break extending from the top left tip of the second "U" in "UNUM" to the denticles.

The Zerbe proofs are more common and much less valuable than the regular proofs. It is not known how many of each variety were made, and various sources quote different numbers. From the ratio with which the coins appear, the numbers of 200 and 12, respectively for the Zerbes and the regular proofs, may be the most accurate. However, if only twelve regulars were made, they make the numismatic rounds with inordinate frequency.

INVESTMENT POTENTIAL: The investor may do well to purchase superb examples picked from original rolls or bags. If this strategy is impractical, the premium for MS (67) coins charged by many dealers seems modest, if the quality is really there.

1921

Typical Mint State Example
MS (63), weak strike, light bagmarks,
good luster.

GENERAL DISCUSSION: The 1921 Peace Dollar differs from all other issues of the series in many ways, although the general design is identical. Van Allen and Mallis list four obverse differences and nine reverse differences between the 1921 design and that used on all subsequent issues. However, one major difference overrides the others — the relief in which the coins were struck. The devices (the head of Liberty on the obverse and the eagle on the reverse) are raised higher from the field on the 1921 issues than those used beginning in 1922. The rims of the 1921s are higher also, imparting a concave appearance to the coin, with the fields seeming to slope away from the rims to a low point and then rising to the devices. On later issues, the fields appear to be level, with the rims and devices abruptly rising from them. If the two different types of Peace Dollars are placed side by side, the difference in overall appearance is readily visible.

This high relief style employed in 1921 caused serious problems in the finished product. Many of the slightly more than one million Peace Dollars dated 1921 lacked a great deal of the design detail that they were intended to have. Almost none of the coins, all of which were produced between December 26 and December 31, 1921, exhibited full detail on the highest points, i.e., the eagle's body and Miss Liberty's hair.

Thus a problem that collectors face today is locating a well struck 1921 Peace Dollar. MS (60) or MS (63) examples of this issue with a typical strike are readily available, but finding an MS (65) coin with virtually full detail is a formidable task. The premium that a well struck coin of this date can command varies exponentially with the amount of detail present. In no other issue of United States Silver Dollar does the strike make so much difference to the price.

Most of the "full strikes" advertised for this date are not technically fully struck, but merely much above average. The term "full strike" as used in reference to 1921 Peace Dollars implies that the coin being offered is a premium example. A more accurate terminology might be "well struck" or "full strike for the date." Unfortunately, the commercial oneupmanship engaged in by many dealers has brought about this imprecision. A full strike by one person's standards may not meet the criteria for that description by another. In other words, some full strikes are fuller than others. Some would argue against the existence of a 1921 Peace Dollar with an absolutely full strike.

Because of the popularity of the date and the general scarcity of circulated examples, non-mint state coins demand a substantial premium, even if well worn.

Occasionally, a roll or two of original coins surface. These groups may contain some well struck coins. Two groups that included an inordinate proportion of sharply struck examples came to light in 1978. One was a mini-hoard of about eighty pieces purchased over the counter by Paramount International Coin Corporation in Englewood, Ohio. These were quickly sold on an individual retail basis, for about five hundred dollars each, by Paramount. The other group was uncovered by R&M Coin Shop in Akron, Ohio, some months before. The 25 or so coins in that holding were sold over the teletype circuit and subsequently retailed by the dealers who purchased them.

Rarely, a single 1921 Peace Dollar becomes available that is virtually fully struck and nearly free of marks. The demand is so great for coins of this description that they invariably bring very high prices. A golden toned, nearly fully struck specimen that lacked significant bagmarks hopscotched among dealers for two weeks at back-to-back California coin shows in early 1979. After being sold initially for $325, the coin was reported to have traded hands for $2,250! This exceptional case is not often repeated on today's coin market; the knowledge and sophistication of the persons involved is much more widespread than it was only a decade ago.

Perhaps the finest non-proof example of a 1921 Peace Dollar to appear in a public auction sale was the lovely example described in the Henry F. Herrman Sale (Steve Ivy Numismatic Auctions, July, 1979) as:

> The most lustrous 1921 Peace Dollar we have seen, and one of the most sharply struck. Radiant beams of intense luster emanate from immaculate surfaces. The hair curls of Liberty and the eagle's feathers are virtually completely struck up. This outstanding specimen will surely set a record price for a coin of this issue sold at public auction.

The coin received a great many bids from seriously interested parties. Only one could be successful in obtaining the prize; he paid $6,000 for the privilege.

Probably the finest known coin of this issue is a fabulous MS (70) owned by a northeastern collector. If a fully struck 1921 Peace Dollar exists, it is this one. A price in the vicinity of $7,500 is reported to have been paid for it.

RARITY IN SUPERB CONDITION: A 1921 Peace Dollar in superb condition is a rare and desirable item, especially if it is nearly fully struck. There is probably no other Peace Dollar that generates such respect as a near perfect example of this issue with virtually full hair and feather detail. There are, however, other Peace Dollars that are much scarcer in superb condition than the 1921, even though they may not command as high a price.

REDFIELD: No.

PROOFS: There are two types of proof 1921 Peace Dollars known, a satin finish variety and a matte variety. The first exhibits some brilliance and luster, while the latter is a sandblast, deep gray type of finish. Both types are extremely rare, though recent discoveries of a few satin finish pieces have made it the obviously more common of the two styles. Prices for the satin type have hovered around the five figure level (e.g., Paramount's Elrod Sale, July, 1976, lot 503 at $8,000, and a private sale in 1978 at $10,000). A specimen similar to each of the aforementioned brought $11,000 in the 1982 ANA sale. A matte specimen sold in Lester Merkin's sale of June, 1971, for $9,000, certainly a more impressive sum way back then than the more recent records for the satin variety. The mattes are readily distinguishable from regular business strikes, but the satins can be deceptive, especially since they were made from dies that were used for business strike production as well. Know your source before purchasing a purported proof 1921 Peace Dollar.

INVESTMENT POTENTIAL: All grades of mint state 1921 Peace Dollars have their positive aspects on today's market. The potential of solid MS (65) or better examples should be obvious; most collectors will demand such quality in the future. Also, one may consider lesser quality mint state examples as desirable investment material, since they have remained at a price standstill while superior examples have skyrocketed. Some adjustment is overdue. Strike is the key to the demand for coins of this issue. If one owns a well struck mint state specimen, he is assured of a strong resale market for his investment.

1921-D

Typical Mint State Example
MS (60), average strike, moderate
bagmarks, frosty surfaces, good
luster.

GENERAL DISCUSSION: The Denver Mint began coining operations in 1906. In 1921, when the Morgan Dollar was resumed, the Denver Mint joined its Philadelphia and San Francisco sisters in its production. The quality of the dollar it produced was far less than impressive. In all fairness to the facility, though, we must point out that the efforts of the other two mints were dismal as well. The new design, which just did not strike up as well as the previous one, and the pressing production demands placed upon all three mints surely contributed to the shortcomings of the final product.

The only other U.S. coins produced at the Denver Mint in 1921 were a small number of dimes and halves.

This issue is readily available in mint state condition. Most examples are no better than an average strike; many are very weak. A fully struck 1921-D with attractive luster and minimal marks is quite scarce.

Circulated examples, and mint state coins of average or inferior quality, are valued slightly lower than common date Morgans of previous years in the same conditions. The dollars of 1921 conform to the same standards of weights and metal content as do the ones of 1878-1904; they are valued less merely because they are considered less desirable by many collectors and investors.

RARITY IN PROOFLIKE: The 1921-D is a very challenging issue to locate with fully reflective surfaces. Many semiprooflikes are offered as prooflike, thus distorting the true rarity picture of the date. In relation to some more common coins in prooflike, which nonetheless bring higher prices, the 1921-D is very underrated.

RARITY IN SUPERB CONDITION: Fully struck coins with minimal abrasions are occasionally offered through major dollar dealers. Coins of this quality are often attractively toned as well. Since superb examples comprise a miniscule proportion of the total mint state population, they will inevitably be removed from the market almost entirely.

REDFIELD: No.

INVESTMENT POTENTIAL: As high quality becomes even more important among present and future dollar collectors, issues such as the 1921-D, common in average condition but rare in superb quality, should be among the best performers in the higher grades. In the lower ranges of mint state conditions, they may prove to be among the worst investments of the Morgan series.

1921-S

Typical Mint State Example
MS (60), weak strike, moderate
bagmarks, frosty surfaces, poor
luster.

GENERAL DISCUSSION: The 1921-S Morgan Dollar is readily available in mint state condition. In condition that is generally demanded by most collectors and investors, however, this issue is surprisingly scarce.

We say "surprisingly" scarce because of the huge production of this date, and the relatively large number of mint state coins that have survived. Based upon characteristics of the typical mint state example, it is surprising that collectible examples are not more highly respected than they are. It is safe to say that the 1921-S Morgan is one of the most poorly produced of the entire series.

The San Francisco Mint had been having its production problems in the years preceding the revival of the Morgan Dollar. All of the minor coinage from cents to halves were predominantly weakly struck and unattractive from 1916 to 1920. When the government added the burden of producing more than twenty million Silver Dollars, any hope of improvement disappeared under the burden of that additional load. The mint did only what was required of it.

As a result, many 1921-S dollars that have never seen a day of circulation may appear only as sharp as one might expect a Morgan in very fine condition to be. The luster is often poor and, if that is not enough, bagmarks are commonplace.

Sharply struck examples are quickly purchased by eager collectors. Superb, well struck specimens are rare; auction records are virtually nil for such coins. Knowledgeable collectors have long been familiar with the difficulty of locating a nice 1921-S. Bruce Todd could not locate a suitable specimen, and his failure was typical of many prominent collectors of the past decades. The $150 realized by the Ronald Keller specimen (Paramount, May, 1973) was an impressive sum for a coin of this issue at that time.

One of the most memorable Morgans of any date that the authors have seen was an incredible 1921-S sold several times at an Atlanta numismatic convention in May, 1978. After seeing so many thousands of typical, weak, lackluster 1921-S's, the sight of an absolutely fully struck, nearly mark free, highly lustrous example was breathtaking. A hint of rose toning added to its appeal. Although not even close to the most valuable Morgan Dollar we have seen, that 1921-S, considering its quality, is one of the rarest.

Another heralded 1921-S traded hands at the 1981 American Numismatic Association Convention in New Orleans. That piece was semiprooflike with some cameo contrast. Dealer Steve Contursi purchased the piece for $2,800 for his private collection. He reportedly declined an offer for $5,000 at the same convention.

RARITY IN PROOFLIKE: This issue ranks with the rarest of the series in availability with prooflike surfaces. Even semiprooflike coins are scarce and command a significant premium when offered. Most prooflike examples, and many semiprooflikes, come from the same reverse die. This die is identifiable by a polishing mark below the eagle's left wing on the reverse (the wing on the viewer's right). This mark appears on the coin as a bright, shiny area of a few square millimeters.

RARITY IN SUPERB CONDITION: Experienced collectors are awed by a 1921-S in fully struck, superb condition. Most coins of this quality are firmly entrenched in advanced collections. The person desiring one on today's market must have plenty of patience and a powerful pocketbook.

REDFIELD: A relatively small number of mint state 1921-S's were included in the Redfield estate. The only effect that the coins had was to add to the already sufficient population of inferior quality dollars of this issue.

PROOFS: Branch mint proofs of this date exist. The exact reason they were struck is not known, but Breen relates in his work on U.S. Proof coins that "Wayte Raymond told me in 1951 that Farran Zerbe had those coins made at San Francisco to go with the Philadelphia proofs from the first dollar dies received at the mint."

INVESTMENT POTENTIAL: There are few enough sharply struck coins to go around now. It is easy to see why the weakly struck coins are undesirable; it is surprising that people actually accepted them as money. The advice for the investor is simple: Strive to purchase examples as sharply struck and mark-free as is practical to locate, but do not wait on a "wonder coin." You cannot make any money investing in coins that do not exist.

1922

Typical Mint State Example
MS (60), sharp strike, moderate to
heavy bagmarks, good luster.

GENERAL DISCUSSION: The dollars of this issue are available in prodigious quantities in mint state condition. Original bags of this date are commonly traded as bulk mint state Silver Dollars.

Since the vast majority of 1922 dollars have been stored in bags since the year they were minted, and have often been transported from one location to another with little regard for their condition, most are severely bagmarked. Many also have a curious spotting on their surfaces; this spotting is opaque, and looks much like dried water spots, as one might see on an automobile's surface after some shower droplets have evaporated. These problems, either individually or in some combination, prohibit most 1922 dollars from surpassing the MS (60) level.

Needless to say, circulated examples are regarded with no respect beyond that accorded common bulk circulated dollars.

Although the vast majority of mint state examples are only of MS (60) quality, most of the individual coins traded between collectors and dealers are of higher quality. Any that have appeared in public auction sales have necessarily been of superb quality; such coins usually bring prices slightly more than one hundred dollars if they are in solid MS (65) or better condition.

RARITY IN SUPERB CONDITION: Only a few out of tens of thousands of mint state 1922 Peace Dollars will qualify as MS (67). Because of the enormous quantity of this issue available, however, superb examples surface with some regularity. When offered, they are met with great demand by type collectors. Bagmarks and opaque spots are the most frequent deterrents to the MS (67) grade.

REDFIELD: No.

PROOFS: There are two types of 1922 proof Peace Dollars, one with a fine grained matte surface and one with a satin finish surface. The matte type is of the same design as the 1921 Peace Dollar, with concave fields and a higher relief than the satin type. Breen lists five of the matte type known, but several others undoubtedly exist; their proof status may not be suspected. Only three were known, according to a June, 1971, Lester Merkin catalog which mentioned the 1922 type of 1921 when describing a proof 1921. The style of the description leads one to believe that it was Breen who wrote it, although this is not verified. Several of the satin types also likely exist, awaiting their discovery.

INVESTMENT POTENTIAL: The investment potential of this issue lies solely in superb specimens. This potential is quite significant, since type and date collectors will have an increasingly difficult time in finding 1922 Peace Dollars of such quality.

1922-D

Typical Mint State Example
MS (63), above average strike,
moderate bagmarks, good luster.

GENERAL DISCUSSION: This issue is not difficult to locate in mint state condition. The strike of uncirculated specimens is usually adequate, although weakly struck coins are seen now and then. This issue is peculiar in one notable respect: mint state examples have two distinctly different surfaces. The most common, occuring about eighty percent of the time, is the normal frosty surface. About twenty percent of 1922-D Peace Dollars have a satiny, almost orange-peel appearance. On extreme examples, the surfaces could be referred to as rippling. The luster is subdued on these pieces; the combination of qualities lends these 1922-D's an unusual appearance that is virtually confined to this issue. This characteristic can be found on other dates, but not to the same extent as on this particular issue.

The grading standards and values are the same for each type. Some collectors perfer the frosty surfaces; others, the satin finish. The choice is purely subjective.

Circulated 1922-D dollars are very common, and command no premium unless in choice almost uncirculated condition.

For some unknown reason, 1922-D dollars with spectacular, natural toning are seen with inordinate frequency, although they are by no means common.

RARITY IN SUPERB CONDITION: The 1922-D is one of the most common of all mint-marked Peace Dollars in superb MS (67) or better condition. Superb examples are often toned, and will be sharply struck and nearly mark free. Such coins are highly respected, as are any superb Peace Dollars. They command substantial premiums when sold.

REDFIELD: No.

INVESTMENT POTENTIAL: For years, the 1922-D and S and 1923-D and S Peace Dollars were valued at approximately the same levels in the same conditions. Today's broader market has seen the 1922-D lag behind the other three issues in value. This is consistent with the relative rarity of this issue. In the future, it should perform in an average fashion.

1922-S

Typical Mint State Example
MS (60), weak strike, moderate
bagmarks, good luster.

GENERAL DISCUSSION: This issue is readily available in mint state condition, but the vast majority of uncirculated examples are very poorly struck and thus not suitable for most collections. The authors have examined original bags of 1,000 pieces and not found a single well struck specimen.

It is not surprising, therefore, that well struck 1922-S Peace Dollars command a significant premium when offered. Collectors may even tolerate a few bagmarks on a coin that is nearly fully struck.

Circulated 1922-S's are common and command no premium, unless in lustrous, well struck almost uncirculated condition.

RARITY IN SUPERB CONDITION: Inadequate striking and abundant and/or severe bagmarks prevent all but a minute percentage of coins of this issue from qualifying for the elite MS (67) or better levels. A well struck, minimally marked 1922-S is the object of many collectors' serious searches.

REDFIELD: Yes. A few mint state bags of this issue were included in the Redfield Hoard. The coins were virtually all weakly struck, and created little interest from knowledgeable collectors.

INVESTMENT POTENTIAL: Even moreso than other dates of Morgan and Peace Dollars, the investment potential of this issue is directly related to the quality of the individual coins purchased. Typical quality 1922-S's have no reason to appreciate in value more rapidly than the Peace Dollar series as a whole, and are not recommended. Sharply struck coins of MS (65) or better grade, on the other hand, will continue to be a difficult item for the serious collector or investor to obtain. As the number of Peace Dollar collectors inevitably increases, a continued demand for this and other Peace issues seems assured.

1923

Typical Mint State Example
MS (60), sharp strike, moderate to
heavy bagmarks, good luster.

GENERAL DISCUSSION: This issue is similar in average quality and overall availability to the 1922. These two dates combined are considerably more common in mint state condition than the rest of the Peace Dollar series as a whole.

Bags of mint state dollars of this date are often traded as common bulk mint state dollars. Circulated examples are common.

The "water spots" discussed in conjunction with the 1922 issue are also often found on 1923 Peace Dollars.

Superb examples are in demand as type coins, and easily command a three figure price if their quality warrants. A few prooflike examples have been seen.

RARITY IN SUPERB CONDITION: In terms of absolute numbers available, the 1923 is one of the most common members of the series in superb MS (67) or better condition. However, in terms of the ratio of superb examples extant to the total number of mint state examples, the 1923 is very low.

REDFIELD: No.

INVESTMENT POTENTIAL: Superb MS (67) or better dollars of this date are the only ones which should be considered for investment purposes. Inferior quality pieces are readily available, and often traded as common bulk dollars.

1923-D

Typical Mint State Example
MS (63), average strike, moderate
bagmarks, good luster.

GENERAL DISCUSSION: Although one of the most common mintmarked Peace Dollars in mint state condition, the 1923-D is considerably scarcer than the 1922-D in all uncirculated grades. MS (60) examples are seen more often than true MS (65)s, which are becoming quite a bit more difficult to find.

Circulated examples are usually valued only as common bulk circulated dollars.

Dollars of this particular issue are notorious for die breaks. These breaks, which are usually most prominent on the obverse, occured when the coin dies used to strike the dollars began to weaken under the constant pressure to which they were subjected. As was often the case with this issue, the dies broke. The resultant fractures in the surfaces of the dies appeared as raised lines of metal on the coins produced from them. The dies in Denver in 1923 must not have been replaced with the proper frequency, since the majority of dollars emanating from these exhibit some degree of die breakage. These breaks may range from a small crack at the tip of Liberty's bust to large arcs that encircle the entire obverse of the coin.

These die breaks do not affect the grade of the coin on which they are present. Some collectors prefer specimens without them; they should examine their prospective purchases for them, or inquire if the breaks are present if they are ordering a coin through the mail.

RARITY IN SUPERB CONDITION: This issue is scarce in superb condition, considerably moreso than the 1922-D. MS (67) specimens are well struck and quite lustrous, with very few bagmarks. The presence of die breaks on an example need not necessarily remove it from the superb category.

REDFIELD: No.

INVESTMENT POTENTIAL: This issue possesses significant investment potential in solid MS (65) or better condition.

1923-S

Typical Mint State Example
MS (60), weak strike, moderate
bagmarks, good luster.

GENERAL DISCUSSION: This issue is easy to find in average uncirculated condition, though it is somewhat scarcer than the 1922-S, to which it is often compared. The San Francisco Mint had little to be proud of in 1923; coins of every denomination it produced were below par. Even the Monroe Doctrine commemorative Half Dollar, one of the few commemoratives produced at a branch mint, received very little quality control. The Silver Dollars fared no better. Of the 24 different Peace Dollar issues, the 1923-S is the worst in average quality of mint state examples.

In a series where strike is an overriding value-determining factor, the 1923-S stands out for its huge difference in value between a typically struck specimen and one which is virtually fully struck. The ratio may be as high as twenty to one! Quantities of weakly struck 1923-S's were not unusual even before the appearance of the Redfield coins in 1976; the additional bags of typical mint state examples of this issue thrust into the market by that Nevada estate liquidation made the rarity of a fully struck coin more apparent. A small percentage, probably less than five percent, of the coins produced by the San Francisco Mint were well struck. A high percentage of the well struck examples are virtually impounded in the collections of knowledgeable Peace Dollar *afficianados*.

RARITY IN SUPERB CONDITION: The 1923-S is among the rarest of all Peace Dollars in superb, well struck condition. A fully struck, near flawless specimen with full luster would undoubtedly command a runaway price if offered at a major public auction sale. The rarity and value of a superb 1923-S is often ludicrously understated.

REDFIELD: The Redfield accumulation contained a few bags of typical mint state 1923-S dollars.

INVESTMENT POTENTIAL: While typical examples remain stagnant, sharply struck coins of MS (65) or better quality should continue to perform well. This is one of the few issues where an investor might consider a coin of MS (63) quality if it is fully struck and reasonably priced. The fullness of the strike will always be the most important factor in determining the value of coins of this issue.

1924

Typical Mint State Example
MS (63), sharp strike, moderate to
heavy bagmarks, good luster.

GENERAL DISCUSSION: While much scarcer than either of its two preceding Philadelphia Mint counterparts, the 1924 Peace Dollar can be considered common in typical mint state condition. The average quality of coins swapped between collectors and dealers is much higher, with a relatively large number of superb examples available from time to time.

Common status is accorded to all circulated 1924 Peace Dollars. Superb specimens are among the most attractive of all Peace Dollars. An occasional example with semiprooflike surfaces is seen, but none have been reported with fully reflective properties.

RARITY IN SUPERB CONDITION: This issue is among the easiest of the series to locate in superb MS (67) or better condition, although one must not take for granted the availability of such a specimen at any given time. Coins of this date which occupy the upper echelons of the quantitive grading scale usually have outstanding luster and minimal marks, and are among the most attractive Peace Dollars available. Like all coins of this issue, superb examples are almost invariably sharply struck.

REDFIELD: No.

INVESTMENT POTENTIAL: Superb MS (67) or better examples should be in consistent demand in the future by both date and type collectors, as well as investors who have learned the wisdom of seeking the finest quality available for their portfolios. Average quality coins of this issue are not investment items; they are speculative in nature, and will perform in direct ratio with the value of silver bullion.

1924-S

Typical Mint State Example
MS (63), average strike, moderate to
heavy bagmarks, good luster.

GENERAL DISCUSSION: Although nothing to boast about, the overall quality of the San Francisco Mint's dollars of 1924 was a considerable improvement over than of each of the previous two years. The strike of most coins was clearly superior, and the luster imparted to the planchets' surfaces was at least marginally better. Although this issue has accrued a reputation for being weakly struck, more above average strikes are seen than weak ones.

The appearance of the Redfield dollars materially affected the supply of mint state 1924-S's on the market. Since the February, 1976, debut of the fabulous accumulation, however, most of the coins have been absorbed, including, of course, the vast majority of the desirable MS (65) or better coins. Most of the coins of this date and mint that Mr. Redfield stashed were sharply struck.

The 1924-S commands a slight premium in circulated grades of very fine or less, and a more substantial premium when in extremely fine or better condition.

Auction records are common for MS (65) specimens, but very sparse for MS (67) or better coins. No price for a truly superb, well struck specimen would surprise the knowledgeable Peace Dollar specialist.

RARITY IN SUPERB CONDITION: The 1924-S is quite rare in superb MS (67) or better condition. The appearance of superb 1924-S's invariably creates considerable excitement among collectors of the Peace Dollar series.

REDFIELD: A quantity of 1924-S Peace Dollars was included in the Redfield Hoard. The number of coins from that source, based on evidence upon the numismatic market, was considerably less than some other Redfield dates.

INVESTMENT POTENTIAL: Recent price increases for this issue have been well deserved. It should continue to garner its proper respect in relation to other semi-key members of the series. MS (65) or better specimens are recommended for investment purposes.

1925

Typical Mint State Example
MS (65), sharp strike, light to
moderate bagmarks, excellent luster.

GENERAL DISCUSSION: Although much scarcer than most common (1922 and 1923) dates of the Peace Dollar series, the 1925 is not difficult to find in mint state condition. When located, mint state examples are apt to be superior in quality to almost all other dates of the series.

This date has the distinction of including some of the finest Peace Dollars available. An MS (67) 1925 is more common than MS (65)s of most other dates. High quality examples are always sharply struck, while exhibiting vibrant luster and pleasantly mark free surfaces. These outstanding examples elicit much respect and demand from type collectors. An added attraction that many of them possess is a subtle hint of light golden toning.

Semiprooflike examples are often available, although the term is too frequently applied to dollars that merely radiate an added amount of luster from primarily frosty fields.

Circulated coins of this issue are common, as are mint state examples of less than MS (65) quality.

RARITY IN SUPERB CONDITION: This issue is among the most common of all Peace Dollars in superb MS (67) or better condition.

REDFIELD: No.

INVESTMENT POTENTIAL: Superb examples of this date offer the double-barreled attraction to both Peace Dollar collectors and type collectors that investors like to see. Coins of less than MS (67) quality, while they may rise in price in the future, will probably not reap the commensurate rewards which superior examples will.

1925-S

Typical Mint State Example
MS (60), weak strike, moderate
bagmarks, poor luster.

GENERAL DISCUSSION: After a temporary improvement in 1924, the San Francisco Mint made a dismal effort in dollar production in 1925. All but a trifling percentage of the coins minted were weakly struck, and most were dull and lackluster.

As any knowledgeable collector or dealer can attest, mint state coins are not difficult to locate, but MS (65) or better coins are very elusive. Coins of typical mint state quality were around even before the Redfield group added to their supply.

Similar to the 1922-D, 1925-S dollars can be found with two different types of surfaces, frosty and matte-like. The matte-like coins are usually sharply struck, while the frosty ones are normally quite weak, with little if any definition imparted to the eagle's feathers on the reverse. Only five percent or less of the mint state 1925-S's encountered on the market have the matte-like surfaces.

Strike is the primary determining factor in the value of coins of this issue in mint state condition. While auction records are scant for superb MS (67) or better coins, they are sufficiently numerous for MS (65) specimens. The prices realized for gem 1925-S's are directly proportional to the quality of the strike.

Circulated examples command little premium unless they are in lustrous, almost uncirculated condition.

RARITY IN SUPERB CONDITION: Superb, well struck MS (67) 1925-S dollars are extremely rare. If a collector restricts himself to coins of this grade, this issue may well be among the last two or three coins acquired. Well struck 1925-S's with few marks are often lacking in the luster category, thus eliminating the possibility of an MS (67) grade. Highly lustrous examples are often weakly struck. A truly superb 1925-S would meet with great demand from advanced Peace Dollar specialists.

REDFIELD: Shortly after the appearance of the LaVere Redfield Estate upon the numismatic market, an increased number of 1925-S dollars could be found. Almost all of the coins that emanated from the fabulous hoard were of typical mint state quality. The few sharply struck specimens which were included were quickly acquired by collectors or investors.

A bag of mint state 1925-S's was rumored to have been sold from the Redfield estate in 1975, approximately one year before the millionaire's silver dollars were marketed *en masse*.

INVESTMENT POTENTIAL: Strike is the most important factor in determining the desirability for investment purposes of this issue. Even MS (63) coins, if fully struck, may have some potential. As with other issues, MS (65) or better quality will no doubt fare the best. Superb MS (67) coins may well become highly respected rarities in the future.

1926

Typical Mint State Example
MS (63), sharp strike, moderate
bagmarks, good luster.

GENERAL DISCUSSION: With the obvious exceptions of the most common dates, the 1926 has always been one of the most available members of the Peace Dollar series to acquire in mint state condition.

The quantitative grade of the typical mint state example nearly reaches the MS (65) level. The strike and luster is normally sufficient to qualify most mint state examples as MS (65)s, but bagmarks often reduce otherwise MS (65) pieces to the MS (63) category.

Circulated examples are little better than common dates, and carry a premium only if they are in about uncirculated condition.

RARITY IN SUPERB CONDITION: The 1926 Peace Dollar is not particularly scarce in superb MS (67) or better condition.

REDFIELD: No.

INVESTMENT POTENTIAL: Judging from the relative availability of coins of this issue in mint state condition, it is surprising that they enjoy the premium that they have traditionally commanded on the numismatic market. Although coins of this date may well rise in value in the future, they may not perform well when compared to most others in the series. Only solid MS (65) or better quality should be considered when adding to one's portfolio.

1926-D

Typical Mint State Example
MS (65), sharp strike, light to
moderate bagmarks, excellent luster.

GENERAL DISCUSSION: After a two year hiatus, the Denver Mint resumed dollar production in 1926. This issue is moderately scarce in mint state condition. The population of mint state coins is well distributed, with original rolls having become very uncommon in the last several years.

The typical mint state quality of coins of this issue is quite high for a mintmarked Peace Dollar. Remarkably, the strike is exceptionally sharp on most examples; a weakly struck coin is hardly ever seen. However, due to improper servicing of the dies used to strike 1926-D's, foreign material accumulated upon the surfaces of the dies, and prevented the peripheral part of the obverse design from being properly struck up upon the surface of the planchet. Coins with this characteristic should not be confused with a weakly struck piece. The hair detail of Liberty and the feathers of the eagle should be examined to determine whether or not the coin in question is sharply struck.

Another characteristic which many consider to be a shortcoming of this date is the abundance of obverse die cracks, to an equal or even greater extent than on the 1923-D. A majority of uncirculated coins of this issue seen on today's market have some die breaks on the obverse. A far lesser percentage, probably in the neighborhood of fifteen percent, suffer from the "dirty die" characteristic mentioned in the previous paragraph.

Circulated coins of this issue, though seldom encountered, command only a slight premium unless they are in almost uncirculated condition.

Surprisingly, auction records for superb examples are almost nonexistent. Private sale records for outstanding specimens have, on rare occasions, exceeded the one thousand dollar mark.

RARITY IN SUPERB CONDITION: Since the 1926-D has the distinction of having one of the highest average mint state qualities of any mintmarked Peace Dollar, superb examples can be found if patience is exercised. The presence of die breaks, unto itself, does not eliminate an example from the superb MS (67) level (see the chapter on grading).

REDFIELD: No.

INVESTMENT POTENTIAL: This issue is a favorite of investors, since it combines both scarcity and high quality. As MS (65) or better coins are available to collectors, coins of lesser grades should be shunned for investment purposes.

1926-S

Typical Mint State Example
MS (60), above average strike, heavy
bagmarks, good luster.

GENERAL DISCUSSION: Peace Dollars dated 1926 which were manufactured by the San Francisco Mint are readily available on the dollar marketplace in mint state condition. A significant portion of the supply on hand originated from the extensive Redfield Hoard.

If this book had been written before the appearance of the Redfield coins, the typical mint state example may have been described as MS (63). This is one, and perhaps the only, case where the quality and number of Redfield coins of a particular date were sufficient to actually alter the typical mint state grade of the date.

From the evidence of the open marketplace, one could arrive at the conclusion that 1926-S was the most abundant Peace Dollar present in Mr. Redfield's bulky accumulation. One could also conclude that this date was in the most hideous condition, at least in respect to the number of bagmarks present on the coins' surfaces. Although the Redfield coins of this issue matched the typical mint state characteristics in terms of luster and strike, they were much more heavily bagmarked than those encountered prior to that monumental Nevada discovery. This is not to say that a Redfield 1926-S is necessarily only an MS (60) — some gem examples were included. Naturally, these were the first to disappear from the market.

Circulated examples command very little respect, and bring only a modest premium even if in the extremely fine to almost uncirculated grade range.

The 1926-S Peace Dollar is comparable, in many ways, to the 1887-S Morgan Dollar. The typical mint state characteristics are similar, especially with respect to the dense bagmarking that curses each issue. They rubbed shoulders in the walls of LaVere Redfield's house, and they are destined to be the last representatives of their respective series to be identifiable as emanating from that source. They were present in seemingly comparable quantities and qualities. Typical mint state examples are abundant; coins of each date in outstanding quality are rare.

RARITY IN SUPERB CONDITION: The 1926-S is very scarce in superb MS (67) or better condition. As a percentage of the total surviving mint state population, superb examples are as rare as many of the other highly respected S-mint Peace Dollars. Whereas strike is the usual obstacle for a superb classification for a San Francisco Mint Peace Dollar, bagmarks are the most frequent spoiler for 1926-S's.

REDFIELD: Yes. An unknown but significant quantity of 1926-S dollars, perhaps among the most numerous of all dates of dollars included in the hoard, came from Redfield. Most of these dollars were heavily bagmarked and/or blighted with surface dirt and grime. Very few were of MS (65) or better quality.

INVESTMENT POTENTIAL: The current affordability of MS (65) or better examples makes them very attractive to investors. The plethora of typical mint state examples on the market will serve to magnify the scarcity of collectible, MS (65) or better coins. Coins of this quality may prove to be wise investments. MS (65) or better 1926-S's are drastically under-rated, and should perform handsomely in the future.

1927

Typical Mint State Example
MS (63), sharp strike, moderate
bagmarks, good luster.

GENERAL DISCUSSION: Coins of this particular issue are readily available on today's market, although they command a lofty premium over common dates. A relatively high percentage of 1927 dollars traded on the modern numismatic scene came from bags sold by dealers in the early 1970's and late 1960's. By that time, the date had already entrenched itself as a semi-key issue. The supply of mint state examples has been sufficiently absorbed to allow the price of uncirculated coins to keep pace with the prices of the series as a whole. The supply of high quality, MS (65) or better, examples has obviously dwindled drastically in recent years.

Alike all Philadelphia Peace Dollars after 1921, the strike is usually sharp on coins of this issue, and the luster is at least adequate. Bagmarks are always present to some degree, usually enough to remove the coin being graded from the MS (65) level.

Circulated coins are scarce, and command a significant premium even if they are well worn.

Although rarely seen, a few prooflike examples of this date do exist.

RARITY IN SUPERB CONDITION: This issue is scarce, though not particularly rare, in superb mint state condition. Since the strike and luster are almost always sufficient for a superb classification, only the absence of bagmarks is additionally necessary for a mint state example to quality for the elite MS (67) label. Fortunately for collectors, a small percentage of 1927 Peace Dollars escaped excessive bagmarking and, for a significant premium, are occasionally available today.

REDFIELD: No.

INVESTMENT POTENTIAL: A much hoarded date in the past, the 1927 has only recently become scarcer in MS (65) or better condition. From this point forward, specimens of that quality or higher should perform in at least an average fashion.

1927-D

Typical Mint State Example
MS (63), sharp strike, moderate to
heavy bagmarks, good luster.

GENERAL DISCUSSION: Examples of this issue are very scarce in mint state condition. For many years it was regarded by experts as one of the most underrated issues of the entire series. Even after the increased sophistication of the modern dollar era has verified the coin's true rarity, enabling it to escalate dramatically in price, many still feel that the 1927-D is underrated in relation to some other dates.

This issue is wrongly reputed to be generally weakly struck, for such is not the case. Advertisements of coins as "full strikes" are common. There is certainly nothing wrong with pointing out a particular coin's strong points, but the addition of a hefty premium simply because a 1927-D dollar is strongly struck is not justifiable. Most of them come that way.

A notation of "nearly bagmark free," however, would entitle the owner to value his 1927-D at a high level, provided, of course, that his claim proved valid. Although not usually numerous, the bagmarks on the surfaces of 1927-D dollars are often severe. An otherwise superb piece may be tragically marred by a single gash on Liberty's cheek, or amid the eagle's feathers.

At every price level that the 1927-D has occupied, mint state examples have been difficult to acquire. No bags have been rumored, even by the oldtimers who seem to have seen everything. Original rolls are rare — the only ones seen by the authors were at a CSNS convention in St. Louis in the early 1970s.

Superb examples are highly desirable and seldom seen. A set at the CSNS convention in Dearborn, Michigan, in May, 1979, included the finest 1927-D ever seen by the authors. The owner, while amazed at the generosity of the offer, refused $1,750 for his specimen. Wholesale "bid" was about $700 at the time for an MS (65) coin. Knowing how difficult a superb 1927-D was to acquire, the owner wisely chose to retain his prize.

Circulated pieces are common in lower grades, but command a substantial premium if found in extremely fine or almost uncirculated condition.

RARITY IN SUPERB CONDITION: Superb 1927-D's are probably more common than the evidence of the modern market indicates; most of the MS (67) coins have already been removed from numismatic trading and rest, virtually impounded, in complete sets of Peace Dollars. Like the 1927 and several other dates of the series, bagmarks are usually the sole deficit from achieving the MS (67) grade. Statistics would dictate that a similar percentage of coins of this date might survive in superb condition. In any case, the appearance of a truly superb 1927-D raises many eyebrows among advanced Peace Dollar specialists.

REDFIELD: No.

INVESTMENT POTENTIAL: Investors should not be frightened by recent price increases. This date, unlike one's local service station, has not "run out of gas." Even MS (63) examples, if fairly priced at the time of purchase may prove lucrative investments. MS (65) coins should do very well. If an MS (67) coin could be bought at a livable price, the owner should consider himself very fortunate, and may look forward to steady price appreciation.

1927-S

Typical Mint State Example
MS (63), average strike, moderate
bagmarks, good luster.

GENERAL DISCUSSION: At the current time, mint state specimens of this issue are readily available on the market. The Redfield Hoard of Morgan and Peace Dollars is primarily responsible for the supply of 1927-S's from which buyers can choose. The demand, at least for the MS (65) or better coins, has outpaced the supply, with price increases having been registered despite the increase in the number of coins.

The Redfield 1927-S's were more sharply struck than the typical pre-Redfield 1927-S. However, many of the Nevadan's coins were heavily bagmarked.

Circulated specimens command a mild premium in the lower grades, and a more substantial one if in almost uncirculated grade.

Semiprooflike examples exist, and they often exhibit evidence of die polishing. This appears as a patch of apparently dense hairlines. Proper examination will reveal, however, that the lines are raised from, rather than cut into, the surfaces. These marks are frequently seen in the upper left obverse field, in front of Liberty's forehead.

RARITY IN SUPERB CONDITION: The influx of mint state coins from the Redfield Hoard offered little in the way of superb MS (67) or better examples. The few that were included were quickly put away. The 1927-S remains a very rare coin in superb condition.

REDFIELD: Coins of this issue were available in significant quantities in the Redfield Hoard. Rolls of coins from that source were seen on the market as late as the summer, 1982.

INVESTMENT POTENTIAL: Coins of less than MS (65) quality should be ignored for investment purposes. MS (65) or better quality should enable this issue to perform in at least an average fashion.

1928

Typical Mint State Example
MS (65), sharp strike, moderate to
light bagmarks, good luster.

GENERAL DISCUSSION: Because of its low mintage, the 1928 Peace Dollar has always enjoyed an undeserved reputation as being one of the scarcest dates of the series. Although it is among the rarest in terms of overall population, in mint state this is not the case. Although the date has risen in value in recent years, along with every date in the Peace Dollar series, a proper adjustment of the relative value of the 1928 compared to some other semi-key dates of the series has taken place. For example, one may study the price histories of the 1928 in comparison to the 1927-S or the 1934-D in MS (65) condition, and note the differences in the price acceleration of the various dates.

Philadelphia's dollar production in 1928 was small in quantity but high in overall quality. A weakly struck example of this issue is hardly ever seen, and the luster of the vast majority of coins is good. Fortunately, most 1928 Peace Dollars escaped heavy bagmarking. Although coins of this issue may bear a few marks which are on the heavy side, they are almost always few in number.

This issue is the only Peace Dollar which is in great demand and short supply in circulated condition. A very high percentage of the total issue of this year is preserved in mint state condition. Even a coin in only good condition is worth well over a hundred dollars.

This is the only Peace Dollar, at the current time, that has been victimized by nefarious alterations. The bogus examples are invariably made by removing the "S" mintmark from a genuine 1928-S dollar. Examine the mintmark area for signs of removal, and compare the characteristics of the coin in question with a 1928-S and a known genuine 1928 Philadelphia Mint product.

RARITY IN SUPERB CONDITION: Since the vast majority of the mintage of this issue has been preserved in mint state condition, and since the typical mint state example is of relatively high quality, it is not surprising that superb examples are generally available to those with patience and a little extra money to spend on a coin of this date.

REDFIELD: No.

INVESTMENT POTENTIAL: The mintage myth seems to have been finally dispelled in the case of 1928 Peace Dollars. A couple of years ago, the writers would not have recommended this issue to investors, citing as our reason the tendency to overrate the date because of its low mintage. Indeed, this issue has not performed on a par with the majority of dates of the series during that period of time. Now, however, since the inexorable influence of the law of supply and demand has finally asserted itself, the 1928 may not be inferior investment material any longer.

1928-S

Typical Mint State Example
MS (60), weak strike, moderate
bagmarks, good luster.

GENERAL DISCUSSION: Mint state examples of this issue are not too difficult to locate on the numismatic market today. The Redfield Hoard contained some bags of 1928-S's; much of the current supply originated from that source.

The strike of the typical coin of this issue is woefully weak; often, virtually no feathers are detailed on the eagle's body. Although not quite as weak as the 1923-S, the strike on the 1928-S ranks among the worst in the series.

The luster is consistently good on mint state examples, and bagmarks are not generally a major problem. However, many of the examples from the Redfield Hoard may have a single scratch, usually about an eighth of an inch long, near the rim on either the obverse or reverse, pointing toward the center of the coin. This mark was probably made by a coin counting machine, although some dealers hypothesize that the marks were made when Mr. Redfield shovelled some spilled dollars back into the walls of his house. Although a more romantic notion than the coin counter explanation, its plausibility seems remote; the marks on the coins are far too consistent in their size, severity and location to have been made by non-mechanical means.

Circulated 1928-S's command a small premium in grades up to and including extremely fine, and a more substantial one if in almost uncirculated condition.

Auction records for superb specimens are few. The finest 1928-S in the authors' memories is a near perfect specimen sold to a Tennessee collector years ago for $300; if placed in an auction sale today, that lovely piece would have the potential to bring over two thousand dollars.

RARITY IN SUPERB CONDITION: A well struck, superb MS (67) or better 1928-S Dollar is indeed a rare item. Despite the influx of mint state examples from the Redfield source, precious few superb coins of this issue have been traded in the last few years. Those specimens which qualify for the superb ranking in terms of luster and minimal marks are often weakly struck, thus greatly reducing their desirability.

REDFIELD: Some 1928-S Peace Dollars were undoubtedly included in the Redfield estate. From the evidence suggested by the open market, the quantity involved was at least several bags of mint state examples.

INVESTMENT POTENTIAL: Once again, strike is the most important determinant of the potential of this issue. Fully struck, MS (65) or better examples should perform in an above average fashion in the future.

1934

Typical Mint State Example
MS (65), sharp strike, light
bagmarks, good luster.

GENERAL DISCUSSION: This issue is scarce in mint state condition, although the collector can be assured, with a modicum of patience, that a nice example can be acquired. A relatively high percentage of the production of this year was not placed into circulation, and survives today for collectors' pleasure.

As can be seen by the description of the typical mint state example, the quality of the dollars of this issue is quite high. A weakly struck example is hardly ever seen; the luster is pleasing, and bagmarks are seldom serious enough to remove mint state 1934 dollars from the MS (65) category.

Mint state coins of this issue are often toned with a natural, light golden color which enhances their overall appearance. Mint state examples of this date are among the most attractive of the Peace Dollar series.

Circulated coins are scarce, and command a significant premium in all grades.

RARITY IN SUPERB CONDITION: As a percentage of the total extant mint state population, superb MS (67) or better examples of this date are among the most common of the series. An occasional MS (69) can be found. Superb examples are often lightly and attractively toned.

REDFIELD: No.

INVESTMENT POTENTIAL: Compared to some of the underrated mintmarked issues, the 1934 does not have outstanding investment potential. It does not take long to realize that mint state examples, even those of MS (65) or better quality, are not particularly difficult to locate. While mint state coins of this date may indeed rise in value in the future, it would be surprising if they kept pace with the series as a whole.

1934-D

Typical Mint State Example
MS (63), above average strike,
moderate bagmarks, good luster.

GENERAL DISCUSSION: This is a very scarce and underrated issue in mint state condition. While recent price adjustments have brought the value of uncirculated coins of this issue more properly in line with that of others in the series, the 1934-D remains, in the authors' opinions, undervalued. While the average mint state quality is not particularly low, MS (65) specimens are often a challenge to locate.

Some feathers on the eagle are almost always struck up, but seldom does one see a 1934-D that could be accurately termed "fully struck." Most mint state examples are lustrous and free of serious marks. There are many lightly circulated examples in existence that are optimistically evaluated as mint state.

Circulated coins of this production are scarce, but command only a small premium in grades of very fine or less. However, as the grade rises to almost uncirculated, the premium accelerates rapidly.

Auction records for superb examples are very sparse. The fact that Wayne Miller's original plate coin was only an MS (65) is supportive testimony to this issue's rarity in superb condition.

RARITY IN SUPERB CONDITION: This issue is extremely scarce in superb MS (67) or better condition, though not quite so much so as the earlier San Francisco issues. Fortunately, strike and bagmarks do not frequently detract from the condition of coins of this issue. The 1934-D is underrated in all mint state grades, especially in MS (67) or superior condition.

REDFIELD: No.

INVESTMENT POTENTIAL: The potential of this issue, in MS (65) or better grades, is apt to equal or surpass any other issue of the series.

1934-S

Typical Mint State Example
MS (63), average strike, light
bagmarks, good luster.

GENERAL DISCUSSION: In *all* mint state grades, this is the scarcest date of the Peace Dollar series, and the most valuable, although some issues are currently exhibiting the potential to surpass the price commanded by the 1934-S in comparable superb condition.

The general consensus on today's market is that the 1934-S Peace Dollar is an overrated issue. The authors adhere to this view, but, at the same time, caution our readers *not* to underestimate this issue in MS (65) condition. The demand for this key date is great, and apparently indefatigable. The overrated opinion came about as a result of the current quality craze in Morgan and Peace Dollars. As the tastes of the collectors became more and more particular, many people realized that there were several issues that were more difficult to locate in top mint state condition than the 1934-S.

The untiring demand that this issue enjoys is illustrated by its substantial price rise in recent years, despite the aforementioned general regard as being an overrated issue.

In circulated grades, the 1934-S is similar to the 1892-S Morgan Dollar. In the lower spectrum of the quantitative scale, i.e., below very fine (20), specimens of this issue command an almost insignificant premium. As the grade approaches mint state, however, the premium increases dramatically. Some nearly uncirculated examples with just the barest hint of rubbing on Liberty's cheek and the eagle's feathers are often offered as fully mint state pieces.

Paramount International Coin Corporation handled two brilliant uncirculated rolls of 1934-S dollars in 1975. They paid approximately ten thousand dollars for each roll. A superb roll of mint state pieces traded hands at the Florida United Numismatists' convention in January, 1978; the price ranged from $1,750 to $2,000 per coin. Other original rolls have been traded, and rumors of a bag of uncirculated coins located in the San Francisco Bay area persist.

Although the Redfield Hoard contained every other S-mint Peace Dollar, no 1934-S's have been verified as emanating from that source.

One of the finest mint state specimens seen by the authors was a coin offered as part of the dollar-rich Stanford Sale (Steve Ivy Numismatic Auctions, July, 1978). It was described therein as:

> Absolutely superb! No significant bagmarks. One hundred percent fully struck,
> with light golden tone. An incredible coin and a candidate for the finest known.

The $2,700 that the coin realized turned a few heads and set a new record price for the date. Many thought it would take years for the buyer to recover his investment. What a bargain it turned out to be! Less than a year after the Stanford Sale, the piece was worth more than double its purchase price.

At the 1981 F.U.N. show in Orlando, dealer Steve Contursi purchased a fabulous, olive-toned specimen for his personal set for over $10,000.

RARITY IN SUPERB CONDITION: The 1934-S is rare in superb condition only because of its overall scarcity in mint state grades. As a percentage of the total mint state population, superb MS (67) or better pieces are not particularly rare. However, due to the great demand for high quality pieces, locating a superb example should not be taken for granted, regardless of the funds available with which to procure one.

REDFIELD: No.

INVESTMENT POTENTIAL: The incessant demand that has consistently met this key issue through the years must give a degree of confidence to the numismatic investor. If he can add MS (65) or better quality to this demand, he can be assured of a logical and likely wise investment. Even if the rumored bag of mint state pieces were to materialize, which is highly doubtful, the market would eagerly absorb the highest quality coins. The experience of the GSA sales and the Redfield Hoard have demonstrated the tremendous power of the American Silver Dollar consumers *en masse*.

1935

Typical Mint State Example
MS (65), sharp strike, light
bagmarks, excellent luster.

GENERAL DISCUSSION: This issue is similar to the 1934 in terms of availability in mint state condition and the characteristics of the typical mint state coin. The 1935 is a bit more common, and comes a little nicer than the 1934.

Some of the finest Peace Dollars available are coins which bear this particular date.

Circulated specimens are moderately scarce in the higher grades and command a modest premium.

The collector need not settle for less than MS (65) quality for this date, and can acquire an MS (67) specimen for a reasonable premium if he so desires. The strike is almost always sharp, and the luster is the finest of any Peace Dollar minted since 1925.

RARITY IN SUPERB CONDITION: This issue is among the most common of the series in superb MS (67) condition. It ranks just after the Philadelphia Mint coins of the 1922-25 era in availability of superb examples, although it is much scarcer than any of those issues in all mint state grades.

REDFIELD: No.

INVESTMENT POTENTIAL: MS (65) coins should perform in at least an average fashion; MS (67) or better coins may do better. Although not prohibitively rare, MS (67) coins will probably enjoy an increased premium in the future.

1935-S

Typical Mint State Example
MS (65), above-average strike, light
bagmarks, excellent luster.

GENERAL DISCUSSION: Dollars of this issue are more consistent in their overall quality than most members of the series. Although a very weakly struck 1935-S is hardly ever encountered, coins that could be termed technically fully struck are also uncommon. The most gratifying property of 1935-S's in general is their attractive luster. Most examples exhibit a brilliance that collectors can only wish for on other issues.

A relatively high percentage of the original mintage has been preserved in mint state condition. Circulated examples are uncommon and command at least a modest premium in all grades.

Coins with a tendency toward prooflike surfaces are occasionally encountered. They are always sharply struck.

A variation in the reverse rays is unique to this issue. On some coins there are four rays beneath the word "One" of the denomination. The four-ray configuration is slightly scarcer than the three-ray which was used on all other Peace Dollar reverses except 1921. Most collectors do not seek one of each variety.

RARITY IN SUPERB CONDITION: This issue boasts a high ratio of superb MS (67) or better examples to the total mint state population. It is one of the easiest Peace Dollars to locate in superior condition.

REDFIELD: A small number, probably just several rolls, of mint state 1935-S dollars were included in the hoard. They were among the first of the Redfield dates completely dispersed.

INVESTMENT POTENTIAL: This has always been a popular date. Even some type collectors with greater than average budgets acquire a 1935-S for their collections. Only examples which meet or exceed the characteristics of the typical mint state coin should be considered for investment purposes.

Bibliography

A Guide Book of United States Coins Yeoman, R.S. (Western Publishing Co., Inc., Racine, Wisconsin, Thirty Seventh Edition, 1984)

Coin Dealer Newsletter (Alan Harriman, Hollywood, California)

Coin World (Amos Press, Sidney, Ohio)

Coin World Almanac (Amos Press, Inc., Sidney, Ohio, Second Edition, 1976)

The Comprehensive Catalogue and Encyclopedia of U.S. Morgan and Peace Silver Dollars Van Allen, Leroy and Mallis, A. George (F.C.I. Press, Arco, New York, Second Edition, 1976)

Encyclopedia of United States and Colonial Proof Coins, 1722-1977 Breen, Walter (F.C.I. Press, Albertson, New York, 1977)

The Numismatist (Colorado Springs, Colorado)